Harvesting Children

Harvesting Children

The Dark Side of Foster Care

Peter White

"Dedication"

This book is dedicated to all foster kids living, dead, and yet unborn...

Foreword

The stories in this book describe families in crisis and what happened to them. They were originally published in The Tennessee Tribune from August 2021-2022. Tennessee's Department of Children's Services (DCS) operates a $1.4 billion/yr child trafficking network, and Harvesting Children details the involvement of its many players.

I started investigating the Tennessee Department of Children's Services (DCS) after an internal survey of DCS employees was leaked to the press. I did a few stories about DCS employees and readers left comments that led to other stories about families. People contacted me via email or left messages at the office. Pretty soon I was overwhelmed with parents and grandparents asking for help. The more stories I wrote, the more leads I got, but couldn't keep up with them all.

People were eager to talk. DCS officials were not. Official obstinacy and their unwillingness to answer questions made my investigations difficult, and the process changed me. I have become an advocacy journalist for the families and the children caught up in the child welfare system.

I wrote this book to tell their stories, to give them a voice, and to understand how such horrible things happened to them. This book also looks at the child welfare system and the people who run it.

For me, it is also a personal exorcism. I lost custody of my kids in a nasty divorce, and they grew up with a mother who turned them against me. They are young adults now, but the parental alienation they endured is still with them. The anguish of not seeing them grow up is still with me, too. A black father who lost his daughter told me, "You never get over it." Like the victims in this book, I know what it is like to be caught up in a system that treats people with contempt who come before it seeking justice.

i

There are two theories about child welfare agencies. Do they rescue neglected and abused children from their deadbeat parents? Or do they run a state security service like a modern-day version of the former East German Stasi? This book takes the latter view. I think, in many ways, DCS is worse than the ills of abuse and neglect it is supposed to cure.

Academics have studied child welfare to death. Auditors have issued damning reports ad nauseam, and year after year, politicians keep throwing money at child welfare agencies; courts issue consent decrees to force them to improve; nonprofits invest time and money; reporters like me write countless articles chronicling child welfare scandals in the U.S.

This book explains how and why these agencies fail. Politicians, scholars, and welfare officials often claim that family reunification is, or should be, child welfare's primary goal. But these agencies spend extraordinary amounts of money taking children away from their parents and succeed at reuniting them only about half the time.

In Tennessee, most of the $1.4 billion Child Welfare budget goes to pay employee salaries. A second big chunk goes to service providers who have state contracts worth millions. Many are non-profits or church-related.

Tennessee is a deeply red state where churches (11,089) outnumber places that sell liquor by the drink (4,613) by two to one. Whisky and salvation have battled here for 150 years. These days, drugs have been substituted for the demon drink of yesteryear, and if you use or fail a drug test, the Department of Children's Services (DCS) will take your kids away.

According to Richard Wexler, Executive Director of the National Coalition for Child Protection Reform, the major problem with child welfare agencies in the US is that they are carceral systems. Like prisons, they rely on hyper-surveillance to wrongfully take children and prosecute parents who are mostly poor.

This view is held by a growing number of researchers, who say Black children are more likely to be removed from their homes and put into foster care than White children. They are also less likely to be reunited with their families. There is a long-standing debate whether this is because of racial bias or because Black families are more likely to be poor and more likely than White families to mistreat their kids.

In any case, the child welfare system has failed to resolve racial disproportionality and disparities for many years. Academics, family advocates, and others are calling for the abolition of child welfare as we know it. I am among them.

The premise behind Harvesting Children is that the state doesn't parent well and should stop trying to. DCS and its cohorts are not saving abused children as much as punishing their parents. Once kids are put in foster care, the state can start collecting child support from their parents. DCS has custody, so by law, they are entitled to it.

DCS caseworkers can't do a decent job because they have too many cases and too much paperwork. They get reprimanded or fired if they fight too hard for the families they are trying to help.

The juvenile court judges who preside over these cases sign emergency removal orders on flimsy or sometimes falsified evidence that provides legal cover for DCS to wrongfully take children from their families before any trial begins.

When most parents go to court, their kids are already gone, and getting them back, if they ever do, is an Orwellian nightmare. The process is rigged, and parents navigating the system face a culture of lying that permeates the department from top to bottom.

The bad actors in this book are identified by name and title. They believe anything is better than the severe abuse or neglect kids supposedly are exposed to before the state takes them away. But these cases rarely involve violence, and the "neglect" often is due to poverty.

Families whose children have been taken are lucky to get them back. DCS sues the others to terminate parental rights after 15 months in custody. Under the Social Security Act, the Title IV-E program was created in 1980 as part of the Adoption Assistance and Child Welfare Act. The federal government reimburses states for half the cost of adoptions. For every adoption, states collect a payment. To stop paying these bounties, Congress would have to change the law.

Child welfare has a withering cast of characters who are all invested in a dysfunctional system. This includes lawyers, Guardians ad Litem, judges, social workers, congregate care operators, foster parents, adoptive families, non-profits, dentists, doctors, therapists, and psychiatrists. These people get involved when the state wants to terminate parental rights.

Family law attorney Connie Reguli describes one such scene in Nashville when she counted seven state functionaries along with the judge and his clerk clustered in the front of the courtroom. Against the phalanx of taxpayer-supported strangers trying to take their children, stood the mother and father and Reguli, their attorney. Three against nine. Doesn't sound fair, does it? It isn't.

"It can't stay the same," Reguli says. "I have grandchildren; you know? And I know that being vulnerable in the United States does not necessarily mean you have a physical or mental disability. You can be vulnerable if you are a victim of domestic violence, if you are poor, if you are a single mom or a single dad. The bell curve for vulnerability is pretty broad, so vulnerable families are at risk.

As you will discover in this book, Connie Reguli has become one of the leading voices, an outspoken advocate demanding change.

"Change comes not just from a voice but from propelling the message across a broader spectrum," Reguli told me. She thinks it will take powerful discussions across many segments of American society to transform the child welfare system.

iv

"Social systems in America have changed, but until we look at the systemic problems, we can't effect that change," she says.

"I mean, why is it all going so wrong? All the results are bad from this 1974 law. The results are bad for foster children. The results are bad for families. The results are bad financially. The results are all bad. We know that. So, we need a change, but until we look at the systemic categories of problems, we can't effect that change," Reguli says.

"We have to understand that the system is broken and the problems are systemic. These stories are not purely academic. One family is affected here, and one family is affected there. But these stories are repeated over and over and over in every community and every state. They reveal problems that are affecting families all across the country."

Child welfare authorities in the US are removing staggering numbers of children just like church and civil authorities did a century ago with American Indian children and like Canadians did with their First Nation children. The rationale was as bogus then as it is now.

The reason so many kids get taken is because their families don't have the money to defend themselves with a good lawyer. They aren't middle class like the people who are prosecuting them or the people who rush to stereotype impoverished parents as sick or evil and, therefore, should have their children taken from them.

But, once taken, most do not thrive in foster care. Being a foster child can be like playing a demented game of musical chairs. In 2021, DCS moved 1,612 children once, 818 twice, and 740 children three or more times. Many of them become maladjusted adults who are psychologically disturbed and end up in prison once they age-out of the system.

Compared to their peers, foster kids are seven times more likely to experience depression, six times more likely to exhibit behavioral problems, and five times more likely to feel anxiety.

Researchers have investigated every aspect of child welfare to find out what is wrong and why it is so bad. The best answer policy wonks can offer is that various unnamed sources "lack the political will" to "do what should be done," by which they usually mean, enact major reform and stop throwing even more money into policing families.

We are always hearing that there aren't enough foster parents, group homes, and adoptive homes to house all the kids DCS takes. The solution is quite simple: stop taking so many kids into custody, provide wraparound services to families, and return the kids to their parents quickly. In the Volunteer State, none of those things is happening with any consistency.

The $1.4 billion DCS budget should be redirected so families get the social services they need. DCS offers services to families it controls but uses a carrot-and-stick approach that is cruel and ineffective. Imagine how ambivalent parents must feel when DCS offers help while simultaneously trying to take their children away forever.

What DCS says it does is often at odds with what it actually does. DCS is hopelessly conflicted about its core mission: should it be reunifying families, or should it be getting as many children adopted as quickly as it can? Most, if not all, child welfare agencies in the US are similarly conflicted.

Two things have become abundantly clear: children who spend too much time in custody are not served well, and most state agencies that manage foster care have been failing to do it well for the last 60 years. Of course, some are better than others. There are a handful of states using a holistic and multidisciplinary approach that lessens the time spent in foster care and increases family reunifications.

However, it's doubtful things will change any time soon in Tennessee. The department should be dismantled and rebuilt from the ground up with completely different leadership. The last two DCS Commissioners spent years in the criminal justice system but not a single day as social workers. A good system should be transparent, which DCS is not, and it needs to stop punishing parents by devoting itself to helping families stay together.

I would like to thank Connie Reguli, Richard Wexler, Maleeka Jihad, aka MJ, Melaniia Jordan, Michael Heard, and activist Joyce McMillan for educating me about child welfare. Their experience and insights are present throughout these pages. Judge Sheila Calloway, Magistrate Mike O'Neil, and Juvenile Court Clerk Lonnell Matthews helped me understand the role of juvenile courts in child welfare cases. Jessica Ramsey provided invaluable insight about Guardians ad Litem, and Senator Ferrell Haile described baby courts, one good thing that is actually helping drug-addicted mothers turn their lives around in Tennessee. Brian Narelle titled the book. I would especially like to thank my editor, Robin Goodrow, who convinced me to share my own story. I am also in debt to the dozens of caseworkers, advocates, officials, non-profits, and families who told me their stories. I hope I have told them well and true.

Peter White
Kingston Springs, Tennessee
October 1, 2024.

Introduction

Orphans used to grow up in orphanages. Two doctors, C. Henry Kempe, a pediatrician, and Federic N. Silverman, a radiologist, published a seminal paper in the Journal of the American Medical Association in 1962 called The Battered-Child Syndrome.

This is how they defined it: "The Battered-Child Syndrome" is a term used by us to characterize a clinical condition in young children who have received serious physical abuse, generally from a parent or foster parent. The condition has also been described as "unrecognized trauma" by radiologists, orthopedists, pediatricians, and social service workers. It is a significant cause of childhood disability and death. Unfortunately, it is frequently not recognized or, if diagnosed, is inadequately handled by the physician because of hesitation to bring the case to the attention of proper authorities."

Kempe's wife, Ruth, was a professor of psychiatry and pediatrics at the University of Colorado School of Medicine. She and her husband founded The Kemper Center for the Prevention and Treatment of Child Abuse and Neglect at the University of Colorado in 1972. It was the first of its kind, providing research, training, education, and innovative program development for all forms of child abuse, neglect, and trauma.

People had a hard time confronting the issue of child abuse because it was overlooked or covered up. The Kempes realized that beating children was not confined to psychopaths or lowlifes. It occurred in families with good social backgrounds, higher education, and good incomes, too. In fact, it was quite common and just not talked about.

Their work changed the way we think about children in our society, and it changed the way states approached child welfare across the country. Reporting requirements and child protection laws now exist in all 50 states because of the awareness the center brought to the maltreatment of children.

Shortly after Battered-Child Syndrome was published, legislators began passing laws, child welfare agencies began building foster care networks, and the federal government started keeping statistics on children taken into custody by state agencies.

The Child Abuse Prevention and Treatment Act (CAPTA) was passed in 1974, and it ushered in a new era in child welfare. CAPTA generated an eclectic constituency of stakeholders from government, charities, law, academia, medicine, law enforcement, social work, community groups, and politics who started describing the problems and developing demonstration programs to solve child welfare issues.

Among other things, CAPTA created funding for out-of-home placement for abused children. Some were housed in congregate care facilities, while others were placed in foster homes with foster parents.

The Adoption Assistance and Child Welfare Act of 1980 created Title IV-E of the Social Security Act and established the first federal rules to govern child welfare case management, permanency planning, and foster care placement reviews. The act required courts to review child welfare cases regularly, and states had to make "reasonable efforts" to keep families together via prevention and family reunification services. States were also required to develop reunification and preventative programs for foster care and assure that children in non-permanent settings were seen at least every six months.

The Adoption and Safe Families Act (ASFA) passed in 1997 and provided federal bonuses to states to increase adoptions. That hasn't been a silver bullet for fixing Tennessee's overcrowded foster system. In 2020, for example, DCS took about 8,000 children into custody but only arranged 1186 adoptions.

At the time ASFA was considered the most sweeping change to the US adoption and foster care system in some two decades. Child welfare agencies no longer had to make "reasonable efforts" to prevent removing children from their homes, and it put their health and safety concerns first, ahead of family reunification.

In 2002, Dorothy Roberts, a law professor at Northwestern University, published Shattered Bonds: The Color of Child Welfare. She said ASFA established "a preference for adoption as the means of reducing the exploding foster care population," but it doesn't provide comparable financial incentives or technical help to states to improve their family preservation programs.

Roberts was especially critical of a new trend in child welfare called "concurrent permanency planning." By placing foster children in pre-adoptive homes, it put kids on two tracks at the same time. One track focused on reuniting them with their parents, while the other sought to find them a permanent home with another family.

"Concurrent permanency planning is supposed to keep children from being stranded in foster care. But this policy puts caseworkers in a schizophrenic position. It intensifies the conflict already inherent in child welfare practice between preserving families and seeking adoptive homes," she wrote.

ASFA institutionalized conflict between birth parents and adoptive parents in child welfare cases across the country, and, as Roberts predicted, it did not work out well for children who were caught in the middle.

The 2018 Family First Prevention Services Act (FFPSA) was designed to help keep children safely with their families and avoid the traumatic experience of entering foster care. The Children's Defense Fund (CDF) called it "the most significant reform to federal child welfare policy in decades."

It calls for children to be placed in the least restrictive, most family-like setting appropriate to their special needs when foster care is needed. Family First calls on states to radically rethink their approach to child protection and family support, and full implementation of the law will be a year-long process, according to CDF.

FFPSA has barely begun in Tennessee. DCS continues to take more kids into custody than it returns to their families. Tennessee had the highest rate of foster care instability in the nation every year from 2016-2020. Foster kids are moved around in Tennessee much more than in other states, and that leads to poor outcomes.

The takeaway from this brief history of federal child welfare legislation is that thinking on the topic goes from its discovery in 1962 to CAPTA and intervention in 1974, to mandating reasonable efforts towards family reunification in 1980, to ASFA in 1997 when family reunification is no longer the primary goal of child welfare.

Lastly, in 2018, FFPSA was designed around family services to keep kids out of the foster care system and the least restrictive environment for foster children. This flip-flopping has happened because when one law didn't solve intractable problems, legislators passed another one. When it didn't work well, politicians passed another one. Child welfare has been around for 60 years, searching for solutions that continue to elude it.

A parallel history has been running from CAPTA's beginning to the present day. In 1973, a landmark lawsuit in New York was launched by Marcia Lowry, an attorney for the New York Civil Liberties Union. The lawsuit was named Wilder, named after Shirley Wilder, a foster child and the lead plaintiff in the lawsuit. She was a thirteen-year-old girl who became a victim of the New York foster care system and eventually died in 1999 from AIDS.

The lawsuit took over 20 years to settle, and the New York foster care system remained virtually unchanged. This case marked the beginning of an era of class action lawsuits filed in an effort to protect children and improve child welfare systems across the United States.

Children's Rights, a national watchdog organization founded in the early 1970s, represented the plaintiffs in Brian A v Sunquist in Tennessee and brought similar class action lawsuits in more than a dozen states on behalf of maltreated children in the US. Those lawsuits exposed states' failure to protect and serve children in their care.

Despite growing awareness about child abuse, we have not managed to end it. Nobody really knows if fewer people beat kids today than 50 years ago, but we know foster parents don't hit as much as parents do. However, there are other ways to maim the young. Research shows that the longer you stay in foster care, the more likely you will be traumatized in other ways and age out of the system permanently damaged as an adult. From this point of view, child welfare in many states is generally bad and getting worse because the number of children in custody keeps growing.

Child welfare advocates knew this back in the 1970s. The legal outcomes of class action child welfare lawsuits are consent decrees, written settlement agreements that include federal monitoring to assess states' progress to improve conditions for children involved in the child welfare system. Consent decrees are expensive and take an average of 17 years to exit from federal oversight.

In 2000, the National Center for Youth Law identified 57 child welfare reform lawsuits involving 36 states, and consent decrees governed at least 35 of them.

In 2021, 70 class action lawsuits in 30 states were either pending or engaged in some aspect of child welfare, and about 20 states were working to implement consent decrees or other related court orders to reform their child welfare systems.

Love them or hate them, when it comes to reforming child welfare systems that can't reform themselves, consent decrees are about the only game in town.

In the 60 years since the Kempes coined the terms "abuse and neglect," they have come to cover a multitude of sins. In a famous pornography case, Jacobellis v. Ohio, Supreme Court Justice Potter Stewart said he couldn't define obscenity, but "I know it when I see it, and the motion picture involved in this case is not that."

Abuse and neglect have become buzzwords, weaponized by welfare agency lawyers to take more and more children into state custody. Dependency and Neglect petitions are the legal means used to separate parents from their children. Overzealous Children Protective Service agents who "see it because they know it" misuse those terms in a variety of ways, which is what this book is about.

The following are just a few stories of the half million children in foster care in the US and how they got there.

Contents

Chapter One: Wrongful Taking

CLARKSVILLE, TENNESSEE–It was a chill, windless Christmas Eve in 2019 when Shakia Richardson started having contractions. But the first-time Mom was ready. The overnight bag was packed, and her partner, Trevon Jenkins, took Shakia to Blanchfield Army Community Hospital at Fort Campbell.

Richardson's primary care physician was off duty on Christmas. After ten hours in labor, Midwife Tiffany Williams delivered the baby, and it was a difficult birth. Sevyn Richardson came into this world with 18 fractured ribs and a broken collarbone on Christmas Day. But nobody knew that at the time. The baby seemed fine, and she and her Mom were sent home the next day.

A few weeks later, the couple's nightmare began. Sevyn got a vaccine and developed a fever, so Mom brought her back to the base hospital. They did an X-ray, found several healing rib fractures, and sent the baby to Vanderbilt Children's Hospital in Nashville.

An odious twist in this story is how DCS used a Vanderbilt MD's report to lend credence to their accusation that the baby had been severely beaten. A bone specialist would later dispute that claim, but the nightmare went on for three long years because DCS refused to admit they had made a mistake.

If it were not for a strong and determined family advocate, Grandmother Shabazz, this story would not have a happy ending. Legislation has twice been introduced to establish family advocates in Tennessee Juvenile Courts who can make all the difference. The proposed laws never made it out of committee.

•••

CLARKSVILLE, TENNESSEE – The Tennessee Department of Children's Services (DCS) took Lacreesha Hill's children away on January 29, 2021. They said the reason was exposure to drugs and lack of supervision.

The parents did nothing wrong. In fact, faced with a medical emergency, they did everything right. The Department of Children's Services (DCS) is quick to remove children, and parents have to jump through lots of hoops to regain them. So, while taking a child can, and did, take less than a day in this case, it can, and did take months for Hill to navigate the serpentine, opaque, and obstructionist procedures DCS placed in her way to get them back. Hill's youngest child, DaCayla, was just 6 months old when DCS took her. She never made it home.

DCS never should have intervened in the first place. It uses drug hysteria to criminalize parents for using them, even when they are prescribed, as in this case, and even when the wrong parent is tested. Furthermore, it shows how vindictive DCS can be even after a tragic death in the family that would have never happened if they had only followed their own policies.

BRISTOL, TENNESSEE – On a sweltering July day in 2021, Angelica Taylor crossed the North Carolina border into Tennessee with her toddler son, Robin. She was pregnant with twins. Taylor checked into a hotel in Bristol but was not feeling well and started to sweat profusely. The hotel manager called paramedics, and they took her across the street to the Bristol Regional Medical Center.

She asked the triage nurse if anyone could sit with Robin while she was being seen. The triage nurse agreed. When she came out of the examination room, a group of security guards surrounded her. A social worker was holding Robin's hand and started to walk away with him. "He's running off with my kid," Taylor screamed.

One guard pushed her to the ground; she was sedated and put on a psychiatric hold.

Three days later, she miscarried and lost one of the twins. After a week, Taylor was transferred to Woodbridge Psychiatric Hospital in Johnson City. She was released from there a week later.

Fast forward to March 9, 2022. Baby Phoenix is born premature, and Mom stays with him in the Neonatal Intensive Care Unit (NICU) for two weeks. Three days after Mom goes home with Phoenix, there is a knock on the door. It is Child Protective Services. They take the baby away.

DCS denied Taylor visitation with the boys in late October 2022, and she hasn't seen either of them since. "They also tried to have me committed again," Taylor said. The judge put a gag order in effect to keep her from speaking publicly about the case. What kind of a world do we live in when people come to a hospital for medical help and get their children taken away?

•••

Apologists for Child Welfare agencies—and there are plenty of them---will claim I've reached into the barrel and pulled out a few bad apples. They'll say, 'You can't judge a book by its cover or mistakes were made,' or some such nonsense. Mistakes were made and nobody was held to account. That's one thing all the stories in this book have in common. Judging from the hundreds of reader comments posted after these stories ran in a weekly Nashville newspaper, they are just the tip of the iceberg.

These particular cases have something else in common. They all show the complicity of hospitals and their staff who alert DCS when they treat a child who might need protection. Hospitals are mandated reporters and required to notify the authorities in the case of suspected neglect or abuse. So are teachers, police officers, and guidance counselors, which seems reasonable. But in doing so, and lacking a proper investigation, otherwise decent people turn the core principle of American jurisprudence on its head. When it comes to Child Welfare, you are guilty until proven innocent.

DCS is supposed to investigate to see if a child is actually abused before they take them into custody. But in each of these cases, DCS showed up and snatched kids without even trying to find out the facts. They took them from the hospital and put them directly into foster care.

DCS is very well connected. It operates in every one of Tennessee's 95 counties. DCS has judges in their pockets and regularly uses local police as muscle if parents resist having their children kidnapped. They have dozens of non-profits on their payroll and hundreds of other service providers under contract. DCS has a Child Abuse Hotline used by tens of thousands of anonymous informers who feed them information. Are you a landlord who wants to get rid of your tenants? Just call the hotline, and DCS will help you put them on the street and snatch their kids while they're at it.

Think of the Stasi in East Germany before the Berlin Wall fell. That's what DCS is like. If you're a member of the working poor or underprivileged, you don't stand a chance against the system. It's ubiquitous, intimidating, and quite devastating to the families who become its victims.

Connie Reguli never set out to be their champion. "This was not a first career. I went to law school after I had worked with my family building this successful restaurant business and really just decided we had too many cooks in the stew. It became obvious that somebody in the family needed to do something else and I was either going to do psychology or law. I wasn't even sure at that point," she told me. Reguli was 38 when she enrolled in the Nashville School of Law, and she proved to be a diligent student with a prodigious memory.

"Everybody cheated in law school. The way they cheated was they got past exams from people, and they didn't study; they just memorized the test. This professor in the civil procedures class told us everything he was going to put in the exam. I made notes. Nobody listened to him. I was the only one to pass the exam. Everybody else failed.

4

"They asked me to go to the dean and basically plead their case. I remember sitting across from him and saying, 'Look, it wasn't me who cheated. My classmates sent me up here to beg for mercy.'"

It worked. The class was allowed to retake the exam. Reguli didn't have to.

"That set the stage for me being the one who is willing to stand up to authorities," she told me.

But she didn't turn into a crackerjack family defense attorney overnight. When she graduated, Reguli went to work for the Davidson County District Attorney. She prosecuted a lot of petty crimes.

"I had to leave the DA's office because I was too reasonable," she recalled laughing. "You know, you get to the DA's office, and they surgically implant that iron rod in your back to make you stiff-necked and terrible to work with.

"I was primarily into domestic violence and child abuse stuff. It was clear that the prosecutor's office was more focused on building their crime statistics than the overall safety and well-being of the community," she said.

There is no denying Reguli has a lot of moxie. Her detractors would call it cheek. Liam Neeson's character in the film Taken tells his daughter's kidnapper that he has a very particular set of skills. "Skills I have acquired over a very long career. Skills that make me a nightmare for people like you. If you let my daughter go now, that'll be the end of it. I will not look for you, I will not pursue you, but if you don't, I will look for you, I will find you, and I will kill you."

Reguli has a very particular set of skills, too. She knows the law, knows court rules, and knows child welfare policies better than the people who are supposed to follow them. She knows what DCS is supposed to do but didn't and what they did but shouldn't have. And she worries about a case like a dog with a bone and just won't give up until the other side lets go.

In 2011, a Maury County mother hired Reguli because DCS had taken her 4-month-old twins. It was Reguli's first broken bones case, and she didn't know what to do. "I didn't know how to help this mother," Reguli recalled. When she lost the case, the mother fired her. "I would have fired me, too," Reguli told me. "I felt so hopeless because I didn't know how to find resources to help her," she said.

Premature infants are prone to have broken ribs when they are born. Babies can't tell you what's wrong because they can't talk yet. Preemies are fragile and often have other problems from underlying medical issues that are not always evident when they are born.

Such cases can be complicated and difficult to diagnose and treat—and even harder to defend in court if DCS takes a baby and accuses the parents of severe abuse. Reguli resolved to never again be left flat-footed when defending a broken ribs case.

"You have different cases going on, but with one of these cases, you are living, breathing, and thinking about it all the time," she told me.

"A couple years later, I'm very aggressively fighting DCS. I'm all-over social media. This young couple from Cumberland County found me, and they had a baby that was born premature—a lot of pre-birth issues. Mom had been in the hospital. At 4 months old, the baby had a swollen ankle. They take the baby to a regional hospital, which does a whole skeletal survey, and they force the mother to go to Vanderbilt.

"Dr. Deborah Lowen comes in, does a skeletal survey, and says the baby has multiple rib fractures at various stages of healing, and they take the baby right there at the hospital. And the Mom's pregnant."

The revolving door between retired US military and defense industry companies has an equivalent in the hospital industry. Dr. Lowen was the head of the child maltreatment program at the Monroe Carell Jr. Children's Hospital at Vanderbilt, but she later switched jobs and became DCS Deputy Commissioner of Child Health.

"They give the baby to a relative. But still, she's on supervised visits. They won't tell her if they're going to take the other baby. I'm just getting involved in the case," Reguli recalls.

She found a radiologist and a pediatrician who had done research about preemies and they sent her a bibliography of research about the underlying medical conditions premature infants can have.

"I was very afraid these parents we're going to end up in jail. This young momma was very afraid she was going to go to jail."

Like she did in law school, Reguli studied hard. She spent hours on the phone with them, picking their brains to understand what all that research meant in layman's terms. More importantly, she learned how to ask the right questions of medical experts in court. And she was convinced the Mom had not abused her baby.

"She wanted to be a momma her whole life. She was like young, sweet, and cute. And if she would have lost this child, they would have taken every child she ever had," Reguli told me.

The Mom delivered a healthy baby, and two days after they went home from the hospital, DCS showed up and took the new baby. Reguli helped them appeal to the circuit court.

"We were there all day. So, then the judge rules in our favor and the babies came home that very day."

That was in 2017, and Reguli thought DCS would certainly appeal the decision, but they didn't. Had they appealed and lost, the case would have set a precedent and looking ahead, the DCS brass didn't want other defense attorneys citing the case, so they chose to ignore it.

"The fracture ribs debacle continues, and we've had other cases like that since," Reguli said.

She is just the kind of lawyer the parents in the next story would have liked as an advocate to navigate the system and help them get their children back. Unfortunately, as most parents usually are, these parents were mostly on their own.

For the most part, the stories here are told as they were first published. Some have been edited and updated. Let's start with the sad, short life of DaCayla Green.

Another Child Dies in DCS Foster Care

Four-month-old DaCayla Green in September 2020. She died June 16, 2021, just after her first birthday.

The Tennessee Department of Children's Services (DCS) took Lacreesha Hill's children away on January 29, 2021, in Clarksville, Tennessee. They said the reason was exposure to drugs and lack of supervision.

Da'Cari, then two years old, most likely picked up a Percocet pill from the floor in the bathroom. Hill had been taking meds after having her tubes tied; she spilled the container and picked them up but apparently missed one.

Lacreesha Hill worked for Duke Energy from home. She wants justice for daughter DaCayla.

There were no illicit drugs found in the home, and she tested negative for opioids.

Da'Cari's Dad, Dominique Green, was watching the kids while Lacreesha was working from home that day.

Dad cleaned up a bit, then gave Da'Cari a shower and put him down for a nap. But his breathing became labored, and he became unresponsive.

Hill called 911; when the ambulance arrived, Da'Cari was barely conscious with pinpoint pupils, a telltale sign, so the EMT gave him a shot of Narcan. He started to come around.

Da'Cari was taken to Tennova hospital in Clarksville. He was then transferred to Vanderbilt Children's Hospital. Vanderbilt ran more tests; there was nothing else wrong with him.

Two-year old Da'Cari Green.

His vitals on 1/30/21: "constitutional: well-developed, well-nourished, and in no distress... Pupils are equal, round, and reactive to light, breath sounds normal, no respiratory distress. He exhibits normal muscle tone, coordination normal, skin is warm and dry, no rash noted."

Toxicology: "Patient's UDS was presumptive positive for opiates. All other testing was negative. He was weaned from Narcan at 3 AM and watched closely for a change in mental status. SW (social worker) was consulted in the setting of ingestion. They felt the patient was stable enough to go home."

After interviewing the parents, Vanderbilt doctors concluded, rightly, that Da'Cari's overdose was accidental. And the social workers also thought he should go home. They felt no need to add more trauma to the family and decided to release the little boy.

Both parents were home at the time Da'Cari picked up what looked like a piece of candy and ate it; the children were not neglected or abused; Mom was working. Dad didn't notice. Things like that happen with young children every day.

Da'Cari recovered quickly, and he should have gone home, but before that could happen, DCS stepped in and took him and his siblings, DaCayla and La'Marah, 10, into custody. That turned out to be a death sentence for 6-month-old DaCayla. A series of blunders, ineptitude, and deliberate delays by DCS over the next four months led to her death and never would have happened if DCS had not wrongfully removed the kids in the first place.

"If DaCayla was alive, she'd be one, but she's gone," Hill told me.

Davidson County District Attorney General Glenn Funk opened an investigation, but DCS will probably never be charged as an accessory to a homicide, although they are certainly guilty. By taking her into custody, DCS took responsibility for DaCayla's safety and failed miserably to provide it.

The Case Against DCS

I'll say it again: DCS never should have intervened in the first place. The parents did nothing wrong. In fact, faced with a medical emergency, they did everything right.

DCS caseworker Brooke Brooks took the children into custody at Tennova hospital in Clarksville on January 29, 2021. It's DCS policy to try and place children with family members. Both maternal and paternal grandmothers live close to Hill. Hill's Mom lives in Oak Grove, next to Fort Campbell, but on the Kentucky side.

Green's Mom lives in Clarksville. Both were willing to take the children. Hill wanted them to go to her mother.

Brooks, or more likely her boss, Heather Jeffries, nixed both of those ideas. DCS doesn't often place children out of state.

L-R, Dominique Green, Da'Cari Green, Grandmother Tanga Lyle on December 18, 2021.

Tennessee doesn't get the federal bounty if a Kentucky grandmother ends up adopting. Kentucky gets it. It can be up to $10,000 but is usually less.

Brooks placed three children with Hill's sister, Teanna Arnold, 35, who lives in Antioch, more than an hour away to the South but in Tennessee. That arrangement violates DCS policy, but Arnold owns a nice big house and works fulltime as a nurse at Centennial Hospital in Nashville. She has two sons, young teens.

"I was going up there every day seeing the kids back and forth every day when I got off work," Hill said.

Tanga Lile, DaCayla and Da'Cari's grandmother, told me that she couldn't visit the kids very often because Arnold's work schedule cut into the 10 AM-8 PM window DCS had allowed for visitation, and Arnold didn't want anybody in the house when she wasn't there.

Arnold asked Brooks for a childcare voucher, but she didn't provide one, so Hill sent her sister three money transfers between March 16 and May 5 to pay for their care, totaling $897. Hill said that her sister took the money but left the toddlers at home with no adult in the house while she went to work. Arnold told her that she had a neighbor who checked in on them occasionally.

It bears repeating that Hill works from home, and Dad was a regular babysitter. They had in place what DCS failed to provide once they took the children. It bears further repeating: DCS never should have taken the children in the first place. Once they did, the kids should have been closer to their Mom. That's DCS policy, but putting infant DaCayla in a nice-looking house where she had her own room seemed like a better idea.

DCS is more than a hundred years out of fashion with that gambit. My ancestors were lace-curtain Irish. Work was hard to find in the early 20th Century, but Irish immigrant families used to put lace curtains in their tenement windows in South Boston. They didn't have a pot to pee in, but from the outside, they looked respectable.

Once Brooks placed them at an inconvenient distance, she should have made sure the toddlers had childcare. DCS caseworkers never visited Arnold's home after they were placed there.

"They took my children away and placed them with my sister. They gave me a parenting plan saying that it was supposed to get dismissed in April if I completed everything, which I did," Hill told me.

That included a drug test, an Alcohol & Drug Education Program, and a mental assessment. Hill jumped through all those hoops while working full-time and driving more than two hours' round trip every day to see her kids after she got off work.

"I did everything," she repeated. Hill came to court with records showing she had done what DCS told her to do. "We complied with them. The case was supposed to be dismissed April 29th," Hill said.

When Hill showed up in court to get "re-instated" as a mom, Brooks wasn't there. DCS Team Coordinator Karmen Davis was there instead

Davis said they were not going through with the reunification because someone had reported the children were being abused, and they had to investigate.

When DCS thought Hill neglected the children they had them out of the home in a New York minute.

Hill's 10-year-old daughter, La'Marah Smith.

Apparently, when they suspect abuse of foster children, they take their sweet time. DCS's failure to return the children when promised proved to be a deadly delay for DaCayla.

"They really should have dismissed it. They didn't follow their own protocol," Hill said. Of all the lame excuses DCS could have made to delay the case, implying Hill had something to do with abusing the children is simply not credible. They hadn't been living with their Mom since January 29, 2021.

Davis assigned a new caseworker, Akendra Patterson, who told Hill she couldn't find Brook's file on Hill's case, so the custody hearing would have to be rescheduled anyway. Hill had to go through all the DCS "education" rigmarole again. Patterson assured Hill everything would be dismissed at the next court date. It was just a matter of a few more weeks. But DaCayla didn't have that much time.

"If they got a call for child abuse and had checked in on the kids, then my child would be alive right now," Hill told me.

Imagine what this forced exile was like for the children. Their Mom visits almost every day, but it just reinforces their separation anxiety because she's not there 99% of the time. Imagine DaCayla crying inconsolably when her Mom leaves her. Imagine Aunt Teanna at her wits end trying to comfort her.

Peggy Gordon is the grandmother of Hill's second oldest child. Gordon lives in Memphis. She took Malaysia, 6, to visit her siblings who were staying with their Aunt Teanna in Antioch. Gordon was there twice. But neither time was Aunt Teanna at home.

"It was evening time when I got there but Teanna wasn't there. Gordon called her. "I told her I said, 'Why are these kids at home by themselves?'"

Gordon told me the two babies looked hungry. "They were not kept up. Their pampers were nasty," she said. Gordon told Arnold's boys to change their diapers and feed them. They gave them bottles. A week later, Gordon came back to pick up Malaysia. "Whenever I went there, they were by themselves," she said.

After several weeks with little or no childcare, imagine that one day, Aunt Teanna arrives home from work and snaps. Shakes the baby to shut her up. It only takes a few seconds to do fatal damage.

Or imagine it was one of Arnold's boys, children themselves, who didn't change DaCayla's poopy diaper and taped her mouth shut and put her in the washing machine because there was no adult in the house to stop them and they were tired of hearing her crying all the time. Or maybe their mother instructed them to "whup" DaCayla if she got fussy.

We don't know exactly what happened to DaCayla or when, but she arrived at Vanderbilt Children's Hospital in a coma on May 19. She had a bruise on her forehead and blood in her eyes.

She was on a breathing machine for five weeks and never came to. "The hospital wanted to make me take her off the plug," Hill recalled. She wanted to do it at 4:44 PM because that was the time she was born. "She fought for a good minute, but she passed at 5:13 PM," Hill said. The autopsy said DaCayla died from blunt force trauma.

DCS acted quickly and removed the remaining two children from Arnold's house and placed them in a foster home on May 19. And for once, DCS showed some common sense and compassion. Caseworker Jasmine Pena helped with the funeral and arranged for Da'Cari and 10-year-old La'Marah to be placed with

Tanga Lyle, Dad Dominque's Mom, in the second week of June. They stayed with her for seven months.

A Broken System

"I can't even remember how many times I went to court. It was court date after court date, and it's still court date after court date," Hill reported. Juvenile Court Judge Tim Barnes finally dismissed the case and released the children into Hill's custody on November 23, almost ten months after DCS took them.

This is the last photo Lacreesha Hill has of all her children together.
L-R: La'Marah, DaCayla (in swing), Malaysia, Da'Cari with back turned.).

DCS controls all that litigation. They change caseworkers frequently. Hill had four. Parents are not informed, and cases get strung out because the original caseworker doesn't show up in court to petition the judge to dismiss them. DCS forces parents to go through 'educational" workshops like Chinese authorities do with their Uyghur Muslims. In Hill's case, they made her go through them twice.

DCS delays and ineptness are actually designed inefficiency to keep children in the system. Federal law requires states to file a motion to terminate parental rights if a child has been in foster care for 15 out of the previous 22 months unless there are compelling reasons not to file. The department's foster care system requires fresh recruits, and the federal rule helps DCS get them. Each one has a dollar sign on their back.

The Department of Children's Services doesn't play nice with children—or their parents – pretty ironic considering the department spent $900 million in 2021 to provide "children's services" to the state's neediest children.

And yet two were given a death sentence: DaCayla Green of Clarksville died in June, and Vincent Carter of Chattanooga died in September 2021. Eight others met the same tragic fate.

DCS spends much of its time and most of that money running a carceral system that preys on poor families by removing young children from their homes to feed a vast network of foster homes scattered across the state. It is an expensive system. DCS's budget goes up every year because they keep sweeping more children into custody. (See https://tntribune.com/dcs-by-the-numbers/)

Alabama gets better outcomes with a much smaller budget. DCS should look to neighboring states and measure success by spending its $1 billion yearly budget, reducing the number of children in foster care instead of increasing it.

DCS started the Hill case in January 2021. They did not release the children to their Mom until November

2021. But DCS did not stop hounding the Dad, Dominique Green.

DCS prosecuted him in Montgomery County Circuit Court for aggravated child abuse and endangerment of a child under eight. He was served on November 9.

DaCayla, Dominique, and Da'Cari Green.

It was about Da'Cari's accidental Percocet overdose back in January 2021. It was a malicious prosecution. DCS had to give the kids back to Hill, but somebody had to pay, and Green was a convenient scapegoat.

It should have been DCS in the dock instead to account for their role in DaCayla Green's cruel and unnecessary death on June 16, 2021. Nobody's holding them to account. And nobody is about to either. The system made sure of that. Bill Lee, Tennessee's rightwing Governor, is an election denier and Bible thumper who fancies himself a criminal justice reformer. He appointed the last two DCS Commissioners, who have decades of criminal justice experience between them but not a single day as a licensed social worker.

A big reason why DCS consistently fails in its mission to help Tennessee's neediest children is poor leadership from people who are used to locking up bad guys, so it's no wonder the department is a mess. We will look inside the troubled department in the next chapter, but not before another story that points out how DCS jiggled the medical evidence in court to justify banishing this Dad from his home for the next two years.

'Twas the Night Before Christmas'

DCS wrongful taking turns two months of hassle into two years of harassment. And it's still going on.

Trevon Jenkins, Shakia Richardson, and baby Sevyn at Blanchfield Army Hospital on Christmas Day, 2019.

Sevyn Richardson came into this world with 18 fractured ribs and a broken collarbone. Sevyn's mother, Shakia Richardson, and her partner, Trevon Jenkins were active-duty military. When her contractions started on December 24, 2019, Jenkins drove her to Blanchfield Army Community Hospital at Fort Campbell, Kentucky. Sevyn is their first child.

What happened afterwards became a waking nightmare that is still going on two years later. Richardson's primary care physician was off duty on Christmas. Midwife Tiffany Williams delivered the baby.

Unbeknownst to the family, Williams was sued for malpractice in 2014. The plaintiff in that suit, Amy Herbst, was a successful Nashville opera singer, whose performing career was ended by the botched episiotomy of her first child. Herbst and her husband, Staff Sgt. James Herbst, filed a $2.5 million lawsuit in Cincinnati federal court against the government and Williams.

Herbst claimed the procedure was carried out without her consent and damaged her digestive and reproductive systems. It also ruined the professional mezzo-soprano's lucrative singing career, and she suffers intense pain during sex, according to the New York Daily News. Five years later, Williams was still employed by the Army as a contract midwife at Fort Campbell.

BeKura Shabazz, Sevyn's grandmother, has been the family's DCS advocate since February 26, 2020.

Richardson had a long, painful delivery. She was in active labor for nine hours. She was given an epidural at 2:06 PM and Pitocin to induce delivery at 7:28 PM. At 9:23 PM, she was dilated 9 cm. Richardson told me that she pushed for an hour.

"I remember feeling her head in my vagina for some time as if she was paused or stuck," Richardson said.

"She should have had a Caesarian," said BeKura Shabazz, Richardson's mother.

Narrow birth canals run in the family. She had the procedure twice with two of her four children. And Shabazz herself was delivered by Caesarian section.

"We have to move this along because the baby is losing oxygen," Richardson remembers a male voice telling the midwife. It was likely the attending physician, Dr. David Paul Tillman.

Baby Sevyn presented "Sunnyside up" and was stuck in the birth canal, so Williams performed an episiotomy; it didn't work. The baby was still stuck in the birth canal. Richardson said that a few minutes passed before Williams cut her again. Finally, the baby came out. Williams reported it was a normal delivery.

However, hospital records show Dr. Thomas Hamilton attended the delivery because Sevyn's heart monitor showed non-reassuring fetal heart tracing or NRFHT. It means her heartbeat was irregular because she was not getting enough oxygen. Sevyn was getting squeezed; indeed, she was slowly suffocating in her Mom's birth canal. That fits Richardson's account that the baby seemed stuck and that both Mom and daughter had a difficult birth.

Two months later, Sevyn got a vaccine and developed a fever, so Mom brought her to the base hospital. They did an X-ray, found several healing rib fractures, and sent the baby to Vanderbilt Children's Hospital.

"When the social worker by the name of Latasha Williams showed up, she had the investigative papers already filled out that the baby was injured through domestic violence. Medical records hadn't been released yet or nothing," Shabazz said.

That's when the grandmother started to question what was going on. DCS was already in the process of wrongfully removing the baby from the parents. This happens frequently all over the United States.

Never in Doubt, Frequently Wrong

"I don't know that anyone has put a number on wrongful removals," said Richard Wexler, Executive

Director National Coalition for Child Protection Reform. He estimates that 75%-90% of all children taken into state custody shouldn't be there.

"Even in more complex cases, there almost always are safe, proven alternatives to foster care," Wexler said. He said most children could have remained safely in their own homes had the right kinds of help been provided to the families.

Wexler said poor children are taken and placed in foster homes far more often than children from middle-class or upper-class families. Investigators confuse poverty with neglect. Wexler noted a bitter irony: Foster parents get funds for the foster child that they may not need nearly as much as the birth parents, who get nothing.

According to DCS 2019 budget figures, DCS family support services received $49.4 million, or about 5% of its total budget of $901 million. Seventy-three percent of the budget, $663 million, went to family management and custody services.

When poor parents lose their children, they are demonized, often criminalized---and certainly overwhelmed by---a child welfare system that includes investigators, hospitals, lawyers, police, judges, social workers, counselors, therapists, educators, and other specialists.

They are supposedly all brought into a child welfare case with the primary goal of reunifying kids with their birth families. In reality, these "do-gooders" are experienced as a phalanx of unwanted meddlers --all of whom must be endured and obeyed--if poor parents are ever to get their kids back.

All too often, they never do. In Sevyn's case, DCS moved against Mom and Dad as soon as they heard the baby had been transferred to Vanderbilt. DCS and Vanderbilt have a cozy relationship. DCS paid Vanderbilt $3.3 million for medical services in 2020.

"Vanderbilt has a specialist called Child Abuse Pediatrician (CAPS). They were first certified in 2009, and these CAPs are the quintessential hit men for putting together the testimony on abuse when they actually don't have a medical specialty," Reguli says.

"These CAPS are not orthopedic surgeons; they are not endocrinologists; they're not X-ray people. All they do is diagnose what they see; that's it. And they say, 'This must be child abuse.'"

The Child Abuse Pediatrician Specialists have now been incorporated into every children's hospital in the United States, all having a financial conflict of interest with the state agencies that use their testimony to put children into foster care.

Most cases DCS investigates arrive via the Child Abuse Hotline. But, the army hospital staff notified DCS in this particular case. So the caseworker, Latasha Williams, jumped in her car and met the parents at Vanderbilt Children's Hospital on a Friday afternoon, February 26, 2020. She threatened them.

"She told us that if we didn't have anyone to come in and watch after 7 PM, then by the time she got off work... it was a Friday. I'll never forget it because it was already 2 or something. The caseworker told us if we didn't have someone to fill those shoes, then Sevyn was going into foster care."

25

Williams wouldn't allow Shabazz to go home with the baby as caretaker. The family scrambled to bring Sevyn's great-grandmother from Virginia, who arrived by American Airlines just after midnight on February 27. Mom and Dad had to stay in a motel. All this cost money. DCS never reimbursed them.

The Protection Agreement Williams forced the parents to sign is how DCS first took control. They also use Permanency Plans and Protective Custody Orders from a judge to maintain it.

Reguli has seen DCS pull out the same tricks from their playbook innumerable times.

"This is a routine strategy and preempts the parents from lawyering up to prepare their defense early in the case. It's always a strategic move for DCS to take control using one of these procedural weapons. The other team is already downfield with the ball before you realize what is going on," Reguli told me.

Heather Jeffries heads Foster Care at the DCS Clarksville office. She gave the order to take Sevyn into custody on March 23, 2020.

Sevyn's parents were tricked by DCS on March 23, 2020. They went to the Clarksville DCS office allegedly for a Family Team Permanency Plan meeting. When they got there, the door was locked, and a Clarksville policeman was stationed outside the door.

DCS took custody of the baby, then only three months old, and she was given to a foster family until a May 4 court hearing. The decision to take the baby was made by Heather Jeffries, who heads Foster Care in the DCS Clarksville office. (See Cover Up).

The Child Removal Network

DCS operates more like a mafia than a child services agency. They have relationships with a host of partners, and DCS officials don't hesitate to use those connections when they move to take a child into custody.

In order to do that with baby Sevyn, they relied on medical records from Vanderbilt, a DCS report from caseworker Williams, and the February 26 protection agreement, which is like a forced confession because it admits guilt at the top of the form.

The presumption is that the parents must be guilty. The same is true of the DCS March 24th court petition to take custody for "neglect and severe abuse"—which Judge Tim Barnes granted. Sevyn had been taken into state custody the day before.

"It felt like they kidnapped her. I felt like we would never see her again. It was defeat, the worst feeling in the world," Richardson told me.

Although Mom gave an eyewitness account of Sevyn's difficult birth, the case came down to a medical opinion about whether Sevyn's broken bones were accidental or inflicted.

This is how caseworker Latasha Williams reported her meeting with the parents on February 27. "No accidental mechanism of injury was provided to explain the patient's injury," Williams wrote.

On page 4 of the custody petition order, she wrote: "Shakia reported that she has no idea what happened to Sevyn." Actually, that is not true.

"When the DCS caseworker came to the hospital she asked me what happened. And I explained that the only physical trauma Sevyn has ever been through was a difficult birth," Richardson said.

The Tribune reviewed hundreds of pages of medical records, statements, and DCS reports in the case. One thing is very clear: DCS preemptively jumped to conclusions and set out to remove baby Sevyn before it even began investigating the case. And it did incredibly sloppy paperwork.

In a rush to judgment, DCS caseworker Latasha Williams wrote a non-custodial family permanency plan, an immediate protection agreement, and a court petition riddled with mistakes. Parents filed a list of 37 errors of fact and corrections with Judge Tim Barnes in Juvenile Court.

Among those errors were: Williams repeatedly misspelled Sevyn's last name as Richardson when it is Jenkins. She wrote Sevyn's birthday as 12/25/17; it was 12/25/19; she wrote Shakia's last name was Jenkins; it is Richardson; she wrote Mom was "overdue by 41 weeks and 6 days"; Mom correctly reported to Williams that she was 40 weeks and 6 days pregnant when Sevyn was born. That's just the first page of errors and misstatements of fact. They go on for four more pages.

Dueling Medical Opinions

Dr. Heather Williams examined Sevyn on February 26 and found her in good health with no evidence of abuse. Except for a fever, all other tests came back negative.

However, two radiologists looked at the X-rays and confirmed what the base hospital had found: broken ribs and collarbone. The collarbone was well-healed and several of the ribs, also. But some ribs were still healing. The X-rays found no other broken bones. And as several specialists noted, baby Sevyn was healthy with no visible signs of abuse.

The case came down to a medical opinion about whether Sevyn's broken bones were accidental or inflicted.

Williams wrote in her report: "As was previously stated, and is further supported based on the birth records, these injuries would not be expected to be the result of birth trauma, especially as radiology has documented a concern that the fractures are in different stages of healing, indicating that the patient may have been harmed at different points in time."

The operative word here is "may". Sevyn may have been harmed at different points in time, and she also might not have been because some ribs take more time to heal than others.

Williams claimed that Sevyn's birth records from Blanchfield Hospital supported her opinion.

Actually, they don't. As noted above, although the midwife reported a normal delivery at the end, she had performed a double episiotomy, and Dr. Hamilton attended the delivery because baby Sevyn was under stress for hours until she was actually born.

If Williams' medical opinion had been left to stand, Sevyn would almost certainly be in foster care today. Richardson went back to court to get permission from Montgomery County Juvenile Judge Ray Grimes for a second opinion. An orthopedic specialist in Chattanooga, Dr. Robert Quigley, examined Sevyn on 5/8/20.

"Rib fractures do not appear to be in a wide range of age of healing. Different fractures heal at different rates. I do not think this review of the skeletal survey means that these injuries for sure occurred at different times. I think that it is possible that these injuries occurred at the same time. However, I state again, there is no way of knowing for sure...that the injuries occurred during birth trauma or from non-accidental trauma," Quigley reported.

Quigley's report was objective. The report from Vanderbilt by Dr. Williams shows confirmation bias. At least, that's how the judge saw things two weeks later.

"Vanderbilt has tunnel vision," said Judge Grimes. He granted a petition to return the baby to the family home on May 4, 2020. But Dad had been ordered out of the home on March 1, 2020. He was not allowed to return until mid-November 2021. "So he's been out of the house for over a year," Richardson said.

The family is still under a DCS edict to have other family members in the home, and they cannot travel out of state. The extended family lives in Virginia. Sevyn's parents are in Tennessee because they were stationed at Fort Campbell.

16-month-old Sevyn with her parents at the Nashville Zoo on April 7, 2021.

"The case is still going on. My grandmother is still here. She is not allowed to go home. If she does go home, my sister comes to take her place," Mom said.

Richardson's family is being severely inconvenienced, but they are lucky. They got Sevyn back after a stout defense against DCS's allegation of physical abuse abetted by a Vanderbilt Child Abuse Specialist who basically agreed with DCS that they broke their baby's ribs and collarbone.

In police jargon, suspicious does not mean guilty. When DCS takes a baby, it means the same thing. Absent any other evidence, and there was none, DCS should have dropped its persecution of the family at the May 4, 2020, court hearing.

"It sucks. It's horrible, but I'm blessed, and I'm thankful. I know a lot of people; they don't get to see their children. So, I just try to be as compliant as I can and still remain reasonable because they have done some horrible things. Horrible things," Richardson said.

Almost two years later, DCS is still doing horrible things. On November 1, Sevyn's parents went to a family team meeting at the Clarksville DCS office. "It was an extremely sour meeting,' Richardson reported.

They asked for permission to let Dad come home. DCS attorney Stephen Marsh said he wasn't comfortable with that and told Mom he was going to get her out of the house, too.

On July 12, 2018. DCS employees Samantha West and Stephen Marsh graduated from the Tennessee Government Management Institute /UT Naifeh Center for Effective Leadership Institute for Public Service.

"And lo and behold, a few days later, there were felony warrants on us for aggravated assault," Richardson said.

Richardson's Mom, BeKura Shabazz, pursued the case with Clarksville PD. She spoke with Sgt. Sunisa Hamilton, a supervising detective.

Clarksville police would not comment publicly on the case. A spokesperson said the case is still under investigation. The Montgomery County Sheriff's warrants office confirmed they do not have any outstanding warrants on Sevyn's mom and dad.

"Once we discovered there could be conflicting information, we prevented that to go through," said Robert Nash, Montgomery County District Attorney. Nash told me the case is not scheduled to go before a grand jury. He won't be prosecuting it.

"DCS ended up digging a bigger hole for themselves. Not only did they (DCS) look stupid, but they lost their trust," Richardson told me.

In May 2022, two years after DCS should have let it go, the judge finally dismissed the case. The family spent $30,000 fighting DCS, not to mention the trauma of separation that still haunts the Mom.

"A house divided against itself cannot stand." —*Abraham Lincoln*

Chapter Two: DCS on the Inside

A man, let's call Bob, works for Child Protective Services (CPS), investigating cases of severe physical or sexual abuse.

"We operate like a secret society in a lot of ways," Bob told me. "Everything we do is confidential." Case managers don't talk about their clients because it would violate HIPAA privacy protections.

"That leads to nobody wanting to discuss anything about the job or what's going on. If somebody gets in trouble, we aren't allowed to discuss it," Bob said. When somebody gets chewed out, everybody is expected to keep silent about what they have seen or heard.

A team leader in East Tennessee, let's call her Jennifer, worked 17 years for DCS. In 2016, she was selected to go to the DCS Leadership Academy. DCS Commissioner Bonnie Hommrich awarded her the very first commemorative coin for outstanding service. It didn't surprise her.

"I am so well-known for helping people and finding resources," she told me.

When Julie Rotella became Assistant Commissioner and moved up to the central office, Marcy Martin took her place as East Regional Administrator. That meant Martin's old job as team coordinator was open.

"It was between me and a coworker named Becky Woods. It was Marcy who had the ultimate say, and, of course, she chose Becky, her best friend," Jennifer said.

"There is so much favoritism, and they do whatever they want, whether it's at the expense of the children and families, and if you speak up, you get in trouble," she confessed.

DCS removed an abused 9-year-old from a foster home in Roane County. When Juvenile Court Judge Brian Hunt heard from an attorney that they left an 18-month-old baby with the same foster mother, he immediately had the toddler removed.

Jennifer was in the courtroom at the time, and although she had nothing to do with the decision to remove the baby, both Marcy and Becky blamed her for making them look bad. "They were furious," Jennifer recalled.

"I did what was right, and the judge obviously agreed. I ended up getting suspended for that." They reported her for "creating a hostile working environment."

"They are going to retaliate. They are going to try and fire me," she told herself at the time.

She appealed her suspension and filed a grievance. And on July 1, 2021, she was moved from Roane to Anderson County. Someone else should have been transferred because she had the most seniority, but instead, they made her a scapegoat. "It was pure retaliation," she said.

During this time, Jennifer's co-workers voted her employee of the month, but she didn't get her photo taken and put up on the office wall, which is customary. Neither Woods nor Martin told her she had even won.

"Everybody knows how bad DCS is," Jennifer told me. "I've always been so loyal, and I've always loved my job so much, but it's become such a toxic environment."

She eventually quit DCS for a better job doing investigations for the Department of Intellectual & Developmental Disabilities (DIDD), which she enjoys and is much happier.

Long-time employees in three different regional offices told me their administrators are bullies who terrorize employees, that they have done it for years, and continue to get away with abusing people despite a number of incident reports in their personnel files.

Foster Care workers in Clarksville wanted to file a class action lawsuit against their boss, Heather Jeffries, for harassment, discrimination, retaliation, and malfeasance. But they couldn't find an attorney to take their case.

The legal barriers to class action lawsuits in a right-to-work state like Tennessee are too steep a hill to climb, especially for state workers who want to sue the government. Jeffries racked up more than three dozen complaints by the people who worked for her. Nothing ever came of them.

Ellen Spivey went through normal DCS channels to file her complaint. An Iraqi War veteran, she interviewed seven times for supervisor positions in Foster Care in Clarksville. Haynes said three times she was not given veteran's preference and would have been selected had Jeffries followed the rules. She dogged internal affairs for more than a year for a resolution. They buried it. She finally quit.

"I worked for DCS for seven years. I thoroughly enjoyed it up until the last year," Spivey told me.

Faced with high employee turnover, mid-level managers kept dumping more cases on their overworked staff. In Davidson County in 2021, according to the Tennessee Comptroller's office, ninety-seven percent of caseworkers quit in their first year on the job.

Ridiculously high caseloads were just one reason former DCS Commissioner Jennifer Nichols got fired in July 2022. The first move made by her replacement, Margie Quin, was to hire outside contractors to pick up the slack. Privatizing child welfare, like privatizing prisons, is like re-arranging the deck chairs on the Titanic. Much of it has already been outsourced. Rather than spending money on much-needed human services and addressing problems within the agency, they spend more on paper pushers and expanding the bureaucracy.

Quin has raised salaries by $7,000, and the turnover rate is better than it was in 2021. During her first year on the job, Quin banked a lot of goodwill with Governor Lee and state lawmakers.

But not enough to put a 20-case limit on staff workloads, which continue to climb. For three years in a row, lawmakers did not fix the chronic problem. The DCS rank and file are still forced to work too many cases and managers still don't take their concerns seriously. When workers don't rush to close cases but instead persist in doing a good job, their managers become vindictive, petty, and tyrannical.

Here are three stories about what it's like to work for DCS in the Clarksville office.

Chaos Reigns in Clarksville DCS Office

"You're protecting everybody else's kids but don't have time for your own." —Autumn Moultry

Angel Miller, a regional DCS director in the Upper Cumberland Region, targeted several longtime employees, suspended three, terminated three, one twice, and pressured four others to resign—all between 2020-2022.

Miller had no comment.

Sarah Shepherd was a team leader in the Clarksville office who resigned in 2020. "I left because she (Carmen Davis) wouldn't stop trying to get me to discipline people," Shepherd said.

Angel Miller is the Regional Investigations Director in the Upper Cumberland Region of the Department of Children Services.

Miller hired Davis in late 2019 to be her assistant, and Davis quickly became Miller's confidante and right hand.

"Carmen Davis is basically Angel's snitch, and she lies a lot," Autumn Moultry

38

told me. Moultry was a Case Manager 4 Supervisor with 18 years on the job. Miller fired her—twice.

Melanie Campbell was a lead investigator who worked for DCS from 2014-2020. Miller fired her in 2020.

Campbell worked in Clarksville. At the time, Campbell had 70 cases, which meant she was required to visit about 200 children at least once a month, an impossible task. Campbell wasn't fired for her job performance but for gross misconduct.

Campbell failed to file a report about one of her clients, a teenager who later committed suicide. Rather than address the unrealistic workload, Miller put the blame on Campbell.

Both Campbell and Moultry appealed their terminations. At least five others appealed their suspensions or terminations between 2019-2021. The state employees' union, TSEA, represents disciplined workers during the 3-level appeals process.

"Nobody wins at the first two levels because it's all DCS people who hear the case," Moultry said. But an independent panel presides over the third level. Moultry said excessive caseloads and management's bad attitude really wore her out.

"It never used to be like that. The first eight 8 years, we enjoyed our jobs," she said. "But now people work overtime, bring work home, but still can't keep up with the number of cases."

"You're protecting everybody else's kids but don't have time for your own," she said.

One worker said case counts in Davidson County are up to 50, and team leaders have had to take some of them over. DCS leadership hasn't effectively addressed the issue.

Autumn Moultry Fired

Moultry's problems started one Wednesday in May 2019 when she filled in for a fellow worker who was in the hospital. The case was in Robertson County, and the judge was a stickler. Moultrie didn't have a crucial report that the court liaison, Melissa Upchurch, was supposed to have gotten the previous week.

"They waited until I got to court to tell me it was missing," Moultry said. The DCS attorney on the case, Julie Wooten, pretended she didn't know anything about it.

"She tried to throw me under the bus," Moultry said.

Both Upchurch and Wooten testified against Moultry at her appeal hearing. Both are part of Miller's inner circle. Miller also testified. An office email was their key evidence against Moultry. Miller claimed Moultry lied to the judge about the email and fired her for it.

In my reporting I cited an "us versus them" dynamic that has created a hostile work environment in DCS offices around the state. I interviewed workers in three different regions, and all reported they endured petty, vindictive managers who played favorites and picked on people they didn't like.

Miller and her minions were in the hearing room for Round 3. Moultry said her resolve began to waver.

"These people were saying terrible things about me, and I thought, 'Am I this really bad person who did all these horrible things?'

Autumn Moultry was an investigations supervisor with 18 years' experience. She said Miller bullied and picked on her for months.

"According to Miller, the judge asked Moultry if she read all her emails. Moultry answered, "Yes."

But Miller wasn't even in the courtroom that day and as it turned out, that's not what the judge asked.

"Play the tape," Moultry said. "Play the tape."

The tape showed that the judge asked Moultry if she "checked" her emails, not if she read them all. The court recording proved Moultry had not committed perjury.

A member of the hearing board noted that the recipients of the 'smoking gun' email were other people involved in that case, not Moultry, who had only been cc-ed. In short, the email was a pretext.

Both Moultry and Campbell won their jobs back, and Moultry collected $30,000 in back pay. But the harassment didn't stop. The unfair treatment continued for another 6 months. Then Miller fired Moultry again in August 2020.

Moultry, Campbell, and other case managers were team players, dedicated to the job and to each other, but they weren't in the in-crowd. When they left, needy children lost their devoted advocates and protectors.

A House Divided

Although morale is low at DCS, it is most likely rooted in organizational changes from the top. DCS has four main divisions: child safety, child programs, child health, and juvenile justice. In 2013, The Office of Child Safety was divided into three branches: assessments, investigations, and training.

"Prior to 2013 everybody worked for DCS under the same umbrella," said James Snodgrass, an investigations team leader and trainer who worked at DCS from 2007-2021.

Snodgrass said regional investigative directors (RID) were hired when investigations were put in the Office of Child Safety. These folks hired their own team coordinators and lead investigators. "They developed a separate chain of command for investigations," Snodgrass said.

Regional administrators took on the assessment load, which had fewer and less critical cases. A turf war broke out between the old guard, who feared losing control, and a new bunch of managers. Battles over space and resources ensued. Snodgrass described it as a tug of war. "Regional administrators wanted the Office of Child Safety to fail," he said.

The 2013 reorganization supplanted Child Protective Services (CPS). The only people whose jobs still have a CPS designation are the CPS directors in each of DCS's 13 regional offices.

There are hundreds of CPS investigators who investigate allegations of abuse and neglect, but their job title is "DCS Case Manager." There are four levels: a caseworker 3 makes more than a caseworker 2, and so on. A team coordinator or program coordinator manages case managers. Nowhere will they be identified as CPS investigators, although that is what they are. Changing their job title doesn't change what they do.

Too many DCS mid-level bureaucrats have become obsessed with discipline and punishment, vindictively wielding their power over workers, even those with exemplary records. In 2008, DCS hired Vanderbilt researchers to study why retention in the DCS Clarksville office was so bad. "Basically, they decided it was a leadership issue," Snodgrass said.

"If you have a supervisor hiding out in their car, ghosting their workers when they need guidance, not monitoring their people, they are not doing what they're supposed to be doing," he told me.

James Snodgrass got good evaluations and received raises and bonuses for his job performance during his 14 years at DCS. "They questioned my integrity," he told the Tribune. Snodgrass resigned last year.

Office hours are from 8:00 AM-4:30 PM.

"But they're sitting in their car with their laptops and not answering their phone calls. They only come into

43

the office when they have to recharge their laptops," Snodgrass reported.

From 2016-2020, Snodgrass was a special response team investigator. He traveled widely, visiting different regions to help out with their heavy caseloads.

Sometimes, he would take over cases from workers who were on medical leave or who had been suspended.

He was not privy to the circumstances surrounding a worker's absence, but in hindsight, he says his role as a "fixer" provided cover for managers who had created their own predicament and were scapegoating employees to take the blame.

When COVID hit in 2020, Snodgrass said the special response teams went "Poof!" and he was reassigned to the Clarksville office.

"The people who were in charge in 2008 are still in charge in 2021, and nothing has changed," he said.

Inside DCS Toxic Workplace

"We have people who are telling us how to do our job who have never done our job." —CPS Investigator.

The caseworker, Bob (not his real name), usually meets a child at school away from the parents. He must earn that child's trust; he must find out what's going on; he must decide if the child should be taken out of the home. Hopefully, he can place an abused child with another family member or somebody the child trusts.

"Sadly, a lot of kids don't have those people in their lives," Bob said. Recent news reports about DCS illustrate chronic problems that have been going on since Bob started as a DCS case manager 20 years ago.

Because there are not enough case managers, workers have excessive caseloads. A second problem is drug-addicted parents.

"The problems are just more exacerbated today because of the drugs. It's an epidemic." It used to be cocaine and pills, but today, it's heroin and fentanyl.

"Fentanyl kills people," he said. When it does, children wind up in state custody.

"Employee burnout is through the roof. We just don't have the resources. I mean the manpower. We just do not have it."

Bob said that case managers and caseworkers have a steep learning curve. The job deals with the victims and their families; it involves school officials, law enforcement, court liaisons, DCS lawyers, other attorneys, counselors, and judges. In short, there is an enormous amount to learn. It takes dedication and experience to rescue children from dysfunctional families. And sometimes there are no good solutions.

DCS has made a concerted effort to hire more case managers, but they can't keep them. DCS hired a lot of people with little or no experience, but the retention rate is 40%. "That's a failure in my book," said one supervisor we will call John.

In January 2021, DCS had 3,547 employees. There was money in the budget for 3,904. DCS was short 357 employees, mostly case managers.

Caseloads

In 2019, the House unanimously passed a bill to lower workloads to 20 cases per worker. The Senate added an amendment that said, "DCS shall maintain staffing levels of case managers so that each region has enough case managers to allow caseloads not to exceed an *average* of 20."

The DCS lawyer who drafted the change explained it this way to lawmakers: "You could do a hard case cap, but if you do that, you're going to have to fund us tremendously beyond what we are now, or we'll be lawbreakers from the moment you pass a hard cap," warned Doug Dimond, DCS general counsel.

In this way, DCS weaseled its way out of the clear intent of the bill, which was to reduce the number of cases each worker had to juggle at any one time.

In 2020, a state audit found that 20% of case managers had more than 20 families in their caseloads, and some carried them for months at a time. In addition, 252 case managers had more than 20 cases a month for at least 6 months; 125 case managers carried more than 20 cases for an entire year.

Supervisor John said DCS upper management announced a big reorganization plan in 2020. They created new positions for a rapid response team and a triage team. Think of it as a cross between SWAT and ER. They were supposed to respond quickly to calls and not let referrals slip through the cracks. The goal, then as now, was to close cases quicker.

But managing a child custody case isn't like emergency medicine or a hostage situation. John said DCS rolled its plan out in Memphis and the Upper Cumberland, but it never went any further. He said they hired a few people but put them in investigations. "We ended up getting more referrals instead of getting new positions filled," he said.

Two Command Structures

Employees describe two different overlapping hierarchies within DCS. One is centralized out of Nashville. Upper management changes with every new administration, and longtime employees consider them temporary help even though they are in highly paid positions.

"I've seen about every way you can do this job, but we have people coming in and telling us 'This is a better way,' and they screw it up," Bob said. "We have people who are telling us how to do our job who have never done our job."

DCS upper management doesn't know or remember what it's like to investigate child welfare cases like the hundreds of employees underneath them. Very few started at the bottom and came up through the ranks. That lack of experience lies at the heart of DCS dysfunction; workers blame management, and DCS leadership retaliates.

In a recent survey of employees from 11 regions, the Central Office, and the Wilder detention facility, DCS employees described emotional exhaustion from the stress of unreachable deadlines and the poisonous work climate. Here is one comment from a case manager about DCS's top leadership.

"The Chief of Staff and Commissioner are so harsh and critical of everyone's work that everyone is afraid of losing their jobs and being humiliated in front of our peers, subordinates, and supervisors. It's emotionally exhausting to work in such a toxic environment." (Central Office)

The other command structure is decentralized and runs through DCS offices covering all 95 Tennessee counties. Regional administrators are keepers of DCS's institutional memory. They tend to be career civil servants with decades on the job. They know where DCS's skeletons are buried because they buried a lot of them.

Thus, a code of silence and secrecy permeates the department, and DCS managers enforce it.

"I don't understand how somebody in that position of power can treat people the way they treat them over the years continually and still be in leadership," Bob said.

He also admitted that if you get caught discussing those things with other people, you will become a target.

"They will retaliate in any way they can. If you show any resistance or stand up for yourself, your team, or anybody, you will be labeled a problem. And if it continues, they put pressure on people until they leave."

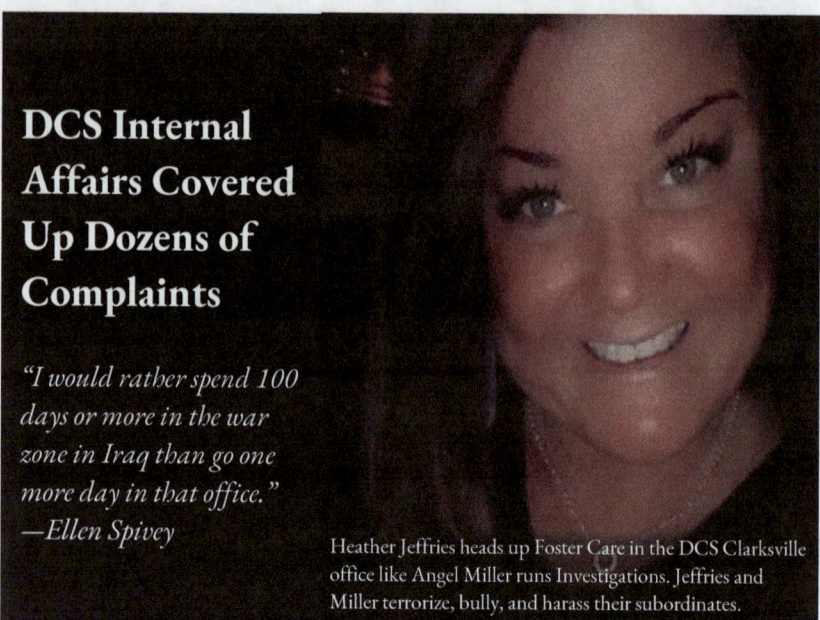

DCS Internal Affairs Covered Up Dozens of Complaints

"I would rather spend 100 days or more in the war zone in Iraq than go one more day in that office."
—Ellen Spivey

Heather Jeffries heads up Foster Care in the DCS Clarksville office like Angel Miller runs Investigations. Jeffries and Miller terrorize, bully, and harass their subordinates.

M. Haynes recalled how Jeffries dictated new policies during staff meetings that were contrary to DCS's written policy. "DCS required certain tasks to be completed within 90 days. Ms. Jeffries wanted us to do it in 30 days," Spivey told me.

"If you pissed her off, you had to come to detention," she said. The detentions started in May 2020, right in the middle of the COVID-19 lockdown when everyone was supposed to be working from home.

"If you were on her lists, then you had to come in and work in front of her," Spivey said. Thirty people met in a crowded conference room with their laptops to complete work that was due within 14 days.

"Multiple case workers contracted COVID, and we still had to come in. You just had to have a mask," she said angrily.

50

"It became less about the children and families, and it was all about reports and numbers," Spivey said.

Haynes filed a complaint in June 2020 about being passed over for promotion. "They didn't do anything," she told me.

Then, in August, Spivey got a call from Internal Affairs that Jeffries had filed a complaint against her for violating HIPAA regulations. Tellingly, Jeffries filed her action against Haynes about something that happened four months earlier and one month after Haynes filed her complaint against Jeffries.

Ellen Spivey, an Iraqi war veteran, was repeatedly passed over for promotion. She filed a complaint with DCS Internal Affairs that went nowhere.

"It was pure retaliation for filing my grievance against her for unfair hiring practice," she said. "I never did what they said I did," she added.

Spivey had two children who needed temporary foster placement, and she wanted to keep them out of state custody, so she told the 76-year-old father to go see her pastor and find out if there was anyone in the congregation who might want to take the two boys, 15 and 16 years old.

"I never revealed their names to my pastor or anything else that violated HIPAA regulations," Spivey said.

The teenagers were eventually placed in state care, and Haynes got two days' suspension without pay from

Jeffries for trying to find them a safe haven. She went the extra mile but got punished for it. Ironically, the DCS recruits foster parents with requirements, explanations, and links on a "Become a Foster Parent" webpage.

DCS Internal Affairs Director Atif Williams would not discuss the case but since Haynes never got back those two days' pay, we can assume Jeffries' complaint was upheld.

Spivey said her pastor backed up her side of the story, but it made no difference to Williams. Spivey's original complaint against Jeffries remained in limbo for months and was never resolved.

The Anatomy of a Cover-Up

Summer slipped into Fall. "Williams told me my case was still under investigation," Spivey recalled. But it wasn't. Williams swept it under the rug and planned to keep it there.

"In December, it got to the point that every day it was something new, something ridiculous. It was petty. They had fired so many people at that point I was walking on eggshells, and I felt like I was going to be the next one. It didn't matter that I was vested. I've seen people who worked 14 years and they walked in and fired them and walked them to the door," she said.

Spivey sent Commissioner Jennifer Nichols her resignation letter on December 8, 2020, giving her notice that she was leaving in 30 days. Nichols forwarded the letter to Williams, who called Haynes the next day.

"Atif assured me they'd get to the bottom of it," Spivey said. She filed the paperwork to reopen her case on December 15.

"Send me your private information, and we'll send you the report, and we'll be in contact," Williams promised her.

In 2019 Atif Williams became Internal Affairs Director for the State of Tennessee, DCS. In 2023 Williams left DCS and accepted a position with a Fortune 500 hospital administration company.

Williams waited until January 13, 2021, to conveniently reopen the case when Spivey was no longer a DCS employee. That two-week delay insured Jeffries would not be held accountable for passing her up.

Seven months went by. Spivey asked Williams for a status report.

Williams sent her an email on July 13, 2021. He said since she was no longer a DCS employee, she was not allowed access to internal reports, nor did she have a right to know what happened to the investigation of her original complaint against Jeffries. It was a perfect Catch-22 with contradictory rules, false promises, and a system hell-bent on protecting itself.

I interviewed more than a dozen DCS employees who have filed grievances against their supervisors. When supervisors discipline their subordinates, the consequences are swift and often vindictive. When employees file complaints against their supervisors, the investigations are slow as molasses and are often never completed.

DCS supervisors can be petty tyrants and get away with it because they know complaints against them will not go anywhere. It's a perfectly corrupt system that protects the guilty and punishes the innocent.

I contacted Williams about the Spivey case. Spivey received a certified letter signed by DCS Affirmative Action Officer Monica Hardaway. The letter said they received her complaint on January 13, 2021. That is not true. Spivey re-filed her case on December 13, 2020, while she was still a DCS employee.

The letter informed Spivey that her second complaint had been dismissed. She wasn't surprised. Not only did Internal Affairs fail to report the findings of her original case but DCS claimed there was not enough evidence to support her allegations in their second investigation. Of course not. They buried it. The intervention of Commissioner Nichols made absolutely no difference to the outcome.

"There's been two investigations, and it's been over 12 months at this point, and nothing is going to be done," Spivey said.

"I would rather spend 100 days or more in the war zone in Iraq than go one more day in that office," Spivey confessed.

When it comes to getting promoted, favoritism and the Peter Principle are standard practice in regional offices across the state. So is bullying. The price to be paid is low morale when merit is ignored. When second-raters are in charge, families suffer, too.

As you've just read, good, hard-working DCS employees were singled out for retaliation and mistreated for speaking out until they quit or got fired. The higher up the chain of command you go, the worse the people are.

Family law attorney Connie Reguli thinks they are a callous lot. I asked her why.

"The culture of the agency is focused on termination of parental rights. I think it's stats that they measure themselves on, just like when I was a DA. Our stats were jail days.

Connie Reguli, veteran family defense attorney, is founder of the Families Forward Project.

And so, we got rewarded for jail days. We didn't get rewarded for protecting the public and justice in the community.

So they are there to terminate parental rights, and that's their main job. That's what they do," Reguli told me.

"The federal government has always paid us only if we pull children from their homes." —Bill Crouch, former Secretary, West Virginia Department of Health and Human Resources.

Chapter Three: How Child Welfare Agencies Operate

When DCS searches homes, it's either done by a caseworker conducting a welfare check or it's an investigator from Child Protective Services (CPS). Many times, their reports paint parents much worse than they actually are, so judges are inclined to let DCS take their children into custody "for their own good."

In October 2022, reporter Eli Hager filed a story about warrantless home searches for ProPublica and NBC News.

"Each year, child protective services agencies inspect the homes of roughly 3.5 million children, opening refrigerators and closets without a warrant. Only about 5% of these kids are ultimately found to have been physically or sexually abused," Hager wrote.

He followed with another news report in December 2022. He said that families investigated by CPS agencies don't have the same constitutional rights that protect Americans when police are doing the investigating.

"The right to remain silent, the right to a public jury trial, the right to face your accuser, and so on are not recognized and enforced by the courts in the child welfare system," Hager said.

In Child Welfare cases, unreasonable searches and seizures are routine because CPS investigators do not need probable cause for a search warrant to enter homes. When they knock on your door, and you let them in, anything they find fault with, they will put into a petition to remove your children. When people say that a man's home is his castle, they haven't dealt with CPS. Less than a dozen states offer jury trials; in 30 states, juvenile court trials are closed.

There is no presumption of innocence in child welfare cases, and you can't plead the Fifth Amendment. They are civil cases, so prosecutors don't have to prove guilt beyond a reasonable doubt. Hager says prosecutors can and do assume the worst when parents won't talk. There is no protection against double jeopardy in these cases either, so what you say in juvenile court can come back to bite you in criminal court, which is why so many parents aren't forthcoming.

DCS caseworker Deandra Miller knocked on Wendy Hancock's door on Wednesday, August 8th, 2018, the same day Hancock reported to Smithville police that her 16-year-old son was missing. (See Chapter Five for more details.)

Miller wanted Hancock to take a drug test. Hancock told her to talk with her attorney. "I don't have to talk to your attorney. I will just go and get a court order," Miller said. And she did. But it wasn't about taking a drug test. That was just a pretext and Hancock later passed the test, anyway. Miller had something more sinister in mind.

Before it was over, at least 15 people were drawn into the conspiracy to prosecute Hancock and railroad her attorney, Connie Reguli. There were police from Smithville and Brentwood, foster parents in Jackson, a DCS foster home contractor, DCS attorneys and caseworkers, clerks, judges, and district attorneys in two counties---each played a part in railroading two innocent people for breaking a law that didn't exist until the judge and District Attorney made it up.

How DCS Takes Children

That's what happened in Wendy Hancock's case. Hancock's 16-year-old son, Chantz, ran away from home and went to his estranged Dad's place. DCS investigators found him there and went along with Chantz's allegation that his Mom, who wouldn't let him have sex with his girlfriend in her house, was a drug dealer.

Connie Reguli, the veteran Family Law attorney, told me that granting an ex parte removal order, based on such an obvious and spiteful lie—and by a judge who had no authority to grant it--was a violation of due process and the end result was that Hancock's two children were wrongfully taken by DCS agents.

"What happens next is that a few well-armed local police show up at your door and leave with your children," Reguli said.

"Under the 14th Amendment, due process requires notice and the opportunity to be heard," she says. There is plenty of case law that grants due process rights to families, but removal orders routinely deny families those rights.

In another case, Reguli posted a YouTube video of police taking a three-week-old baby from its mother in a Nashville parking lot in October 2020. Both mother and baby were fine, but DCS put the baby in foster care that very night. Reguli kept insisting on an evidentiary hearing. Rather than let a judge weigh the facts in the case, DCS finally dismissed it after keeping the mother and baby apart for ten months.

Frequently, DCS doesn't investigate the allegations but gets juvenile court judges to issue emergency removal orders to take children from their homes before the parents even know about it. As one can imagine, it hits them like a freight train. With sickening regularity, DCS attorneys file petitions based on accusations taken from third parties, often anonymous, and swear they are true in court documents. When defense attorneys do not aggressively challenge those petitions, and most don't, judges will routinely grant custody to DCS.

Once that happens, it is an uphill battle for parents to regain custody of their children because the old saw about winning is also true in foster care cases: possession is nine-tenths of the law.

"Sometimes I get labeled as someone who doesn't believe child abuse happens," she said.

Reguli knows better. Her very first jury trial as a prosecutor involved the murder of a baby. "We won that case," she told me.

Academics like Dorothy Roberts and Alan Dettlaff, who are abolitionists like Connie Reguli, sometimes face similar criticism. Both have written books highly critical of child welfare. But they would never say child abuse doesn't happen, and neither does Reguli.

DCS Gets Federal Money Just Like Local Police

"Back in the 1960s," Reguli tells me, "they put a stipulation on getting welfare that you had to have suitable housing to get benefits, and if you didn't, they would take your children."

President Lyndon Johnson had a vision for a Great Society that promoted civil rights, health care, and a number of welfare programs in what became known as the War on Poverty. That's how we got food stamps and federal college grants.

The last major piece of domestic legislation Johnson passed was the Omnibus Crime Control and Safe Streets Act of 1968. It was the centerpiece of a lesser-known war, one that has since eclipsed the War on Poverty. Johnson wanted crime control to become a federal priority. He called for a War on Crime and had the Department of Justice create grant programs for the new Law Enforcement Assistance Administration.

Since then, according to Harvard Assistant Professor of History Elizabeth Hinton, federal influence in civilian police operations has only grown while "the Office of Economic Opportunity at the Center of the War on Poverty never grew into a more permanent agency."

In a 2015 article in TIME, Hinton noted some scholars say that crime control is Johnson's most enduring legacy. It's how local police get tanks, helicopters, robots, and military gear like rifles and new Kevlar vests.

"Over time, national policymakers retreated from and eventually dismantled many of the social welfare programs of the Great Society;

59

the War on Crime, on the other hand, became the foremost policy approach to the social and demographic challenges of the late twentieth century," Hinton wrote.

During the last fifty years, Richard Nixon called for a War on Drugs, and George W. Bush called for a War on Terror. Black Lives Matter activists would say these wars have coalesced and been brought to bear mostly on Black communities. In 2014, that's how we got riots in Ferguson, Missouri, after an unarmed black teenager was killed by a local police officer. Police responded with military guns, and they used tear gas, dogs, smoke bombs, and tanks to restore law and order. And then, in 2020, a policeman in Minneapolis murdered George Floyd.

Reguli says all these wars got "twisted around" in peoples' minds. Regarding child welfare, policy wonks decided they couldn't call the Child Protection Act a welfare bill, so they called it the Child Abuse Protection Act instead. The Child Abuse Prevention and Treatment Act (CAPTA) was first enacted in 1974 and has been amended several times.

"We're still going to take children from poor families. We're going to pay a different kind of welfare to foster parents to raise these children," Reguli explained. "They think poor people are stupid, anyway," she said. "With all these wars, people grew dependent on the federal money that flowed from them. Then they started privatizing it, and at the state level, they couldn't do anything because they knew their agency had to have that money. Until the federal government rewrites CAPTA, we're still going to be fighting the same financial battles. Right now, they can't do anything to stop it," Reguli told me.

How DCS Can Get You Fired

In the course of its investigations, DCS will sometimes identify someone as having abused or neglected a child, even if no children were taken into custody. Without going through juvenile court proceedings, DCS will put you on its list of child abusers. Once you're on that list, you can't get off.

DCS will review the case file administratively and send you a letter telling you you're on their list of perpetrators. You can make a written request for a hearing if you want, but there is no guarantee you will get one. If you get a hearing, you can bring your own lawyer, but you will almost certainly lose because DCS runs the show.

"So DCS has its own administrative court, and the people who work for it are paid by DCS. The administrative judges are hired by DCS, the prosecuting attorneys are hired by DCS, and they can just look at the investigative part of it. And even without having a hearing, they can administratively say that abuse or neglect has occurred. They can say that without even a hearing," Reguli said.

But not to worry! Here are Do-It-Yourself instructions from DCS about how to fight back:

"You can request that the administrative Judge reconsider their decision. Next, you can appeal to the Commissioner of DCS, requesting that they overturn the decision. The next step is to file an appeal for judicial review. This appeal can be filed in Chancery Court either in the county where you reside or in Davidson County, the official residence of the Commissioner of DCS. You can obtain a review of the decision of the Chancery Court by appeal to the court of appeals."

Theoretically, you could take your case all the way to the Tennessee Supreme Court. Reguli has practiced family law in Tennessee for over 25 years and won more cases than she lost. But she won just two cases in the administrative legal process. Practically speaking and by design, that avenue is generally a dead end.

"It's very difficult for a parent to win because DCS has a low burden of proof, and parents rarely have aggressive representation at this stage," Reguli said.

Most state agencies have their own administrative court process. The Tennessee Department of Human Services (DHS) has one regarding

61

child support. It, too, is a kangaroo court with a pre-determined outcome in most cases.

DCS used to conduct Child Abuse Registry Committee Reviews. But in 2017 the state legislature voted not to approve due process procedures for the release of Child/Abuse/Neglect Records rules. So, DCS can no longer conduct the Child Abuse Registry Committee Reviews, and once you're on their list, your name "will remain on the Child Abuse Registry indefinitely."

"And being on the registry means you cannot teach; you cannot work at a daycare. You cannot go to your kids' school events. You can't go on field trips with your kids. So, you can't be a nurse. You can't practice medicine, you can't be a psychologist, and you can't be a therapist. It's pretty aggressive," Reguli warned.

DCS Gets Bad Grades

Every year, DCS produces an Annual Progress and Services Report (APSR). The Youth & Families Children's Bureau (CB) of the U.S. Department of Health and Human Services (HHS) uses APSRs and other data that states submit for its reports. The Children's Bureau publishes annual reports like NCANDS, AFCARS, and Child Maltreatment Reports. It also does Child and Family Service Reviews (CFSR) every ten years or so. The bureau assesses every state and then issues a final report that is based on self-reporting by child welfare agencies. In Tennessee, DCS incorporates internal and external stakeholders in the CFSR process.

There have been three CFSR rounds. The third round ended in 2017, and a fourth will be completed by 2025. A CSFR Program Improvement Plan (PIP) is how the state intends to improve its performance. The Children's Bureau's Tennessee Statewide Assessment for Round 3 is 234 pages. The Bureau's Tennessee Final Report for 2017 runs 39 pages. Tennessee's 2018 PIP runs 37 pages.

If you think deciphering child welfare acronyms is tough, you should try reading some of the reports. For example, Tennessee's APSR for FY 2022 is 143 pages. The evaluation process takes time and involves stakeholders who review a number of actual cases.

It's a pass/fail system of performance in seven subject areas: two safety outcomes, two permanency outcomes, and three well-being outcomes. The performance ratings are subdivided into 18 items and sub-items with three possible grades: pass, fail, or needing improvement.

The Child and Family Services Reviews are based on DCS self-reporting, case reviews, and feedback from stakeholders and others who interact with DCS. Focus groups and surveys are included, and input from all these sources comprises the Tennessee Final Report of 2017.

DCS assessment of its performance on outcomes and the functioning of systemic factors in relation to title IV-B and IV-E requirements and the Title IV-B Child and Family Services Plan of the Social Security Act.

The results of case reviews of 75 cases (40 foster care and 35 in-home) conducted via a State Conducted Case Review process in all 12 regions in Tennessee between April 1, 2017, and September 30, 2017.

Interviews and focus groups with state stakeholders and partners, which included:

- Attorneys representing the agency, parents, and children and youth
- Child welfare agency commissioner, senior and program managers
- Child welfare agency supervisors and case workers
- Community Advisory Board
- Court Appointed Special Advocates (CASA)
- Foster and adoptive parents and relative caregivers
- Foster and adoptive parent recruitment and retention staff
- Foster Care Review Board
- Interstate Compact on the Placement of Children (ICPC) staff

- Information systems staff
- Judges
- Other state agencies receiving federal funding
- Parents
- Service providers
- State-licensed/approved childcare facility staff
- Training staff
- Youth served by the agency

Highlights of CFSR Round 3 Tennessee 2017 Key Findings

<u>**Performance Measurements**</u>

A. No available data to compare with national standards.
B. The state achieved substantial conformity for one of the seven outcomes.
C. The state achieved substantial conformity for four of the seven systemic factors.

Thirty-seven items in the 2017 report either failed or needed improvement. Fifteen were in substantial conformity or noted as strengths.

Highlights of CFSR Round 2 Tennessee 2008 Key Findings

<u>**Performance Measurements**</u>

A. The State met the national standards for two of the six standards.
B. The State achieved substantial conformity for none of the seven outcomes.
C. The State achieved substantial conformity for five of the seven systemic factors.

Forty-four items in the 2008 report either failed or needed improvement. Twenty-five were in substantial conformity or noted as strengths. Comparing key findings in 2008 with 2017 is impossible without 2017 data for the six national standards. An easier grading system was adopted in 2017 after states gave feedback following the

2008 CFSR. But the 2008 and 2017 findings were not so different in that they were both terrible. These reviews are like audits but not nearly so tough. DCS has significant input in determining the results. It's kind of like getting a cheat sheet for a final exam---but you still manage to fail the test.

Like we've discussed, the purpose of the CFSR is to improve performance. Things like timeliness of investigations, permanency, how close siblings are placed when they are sent to foster homes, visits with siblings, training, services provided to foster children and kids still in their family home, and dozens of other items are examined. The assessments take place in every region where DCS operates and include people who are knowledgeable, and the results show they were up to the task. DCS clearly has a long way to go before it can lay claim to its motto, "Children First."

Is the glass half full or half empty? The CFSRs support either view. A person could reasonably conclude that DCS isn't saving Tennessee's neediest children as much as it's failing them.

The following article supports that view, and four other stories chronicle how the child welfare apparatus failed families instead of helping them. Unlike the CFSRs, I name the guilty parties and tell how they victimized and persecuted these families. For the most part, these stories appear as if they were first printed in the Tennessee Tribune. Some have been updated.

DCS Needs a Major Overhaul

This beautiful image hides an ugly truth: DCS takes kids away from their parents and puts them into foster care. Most children do not do well there.

For several years running, the Tennessee Department of Children's Services placed more children in foster care than kids it returned to their families. In 2014-15, 3,078 children of 8093; in 2015-16, 2,895 of 8,001; and in 2016-17, 1,365 of 14,421 children returned home. We asked for more recent data but did not hear back from DCS by press time.

Former Commissioner Jim Henry (2013-2015) supported a number of reform initiatives like In-Home Tennessee to improve how the child welfare system works with families. He promoted and found money for Community Advisory Boards and community-based child abuse prevention.

In 2014, Henry signed 42 contracts with 25 community-based agencies that provided support services to 3,200 children. Henry had the right idea: keep children out of the system by providing families with much-needed services at home.

Those efforts started to pay off. The number of children taken into DCS custody in 2013 was 8,426. In 2014, it was 8008. In Commissioner Bonnie Hommrich's first year as DCS Commissioner (2015), the numbers dropped again to 7,856.

But during Governor Haslam's administration, DCS moved away from reforms like advisory boards and instead built a formidable custody apparatus with federal and state funds.

The department operates like the mafia; it has tentacles everywhere. Judges are afraid of it; hospitals are, too; police departments do their bidding. Parents are terrified once DCS takes their kids, they will never get them back. DCS is also ubiquitous; it operates in every Tennessee County. From 2015-2022, DCS took more children into custody than the year before. Its budget increases every year.

DCS likes to brag that it's done this and that and more of the other, but it hasn't produced better outcomes. Many DCS caseworkers hate working for an agency that is focused more on procedure and control and increased revenue than actually helping needy kids.

As I reported, long-time employees who tried to help their clients often found themselves at odds with vindictive supervisors who harassed them until they quit. They are replaced by inexperienced caseworkers who are not trained to be effective social workers. Instead, they learn quickly to apply often arbitrary rules or face disciplinary action from autocratic supervisors. At least 20% of caseworkers leave every year.

In Chapter Two, I described how DCS mishandles cases, does sloppy investigations or none at all, and it operates with reckless disregard for the families and children they are supposed to serve. It is not just a dysfunctional system; it's dystopian.

The two main reasons given for moving children out of their homes and into foster care are severe abuse and neglect. It turns out children are more likely to suffer sexual abuse in foster care, often from other foster kids, and numerous studies show foster kids do not "do better" than kids who grow up with their families, regardless.

One 2007 study by an MIT researcher, Prof. Joseph Doyle, looked at outcomes for 15,000 children in foster care. He compared them with comparably mistreated children left in their own homes. On multiple measures, the children left in their own homes did better. (see findings below)

FINDINGS FROM THE MIT STUDIES:

Compared to the comparably- maltreated children left in their own homes, the foster children were:

- Less likely to hold a job for at least three years.
- More likely to become pregnant as teenagers.
- More likely to be involved in the juvenile justice system.
- More likely to be arrested as young adults.

Source: National Coalition for Child Protection Reform

A year later, Doyle did another study of 23,000 cases to find which children were more likely to be arrested as adults once they aged out of the system. In that study, children left in their own homes also fared better.

A University of Minnesota study tracked outcomes of foster children from birth to age 9. They compared children in foster care and children under similar circumstances and found that the children left in their own homes also did noticeably better.

University of Florida researchers looked at two groups of mothers who abused drugs during pregnancy. One group kept their babies, and the other had them taken away.

After six months, they tested the babies using the usual measures like rolling over, sitting up, and reaching out.

"Typically, the children left with their birth mothers did better. For the foster children, the separation from their mothers was more toxic than the cocaine," wrote Richard Wexler, Executive Director of the National Coalition for Child Protection Reform.

The effects of foster care on older children aren't any better.

Consider the findings of a 2005 study in Oregon and Washington conducted by the Casey Family Programs and Harvard University. The subjects were 659 young adults between the ages of 20 and 33 who had been placed in family foster care between 1988 and 1998.

Richard Wexler is a noted child welfare advocate and executive director of the National Coalition for Child Protection Reform.

"The only way to fix foster care is to have less of it," Wexler says.

Overall: Over half of the alumni (54.4%) had current mental health problems, while less than one-quarter of the general population (22.1%) had current mental health problems.

Post-traumatic stress disorder (PTSD): The prevalence of PTSD within the previous 12 months was significantly higher among alumni (25.2%) than among the general U.S. population (4.0%). As a comparison, American war veterans have lower rates of PTSD (Vietnam: 15%; Afghanistan: 6%; and Iraq: 12% to 13%). PTSD, depression, and social phobia may be the most significant mental health conditions of alumni.

Major depression: The prevalence of major depression within the previous 12 months was significantly higher among alumni (20.1%) than among the general population (10.2%).

"There are cases in which the trauma of removal, bad as it is, is less bad than leaving the child in her or his own home," Wexler explained. But there are relatively few of those severe cases. Wexler said multiple studies show that the only way to fix foster care is to have less of it.

The state legislature could definitely do better than it does. Rep. Gloria Johnson and Senator Heidi Campbell introduced legislation in 2020 to cap caseloads at 20 per worker and deal with other problems at DCS. Three years later, the bill has still not passed. In February 2024, Johnson's latest bill to put a cap on workloads failed in the House Children and Families Subcommittee.

Plenty of bad child welfare bills did pass. Budget hearings happen at the end of every calendar year when DCS leaders have to defend their poor record in front of the people who sign their paychecks. Invariably, they ask for more money. They always get it. (See Chapter Six.)

Mom gives up 3 kids in custody fight to get baby back from DCS

DCS Used Custody Fight to Remove Kids in Two Counties and then accused Mom of drug use.

The Lassiter/West blended family L-R, Althea (8), Cullen (4), Luke, Boston (15), Abby holding Lucy, and Sullivan (10)

NASHVILLE, TN – No mother should have to choose between her three older kids and her 4-week-old baby DCS took away from her in October 2020. But that was the hard choice Abby West had to make.

"I think the goal of giving me an attorney in the divorce was to get me to sign the settlement agreement," said West, mother of 4. The judge awarded West $5,000 to hire a lawyer and $300 in monthly support during the divorce trial. The agreement West ended up signing is not in line with Tennessee case law that gives parents equal time with their children after a divorce.

But it meant West could start having parenting time with her three older children, so she signed it. She now gets them for only 104 days out of the year, while her ex-husband has them for 261 days.

"Three months later, DCS non-suited Lucy's case," West told me. DCS dropped its prosecution of West after snatching baby Lucy and then harassing her mom for 10 months while the divorce was underway.

DCS acted like a meat hunter, closing in on wounded prey.

"Non-suited" is the closest thing you'll ever get to an apology from DCS for wrongfully taking your children. When divorcing parents can't agree on terms, and DCS gets involved, it usually takes Mom's side; sometimes it takes Dad's; sometimes DCS takes the kids away from both parents.

I reported about DCS manipulation of police, hospitals, judges, and court proceedings in Tennessee Juvenile and District courts. (See Black Father Fights to Be a Dad at the end of this chapter.)

In a Montgomery County DCS case, Ralph Ulysses has gotten two judges to recuse themselves because they refused to hear a motion to remove a restraining order that should have been heard by October 2020 and was still in effect a year later. Because of this, Ulysses has not seen his daughter since Feb 2021.

Ulysses hoped Juvenile Court Judge Wayne Shelton would finally vacate the restraining order and change the venue to Davidson County. Abby West has already been there, and it was no easy walk in the park.

"My divorce and custody battle definitely had an effect on Lucy's case. That could be why DCS responded so dramatically and rushed in the way they did," West said.

The DCS case against West started on September 11, 2020. DCS investigator Sylvia Vanderbilt went to West's home in Donelson to tell her that traces of methamphetamine were found in Lucy's umbilical cord.

On October 2, Child Protective Services (CPS) investigator Teena Jones visited West at home. It checked out fine. West peed into a cup and signed an agreement not to be around drug users and to be subject to random drug screens.

Lucy Lassiter at two weeks old. Two weeks later, DCS took her.

Jones told West the case would be closed. But it was only the beginning. On October 5, CPSI Alexandrea Hickson came to the home, and Mom again peed into another cup. Hickson told her that it was positive for THC. West explained to Hickson that she bought the CBD over the counter. The drug screen showed traces of THC, and even small amounts can inhibit development in nursing babies. Once Hickson made an issue of it, West stopped taking CBD.

Sometime between October 2 and October 5, DCS learned West's partner, Luke Lassiter, baby Lucy's father, had a DCS case in Hickman County. They probably heard about it from Adam West, Abby's ex. He called DCS the day before Lucy was taken.

Baby Lucy was taken into custody around midnight in a Berry Hill Wendy's parking lot on October 6, 2020. She was just one month old. Family Law Attorney Connie Reguli filmed the whole thing. (See https://youtu.be/bTjVf-hgjuE)

"You're going to see what a real government kidnapping looks like... taking babies for profit," Reguli announces into her cell phone camera and then turns and walks into the parking lot where several police squad cars are blocking West's car. Lucy's dad, Luke Lassiter, is standing by his truck.

When first questioned, a young cop is unclear why they are even there. When questioned who Reguli is she answers that she's the father's attorney.

"I do a lot of cases with DCS... this child snatching stuff, I don't tolerate it," she tells the cop. One by one, Reguli talks to four officers and asks them why they are blocking them in. One of them answers it's a missing child.

"She's not missing. She's right there with her Mom," Reguli tells him.

The police immediately got on their cell phones but couldn't' reach DCS and Reguli tells one of the officers that DCS never called her and she represents Lucy's Dad, Luke Lassiter. Thirty minutes go by before DCS caseworker Kimberly White shows up with a non-exigent removal order—which means it's not an emergency. But DCS was obviously in a rush to take the baby.

Reguli gets on the phone with DCS supervisor Sylvia Vanderbilt. She asks her what the allegations are and if DCS held a safety placement meeting with Lucy's parents. They are required by policy to have such a meeting. Vanderbilt hangs up on her.

And then "under the color of law" baby Lucy is taken into custody. "This is what they do," Reguli said again, speaking into her camera. "And they get the cops to come out and help them...they violate a lot of constitutional rights; I'll tell you that." The video of the event has had 214,000 views on YouTube thus far.

DCS Case Against Lucy's Mom and Cullen's Dad: drugs they didn't take

West once did have a drug problem. She relapsed in 2017 and realized she needed to do something about it. She sent the three kids to their Dad, got clean, and told the Tribune she hasn't used for three years and has been clean for 10 of the last 15 years.

But she didn't trust DCS or the lab they used, so she had a hair follicle test done on October 6. A week later, it came back negative. By then, DCS had already taken Lucy. Hair follicle drug tests involve removing a small hair sample for laboratory testing. Results can show if a person has been using certain drugs or prescription medications in the previous 3 months. It can detect cannabis, amphetamines, and more.

"Over the course of the nine months, I took 32 tests. They were all negative for drugs. Two were considered positive because a protein called Creatine was found in two of the samples," she said.

West disputed the positive findings. She had stopped taking CBD and took her own test that was negative just a few days before DCS tested her again, and they said she was positive. They kept bringing it up over the next few months and Magistrate Carlton Lewis ordered West to take drug tests with Aver health. She wasn't taking drugs, so slowly, West made headway against DCS's allegations.

Dr. Ann Charvat, West's Mom, had custody of Lucy. She testified twice at hearings in Juvenile Court. Magistrate Lewis seemed intimidated by her.

Charvat spent a career helping people, has a PhD in sociology, and has been an expert witness in more than 100 capital cases. She is no slouch and Dr. Charvat was Lucy's grandmother. She was not the least bit intimidated by Magistrate Lewis. Lewis fought with Charvat and, at one point during the proceedings, called her a liar.

Given his hostility and obvious bias in favor of DCS, Lewis eventually recused himself in May 2021. On May 18, 2021, West signed the divorce agreement in Circuit Court. In June, West filed a motion for unsupervised visitation in Juvenile Court so her mother, Charvat, could go home to Illinois.

Grandma Ann Charvat with Abby West and her four kids.

Lassiter filed a joint discovery motion for West, Charvat, and himself in Davidson County Juvenile Court. Family law attorney and video vigilante Connie Reguli represented Charvat.

DCS wanted no part of Reguli. She would have cut them into a thousand pieces for repeatedly misleading West and Lassiter, running roughshod over them in four different courtrooms in two different counties, and all the while violating DCS protocols with impunity. DCS can dish it out, but they can't take it.

On July 1, 2021, DCS submitted a motion to Juvenile Court Judge Sheila Calloway to non-suit the case.

77

Calloway granted it. It meant DCS was throwing in the towel, and after ten months of hell, Abby, Luke, and Baby Lucy could finally go home.

In October 2021, West filed a civil rights complaint in federal district court against ten DCS employees, the MNPD, Vanderbilt Medical Center, and Averhealth, the lab-testing company.

Luke Lassiter Had One Good Judge

Lassiter is appealing his DCS case in Hickman County. He gets his son, Cullen, now 4, every other weekend. He wants him back full-time. Cullen's uncle, Grant Crawford, is willing to give Lassiter custody, but DCS won't let him, and Lassiter can't get his custody petition heard.

Family Law Attorney Connie Reguli with Lucy Lassiter.

Hickman County has just one Juvenile Court judge, Amy Puckett, and she has recused herself from the case. Lassiter received notice from the Tennessee Supreme Court appointing Judge Douglas Chapman from Maury County to his appeal case.

"So right now, my custody petition is floating in the wind," he told me.

The case started in November 2019 in Hickman County when Cullen's maternal grandmother and his Mom's brother, Grant Crawford, picked up 2-year-old Cullen from daycare while Cullen's Mom,

Christina Crawford, was at work. Without talking to Cullen's Mom or Dad, they gave him to DCS, which put him in foster care. They had reason to take such drastic action. Though Crawford worked, she was a heroin addict. Lassiter had been out of the house for a year, and Crawford didn't let him see Cullen during all that time.

"They coerced us in court," Lassiter said. Cullen's grandmother didn't want to become a foster parent. "If you don't sign temporary legal custody over to Grant (Luke's Uncle), he'll be placed in a foster home and be lost in the system," DCS attorney Keller Mizzell warned Lassiter.

Somebody in the gaggle of DCS workers gathered outside the courtroom pressured Lassiter to sign the custody papers, threatening, "We are going to send him to some foster home, maybe in Memphis." There's nothing like a little race-baiting to put the fear of God into a reluctant defendant terrified by what might happen to his child.

DCS took Cullen because his hair follicle tested positive for heroin. But DCS can't terminate parental rights unless both parents are convicted of severe abuse or neglect. Only Mom used heroin. Lassiter doesn't. DCS knew that, so they framed him for smoking pot while Christina was pregnant with Cullen three years before. They had no evidence, but that didn't stop DCS.

Christina and Cullen had tested positive for THC when he was born in 2017. DCS found the case unsubstantiated and closed it at the time. Three years later, DCS resurrected the "unsubstantiated" finding to file a new petition against Cullen's mom for severe abuse and neglect, this time naming Lassiter as a respondent. It was not about the mom. She was out of the picture since Cullen had been removed from her care 2 years earlier. Now, the focus was on Lassiter. DCS wanted him out of the way.

Lucy Lassiter, Abby West, and Luke Lassiter, Halloween 2021.

Lassiter said he was never asked to take a drug test.

"There were no allegations against me. Not a single one. But somehow, now I'm guilty," he said.

"I'm a severe child abuser because my son's Mom smoked a joint while she was pregnant, and that's the allegation I'm fighting in the Court of Appeals," Lassiter reported.

Juvenile Court Judge Puckett let them get away with that. She forced Lassiter to agree to random drug screens in order to see Cullen every other weekend. They used the same tactic with Abby West. It was unwarranted in both cases.

"I've never failed one. I've passed every single drug screen they've given me, including a nail follicle test," he said. Even so, DCS wouldn't let Lassiter visit with Cullen until Circuit Court Judge Michael Spitzer found DCS in contempt. After that, he got Cullen every other weekend

In his appeal, it should have been easy to show DCS decided Lassiter was guilty by association. His court-appointed lawyer made no oral argument, and Lassiter lost the appeal.

For two years, Cullen had been visiting with his dad every other weekend but now he is not allowed to. All too often, judges let DCS get away with wrongfully taking children and treating parents with utter contempt.

Judges either cooperate willingly or acquiesce because they are afraid to make waves. Judge Michael Spitzer is one judge who stood up to DCS bullying and found them in contempt. When a judge holds a private citizen in contempt, they go to jail.

When DCS gets found in contempt, they just shrug it off and keep on snatching babies and terrorizing families. It doesn't change their behavior.

•••

The next story is about a father who has joint custody but has not seen his daughter in three years. One judge placed a temporary restraining order on the father, and another allowed the Mom to move out of state with the girl.

Dad, who is black, has "visited" her ten times via video link at a therapist's office.

"It's mostly a lot of lying," he told me. Mom has turned his daughter against him. It's called parental alienation. "You never get over it," he told me.

Black Father Fights To Be a Dad

Ralph Ulysses and his 11-year-old daughter have not seen or spoken to each other since February 2021.

CLARKSVILLE, TN – Genevieve was eleven years old and couldn't legally speak for herself. When she turned 12, she was able to tell a judge that her mother abuses her. Genevieve could have testified how her mom committed her to Cumberland Hall Hospital in Hopkinsville, Kentucky because she was "suicidal and homicidal." But she never told that story in court.

"My daughter wasn't having a psychiatric crisis. My daughter was reacting to abuse," said the girl's dad, Ralph Ulysses.

On September 18, 2020, Genevieve's mother, Christina Blankenship, took her to the Tennova Hospital in Clarksville. They found opiates in her blood. According to Ulysses, the girl told the triage nurse that her mother was abusing her. Mom reported that Genevieve threatened to kill her and commit suicide.

"Mom was using her power as an adult to tell my daughter's story to make it seem like she was the victim," Ulysses said.

Dr. Srikar Koranam placed the girl in a psychiatric hold. Youth Villages, a DCS contractor, gave Genevieve two evaluations within 24 hours. Both concluded she did not need to be committed but should be released to her dad "for respite."

Doctors can override social workers, and Dr. Koranam did just that. But no mental institution in Tennessee would take Genevieve because two separate evaluations concluded she wasn't crazy.

On September 22, 2020, Tennova Hospital transported the girl to Cumberland Hall Hospital in Hopkinsville, Kentucky, where Mom had her committed. Cumberland Hall diagnosed Genevieve with disruptive deregulation disorder, that means she couldn't control her emotions.

"The problem with that diagnosis is that my daughter spends 7 hours a day at school, 5 days a week. 35 hours a week, and not once in 6 years has she ever be in trouble for not being able to control herself," Ulysses stated.

"The only place where she can't control her moods is in her mother's household. I have no problem with her being 'dis-regulated,'" he said. Genevieve had no problems at summer camp or when he brought her to work. Ulysses works for a large insurance company as a senior insurance underwriter. Mom is unemployed.

"Why hasn't anybody pressed the play button?"

–Ralph Ulysses says Mom's Recording of a Murder Plot is fiction.

On September 25, 2020, while Genevieve was still at Cumberland Hall, Mom took out a restraining order

83

against Dad, claiming she had a recording of a conversation between father and daughter discussing a murder plot to shoot Mom and her husband, Matthew Blankenship. "Preposterous and absurd," Ulysses said.

When I interviewed Ulysses, he asked, "Why hasn't anybody pressed the play button?" Ulysses said the recording, if it exists, would disprove Cristina's claim of a plot. A year later, the matter was still not heard in the juvenile court.

For more than a year, Genevieve and her dad have been living a waking nightmare. DCS has tried to pathologize both the girl and her father.

Ulysses has filed 14 referrals for child abuse with DCS that they failed to investigate. Ulysses said Clarksville Team Coordinator Heather Jeffries personally buried two of them.

"They had to cover up their inability to look into child abuse before it became bad enough to put a child into a mental institution. They participated in the abuse themselves," he said.

DCS claimed Genevieve never made statements about being abused. They said Dad was making allegations out of the blue.

"They said I'm disgruntled, difficult, blah, blah, blah," he said. DCS was parroting what Genevieve's mom and her husband had told them.

"But when they released their records, it turns out my daughter had been making these allegations. She made them to DCS; she made them to Youth Villages; she made them in school, and DCS ignored all of this."

Heather Jeffries heads up Foster Care in the DCS Clarksville office like Angel Miller runs Investigations. Multiple witnesses said Jeffries and Miller terrorize, bully, and harass their subordinates.

"Heather Jeffries has quarterbacked this entire thing," Ulysses told the Tribune. She took over the case last year when Cumberland Hall wanted to discharge Genevieve for her own good. Jeffries pressured them to keep her there longer.

"The entire time my daughter was at Cumberland, she refused to visit with her mom, and she alleged abuse almost nonstop so DCS couldn't release her to her mom," Ulysses said. Because of the bogus restraining order, she couldn't be released to her dad either.

> *"Heather Jeffries has quarterbacked this entire thing."*
>
> –Ralph Ulysses

The case was becoming troublesome. Jeffries tried to send her to an aunt in Florida. On October 14, 2020, DCS asked Juvenile Court Judge Tim Barnes to place the girl with her maternal aunt. The aunt drove to Clarksville from Orlando, expecting to be given custody on that same day.

After Ulysses objected, Barnes blocked the out-of-state placement, ruling it would be illegal to do exactly what it looked like it was---an attempted kidnapping by Mom and DCS's Jeffries to send Genevieve away.

Barnes took the girl into state custody on November 2, 2020, and two DCS caseworkers drove her to Parkridge Valley Hospital in Chattanooga. Their records indicate it was an initial admission, but it was Genevieve's second commitment in less than two months.

Parkridge didn't know about the girl's previous time in Cumberland Hall, and DCS didn't tell them. In fact, DCS claims it has no case records from the time Tennova found opiates in Genevieve's blood until the time she entered Parkridge. Parkridge Valley records show she was admitted because "her parents are worried about her."

"That's utter and complete bull," Ulysses said.

"They want the record to start at Parkridge, so they control the narrative," he told me.

Dad described Genevieve as a gifted child with a high IQ. In six weeks, she ran up a $35,600 bill at Cumberland Hall, which Blankenship couldn't pay; TennCare wouldn't pay it either because it was out of state, and Ulysses' insurance wouldn't cover it because there was no medical necessity and no prior authorization for the commitment.

"The judge, along with DCS, they have these outside providers that they work with, and the state can be billed for it," he told me.

DCS paid Parkridge Valley Hospital $9.2 million in 2020. While she was incarcerated there, Genevieve was treated by therapist Christy Belew, and Genevieve told her dad that the therapist tried to brainwash her into accepting her fate—and willingly go back to her Mom's house—or face indefinite detention. Genevieve held out for six weeks. She finally acquiesced and went to her Mom's house on December 17, 2020.

Youth Villages	$81.2 million
Omni	$62.4 million
Keys Group Holdings	$35.5 million
Camelot	$33 million

Top Four DCS Contractors in 2020

On February 24, 2021, Genevieve was talking to her Dad on the phone, and she asked him," "What am I going to do if they remove you from my life?" He answered, "I would die before I would let that happen."

By this time, Dad had a pretty good idea of who he was up against. Mom was conspiring with DCS; DCS lawyer Margaret Parker was conspiring with Judge Barnes and the guardian at litem, Erin Poland. They were all trying to keep Ulysses away from his daughter and declare him a threat to her well-being.

But the record shows he was not a threat

On February 25, 2021, Ulysses had a trove of subpoenaed records to show Judge Barnes what Jeffries and her minions had been up to. He hoped Barnes would at least dismiss the restraining order so he could go back to 50-50 parenting time. But his motion to vacate the restraining order never came up at the hearing.

(Panel of Three) Erin Poland (left) was appointed Guardian ad Litem by Juvenile Court Judge Tim Barnes (right). DCS attorney Margaret Parker with unidentified Texas Stars fan.

"They were backtracking to use the legal process to clean up their own mess and scapegoat me for their missteps," he said.

DCS did not release two months of records crucial to his case, but they sent Ulysses's records from a different case instead. Ulysses sent those to Representative Mary Littleton, Chairwoman of the Children and Family Affairs Subcommittee that oversees DCS operations in the Tennessee legislature.

When the Feb 25th hearing began, DCS attorney Parker immediately started attacking Ulysses. She told Judge Barnes that he violated HIPAA regulations. Barnes agreed with Parker even though it was obvious that DCS had released the private information. Neither DCS nor Barnes liked Ulysses blowing the whistle on them.

The HIPAA accusation was a red herring but effective because Barnes did not take up the motion to vacate the restraining order. Cases involving protection and restraining orders are usually heard within two weeks. More than a year went by, and the order was still in place.

"They are doing everything they can to keep it from coming up," Ulysses said.

Ulysses is a lot like a determined boxer who keeps getting rabbit-punched by a dirty fighter, and the referee does nothing to stop it. But Ulysses wouldn't go down without a fight.

And he managed to win a round. Ulysses filed a motion asking Judge Barnes to recuse himself. He had plenty to say about the judge's biased mishandling of the case. According to Ulysses, Barnes presided over a kangaroo court with paid informants from DCS helping him do their dirty work, and he called him on it.

Barnes did recuse himself, and a new judge, Sharon Massey Grimes, took over the case. Ulysses wanted her to vacate the restraining order, but Grimes refused. Grimes presided over just one hearing, and then veteran Judge Wayne Shelton took the case in January 2022. In June, Shelton granted Christina's motion to relocate to Florida. Dad objected as the motion was not filed with the clerk. He wanted to reschedule the hearing.

"There's nothing you can do about it," Shelton told him. I retire in 14 days." And that, as they say, was that. Father and daughter have yet to be reunited.

•••

Secrets and Lies

A Tennessee Comptroller's audit in 2020 and a performance update in 2022 found many deficiencies in DCS operations, some going back years. The gist was that DCS is incompetent, not venal. In truth, it is both.

A culture of lying permeates DCS from top to bottom, a culture hell-bent on protecting itself at all costs. DCS Commissioner Jennifer Nichols went before a joint legislative committee on February 9, 2022. "The majority of children who enter DCS custody, actually about 80%, are reunited with their families," Nichols testified.

But Tennessee's reunification rate was between 55.2%-57.8% in the years 2015-2019, according to the federal Adoption and Foster Care Analysis and Reporting System (AFCARS). According to Child Trends, the most recent reunification rate in Tennessee is 47%. So Nichols looked those legislators straight in the eye and lied to their faces. Those lawmakers didn't blink and accepted her words as gospel.

Following the example set by their bosses, caseworkers routinely lie under oath so kids remain in custody long enough to terminate parental rights. Reguli has been watching this phenomenon go on for more than 20 years. "DCS employees do not face any consequences for false testimony, false reports, or false affidavits. They are more likely to get promoted," she says.

Politicians regularly hold hearings with DCS officials about the challenges they face. The tone is always reverential, and they flatter the brass with compliments about what a difficult job they are doing and how fortunate the state's neglected children are to have their protection. All too often, it's hogwash. (See Muzzled in Chapter Six)

These hearings are mostly for show and generally follow some bad news about the department. Things are admittedly bad but supposedly getting better, especially with all the new programs DCS has initiated or re-tooled. The Governor has put more money into the DCS budget next year—even though he fired the last Commissioner for incompetence. And so on.

Governor Bill Lee appointed DCS Commissioner Margie Quin in July 2022. Quin testified to legislators twice in late 2022, showing just the right blend of horror at the department's failures and the sober face of a new sheriff in town. The upshot: she asked for a $300 million increase in the DCS budget for FY 23-24. She got it and more.

How Parenting Plans Break the Parent-Child Bond

Sometimes, DCS tries to get parents to sign a safety plan before they take a child. If they won't sign, DCS goes to a Juvenile Court to get an emergency removal order. Once DCS takes custody of a child and a judge rules they have good reason, DCS makes parents sign a permanency plan. If parents complete the plan requirements, DCS is supposed to return the children. Permanency Plans sometimes require drug counseling, attending school, or parenting classes. Parents have to attend Family Planning Meetings with caseworkers who measure their progress. The rehabilitation is supposed to lead to family reunification. It frequently doesn't.

Reguli says the state turns days into weeks, and weeks into months, keeping children in the homes of strangers often for more than a year before they even have a trial. "This is a fundamental problem, and over time, things have only gotten worse in many states," she reported. Parents run like hamsters on a wheel to complete some program or other, and sometimes the same one twice. This "rehabilitation" is positively Orwellian because DCS officials keep moving the goalposts, putting up more obstacles, and many parents never regain custody of their children regardless of what they do.

Some caseworkers violate DCS policies and play fast and loose with the rules in order to keep control of the children they take. After fifteen months in custody, DCS can sue to terminate parental rights. States get a federal reward for every adoption they finalize. If a child is Title IV-E eligible under the Social Security Act, the federal government reimburses the state for at least half of the adoption costs. In 2017, Tennessee received assistance payments of $467,500 for 1,260 adoptions ($371 average). In 2021, it received $, 1,349,500 for 1,201 adoptions ($1,123 average), and so it goes.

"They may not be arrested for it – but they should be." – Jon Hageman, foster father.

Chapter Four: Where Do All Those Kids Go?

They go to a foster home or group home, back to their birth family or a relative, to a congregate facility with other high-needs children, or they go to a locked detention center or jail. Some run away and are never heard from again. DCS was created in 1996 by an executive order combining child welfare and juvenile justice services in Tennessee. Six agencies that hadn't worked together before, or previously shared information, became one big inefficient agency.

In 2000, Children's Rights, a national non-profit that advocates for children in foster care, filed a class action lawsuit, claiming over-utilization of emergency shelters and congregate care facilities, untrained caseworkers, high levels of placement instability, inadequate efforts to achieve permanency, inadequate educational services and disparate treatment of African American children in foster care.

The Brian A. class action lawsuit was settled in 2001, which resulted in broad-based system reform and an infusion of significant new state funding. The settlement agreement required the state to accomplish the following:

- Decrease the lengths of stay of children in state custody;
- Decrease the number and rate of children re-entering state custody;
- Reduce the number of placements moves experienced by children in state custody;
- Reduce the number and rate of children being restricted from their own families, communities, and family placements; and

- Reduce all disparities associated with race/ethnicity, gender, or age.

Federal oversight of DCS officially ended in 2017 but DCS had effectively been back in control since 2010. Six or thirteen years later, depending on when you start counting, DCS is not in compliance with any of the five court-mandated outcomes agreed upon in 2001.

Ira Lustbader, the lead attorney for Children's Rights in the Brian A case, defended the settlement and told me he had no plans to re-open the case.

In Tennessee, DCS has more than 5,000 foster families and group homes. It is constantly looking for more foster homes and foster parents. Some foster homes are mom-and-pop operations that pay off their mortgage with the money they get from DCS. Every two years DCS does a reassessment and inspects them.

Some people foster kids for years, while others stop, sometimes after adopting them. Managing foster homes for DCS is like filling a bathtub without a stopper. With more children coming into the system than leaving it, DCS can't always find a suitable placement, so they would put kids in church basements, one of twelve DCS regional offices, or at the Davy Crockett Tower in downtown Nashville--- places less appropriate than where many of those kids came from. Many of them are teens with special needs. At a time in their lives when traumatized kids need the most consistency, the revolving door of adults in their lives and the high turnover of staff only adds to their trauma.

Private contractors in Tennessee are a significant and growing part of DCS operations. They charged DCS $14 million for services to foster children in 2021 and $355 million to house them. Non-profits like Youth Villages are big players, and they have partnered with DCS for years with very mixed reviews. In October 2017, DCS and Youth Villages entered into a 5-year, $15 million contract to provide intensive in-home services and assessments to its foster youth. In contrast, DCS spent just $3 million on family services for the entire state.

In late 2022, newly appointed Commissioner Margie Quin asked for an additional $11.4 million in her fiscal year 2024 budget to hire private case managers. The total budget request was $1.4 billion, the largest since DCS was created in 1996.

DCS requested $156 million in new funding for fiscal year 2024, which began July 1, 2023. The budget request includes $15.8 million to increase case manager salaries, a $30 million increase for contract providers, $5.7 million for adoption services, and $7.4 million for "prevention" services. Whether those services will be free, voluntary, and offered to families who have not lost custody of their children is unclear.

In its 2021-22 Annual Report, the first under Quin's leadership, DCS talks about compliance with The Family First Prevention Services Act of 2018. During the fiscal year 2022, an In-Home policy and practice workgroup "re-emerged," and an In-Home Resource Linkage program (RLC) was offered in all 95 counties. The purpose and goal of RLC is "to safeguard and enhance the welfare of children, preserve family life, and prevent harm and abuse to children by strengthening the natural abilities of families." The report noted that their advocacy and coordination work is "paying off," and they are "reaping the seeds that they have sown."

It goes on: "For each month of FY 21-22, an average of 146 Family Support Services (FSS) cases and Family Crisis Intervention Program (FCIP) cases opened in the state every month. An average of 240 FSS and FCIP cases closed in the state every month. July 2021 had 1851 FSS and FCIP cases in the state, and July 2022 had 1546 FSS and FCIP cases in the state. The supportive services provided to these families reduced custodial episodes and trauma that children experience when removed from their homes."

With all the jargon and acronyms in play, it's hard to understand precisely what all this means. The number of cases from 2021 to 2022 decreased, a good thing because it means the number of children taken into custody also decreased. But in reality, between July 2021 and July 2022, 305 families stopped getting services.

It all sounds good on paper, but who received what services from whom and at what cost is not specified. How families were chosen and how DCS identified them is vague, and no concrete examples of prevention were provided.

I asked DCS several times to identify the funding sources for family services and whether the families who received services had children in custody already or were at risk from having them taken. They didn't respond.

A large chunk of the DCS budget increase will be devoted to a new technology system. Quin told legislators that $69.3 million was needed to overhaul an outdated online system that is responsible for tracking tens of thousands of foster children, foster parents, and provider's cases. Quin said the state was already paying millions to maintain the outdated system called TFACTS. It was put into service in 2010 but never worked right. (See Chapter Eleven)

Is Anybody Else Watching?

The department provides different levels of care, up to and including one locked facility for youth deemed too violent or too disturbed to live safely with their parents, a foster family, or in a group home.

Less than 200 youth are in secured facilities, a small percentage of the 6,000+ children DCS takes into custody every year, and an even smaller percentage of the total number—about 9,000--if you count holdovers from previous years. So, yes, there are at-risk youth in the system, but a very small percentage of all the children in custody overall.

A 2022 state comptroller audit found DCS operations woefully deficient at the Wilder Youth Development Center. Wilder is the only hardware-secure facility for teenage boys who were found guilty of two violent or other serious crimes. The majority of them are Black with disabilities. In recent years, there have been multiple riots and escape attempts at Wilder, and the facility has been decimated by turnover.

Dozens of juvenile inmates broke out of their pods one Sunday night in September 2019. They tore up the facility, causing $100,000 in damages. Eleven 18-year-olds were arrested. Several others were moved to unknown locations.

A small team led by Attorney Jack Derryberry, Legal Director of Disability Rights Tennessee, investigated Wilder after the 2019 riot. Their April 2022 report, Designed to Fail, concluded guards routinely abused and mistreated the teenagers. Wilder used to house between 80-120 youth, but as of May 2022, it held only 32. DCS did not respond when asked where they placed some of those Wilder inmates.

In September 2023, the department announced plans to rebuild Wilder and construct a new youth center in Nashville. The new facilities are expected to increase the number of beds by more than 150 across the state.

In 2020, investigative reporter Jeremy Finley interviewed six families who said DCS withheld information about children with histories of violence or sexual behavior.

"They may not be arrested for it – but they should be," said Jon Hageman, a foster father. He told Finley that when a teenager was placed in his home, the state provided a checklist citing he had no history of destruction of property or violence. Not long after the 17-year-old came to live with Hageman's family, he flew into a rage, breaking a TV, punching a door, and smashing dishes. Hageman no longer trusts DCS because they lied to him.

Finley also interviewed a former DCS employee who said youth with violent histories were routinely placed with unsuspecting foster families who were not trained to handle high-risk placements. He told Finley that he came forward after years of seeing how DCS treated foster parents. "It was very disturbing to me," he said. Several foster parents have complained publicly about DCS, while others are too afraid to speak out.

Runaways

State and federal data indicate children in foster care run away from placements fairly frequently—more often than their peers in the general population run away from home.

According to the Adoption and Foster Care Analysis and Reporting System (AFCARS), approximately 402,000 children were in foster care in 2013. State agencies reported 4,500 of those children as having run away (1%). The majority of those who were identified as having run away from foster care were between the ages of 12 and 17.

These national statistics show:

- Most of the runaway foster youth entered care after they turned 12 years old.
- Most children who run away from their foster care placement have been placed over 3 times.
- Girls are more likely to run away from care than boys.
- Runaways are more likely to be African American or Latino.

Most runaway youths (regardless of whether they ran away from their biological parents or foster parents) struggle with substance abuse and mental health issues.

Youth who identify as LGBTQ are more likely than their peers living in permanent care to run away from a foster care placement or be kicked out of their placement by their foster parent.

In 2018, 437,283 children were in foster care in the U.S., and 4,247 of them ran away (slightly less than 1%). In 2020 in Tennessee, 8,839 children were in custody, in 2021, 8,713 were in state custody. How many foster kids ran away in those years? I asked DCS but did not get a reply.

In April 2023, the Colorado Sun reported that 20-30 kids run away from foster care in Colorado each year and are not found. Their child welfare cases were closed. A U.S. Department of Health and Human Services audit of Missouri, released in 2021, found that in 2019, 978 children went missing from the state's foster care system. Nearly half of the cases reviewed weren't reported to either law enforcement or the National Center for Missing & Exploited Children, according to the Missouri Independent.

Researchers from the University of Denver's Evaluation and Action Lab say a key reason they run is that they are looking for "connectedness," often by running to family members. Also, they are living in "fight, flight or freeze" mode, a constant state of stress.

The study found children are typically "dysregulated at the time of a run" and can't access the part of the brain that makes rational decisions or understand consequences. Some run to find drugs or alcohol, often a way of coping and medicating themselves. Many run to a place of familiarity, the study found.

The KIDS COUNT Data Center says that while absent from care, youth are at high risk of being sexually or physically victimized, engaging in delinquent behavior, using drugs or alcohol, or being the victims of human trafficking.

Among the 4.2 million youth and young adults who experience homelessness in the U.S. each year, many are runaways from birth families and foster homes. In March 2023, the National Conference of State Legislatures reported that 700,000 homeless youth are unaccompanied minors—meaning they are not part of a family or accompanied by a parent or guardian.

The next story is about caseworker Reba Terry lying to the family of a black boy and, conspiring behind their backs to let the white foster parents adopt him. It also shows how DCS uses parenting plans to manipulate families and then do whatever they please.

•••

DCS Trolls Black Babies For Cash

Connie Reguli defends Black family in custody case.

Loren Mitchell with her two sons, Michael and Skyler.

NASHVILLE, TN– Fourth Circuit Court Judge Phil Smith and Department of Child Services (DCS) attorney Shay Jolly took away an African American baby from his family and gave him to a white foster family in Old Hickory, a Nashville suburb set along the Cumberland River.

The State of Tennessee will get at least $5,000 from the federal government for such a move—a bonus every state gets when someone adopts a neglected or abused child who is not related by blood. The adoption incentive can be as high as $6,000 per child. But if a child is placed with a relative the state gets no bonus.

Skyler Mitchell is 17 months old. But In September 2020, when he was three months old DCS took Skyler from his mother, Loren Mitchell. Skyler was placed into foster care with Adron Wayne Ray III and his wife, Abigail Bargatze Ray, who are white. They have two children of their own.

Under DCS policy, foster parents are required to "work with the birth parents" and are prohibited from

101

seeking a termination of parental rights and adoption on their own. It's in their contract.

Loren Mitchell, Sklyer's mother, is mentally disabled and cannot care for Skyler. Her older son, Michael, 7, lives with his Aunt Angela Moyo Jr. and his paternal grandmother, Angela Moyo Sr.

They want to keep and raise Skyler, and they are qualified to do so. Under the rules governing the placement of abandoned or neglected children, Skyler's relatives, who are also African American, have top priority to become his caretakers.

Adron Ray and his wife Abigail are Skyler's foster parents who are trying to adopt him and terminate Loren Mitchell's parental rights.

On September 18, 2020, Angela Moyo Jr. appeared in Davidson County Juvenile Court to discuss Skyler's placement for the first time.

"I told them all that Skyler is loved, he is wanted, and that I was doing everything possible in order to get him," Moyo Jr. said.

That meant getting a new apartment ready for both the boys and herself. Her niece, Loren, was on board with that plan and so was DCS, supposedly.

On February 10, 2021, Moyo Jr. emailed caseworker Reba Terry to tell her she had found a home for the boys. Moyo Jr. said she emailed, called, and texted the caseworker to schedule a home inspection.

"Reba Terry is the DCS social worker who should have expedited the relative placement," said Connie Reguli, Moyo's attorney. But instead, Terry dragged her feet for six weeks. There was plenty DCS should have been doing to reunify the family.

Angela Moyo Jr. was denied custody of Skyler Mitchell although she is caretaker to his half-brother Michael.

According to the Tennessee Department of Children's Services Child and Family Service Plan, DCS supports relatives "who take on the responsibility of raising related children when birth parents are unable to do so"

"Kinship placements and the kinship resource home approval process will continue to go through modifications to improve the timeliness to approval and to provide financial assistance within a shorter period of time. There is a drive to increase the number of Kin/Relative placements within each region and statewide," reads part of the service plan. In Skyler's case, DCS not only failed to do that, but it also failed to deliver the following services it is required to offer children under the age of five:

1. A series of case reviews to target cases for needed work toward permanency and to ensure the length of stay is reduced. Permanency Reviews are conducted on all cases where children have been in custody for over 6 months.

2. A special 9-Month Legal Review to ensure casework activities are on track toward reunification or shifting gears toward alternate permanency arrangements, including TPR (termination of parental rights).

3. DCS strives to ensure kinship placements for all children in DCS custody. Oftentimes, relatives are better equipped to care for younger children as their needs are different from older children.

On March 23, the fosters, DCS caseworker Terry and her supervisor, Tonya Russell, Angela Moyo Jr. (Skyer's aunt), and Loren Mitchell (Skylar's birth mother) held a progress meeting by phone about what remained to be done before Angela could become Skyler's guardian. Moyo Jr. repeated her desire to be Skyler's caretaker, and she asked why DCS hadn't done a home inspection yet.

Caseworker Reba Terry did the home inspection the next day, and it was fine. All of the conditions of the permanency plan had been met and there only remained fingerprinting and signing some paperwork before Skyler would start a new life with his extended family

On April 8, 2021, Terry met Angela for her to sign some final paperwork. Both birth mother Loren and Auntie Angela Moyo told the Tribune they were expectant and thrilled they would no longer have to plan visits with Skyler because he would soon be living with Angela.

According to the aunt, immediately after Caseworker Reba Terry left with the signed permanency plan paperwork on April 8, she called Adron Wayne Ray III and his wife, Abigail Bargatze Ray, and told them that Moyo was about to take custody of Skyler.

DCS caseworker Reba Terry was assigned to the Mitchell case. She was supposed to be helping baby Skyler reunite with his family but instead she secretly helped the foster parents keep the boy.

"I didn't realize it at the time, but Reba Terry was informing the Rays (fosters) of every step that I took towards getting Skylar into my custody," Moyo told me.

"Reba Terry sabotaged the relative placement," Reguli said.

What happened on April 9, 2021, and in the following days is a twisted tale of deception, corruption, and outright chicanery on the part of the fosters, a number of DCS employees, and Judge Phil Smith, all of whom worked in concert to deny a family placement that was both imminent and lawful in Juvenile Court in order to give a Black baby to a white family in a higher court—for which the state of Tennessee could collect a cash bounty.

The lawyer representing Adron Wayne Ray III and his wife, Abigail Bargatze Ray, is attorney Wende Jane Rutherford. On April 9, 2021, Rutherford filed for an

105

ex parte restraining order to keep DCS from awarding Moyo guardianship of Skyler. Judge Smith signed the order. The Rays also filed a petition to terminate Loren's parental rights, setting the stage for the baby's adoption, and an ex parte restraining order.

On April 14, DCS held a WEBEX meeting with the Rays, Angela, Loren, Reba Terry, and DCS attorney Shay Jolly. It was a pivotal moment in the case. Loren reported she had completed her domestic violence class, her parenting class, her parenting assessment, and said she was working on housing.

Angela said that everyone on the call acted like everything was going along like it should and DCS was still looking to place Skyler with her.

"I had been telling them and been in constant communication with them and the foster parents, and everybody agreed at that point—Angela is going to get the baby.

Loren always said, 'I want my sister to have my baby.' I always said I wanted Skyler. DCS, everybody was like, 'ok, this is what we're working towards.' After the call, I remember feeling like, 'ok, we are still on track. We just need to get over these few hurdles and we could get Skyler back'."

But that wasn't going to happen. The foster parents, Adron Wayne Ray III and his wife, Abigail Bargatze Ray, knew they could block the relative placement by filing their petition the week before but said nothing about it. Angela said that neither they nor DCS mentioned it during the call. It came as a terrible shock a few days later when Loren was served with papers.

DCS could have easily placed Skyler with Angela if they acted quickly, and they should have but they didn't. Instead, they were deceitful, as were the foster parents scheming behind the scenes.

Skyler with his mother, Loren Mitchell.

DCS would soon betray not only Sklyer's family but also its own first principle of reuniting families.

Angela and Loren both told the Tribune that DCS betrayed their trust, lied to them, and deliberately deceived them. The family placement did not happen as previously agreed to, and they are furious about it.

On May 18, 2021, DCS attorney Shay Jolly entered into an Agreed Order with the Rays that DCS would not remove Skyler from their home.

So, in a little more than a month, DCS abandoned its relative placement goal in Juvenile Court and joined the Rays in the 4th Circuit Court as a co-petitioner to terminate Loren's parental rights—something that would not be necessary if Aunt Angela Moyo was given guardianship of Skyler as she'd hoped she would.

It is not clear exactly when or who decided to abruptly change Skyler's permanency plan, but caseworker Reba Terry played a key part, as did DCS lawyer Shay Jolly.

Loren Mitchell did not enter the May 18 agreed order. In July 2021, three months later, she still had no attorney, and there was no Guardian ad Litem for Skyler, both of which are required by state law.

"He (Judge Phil Smith) should not have signed that restraining order," Reguli said.

Under a 2016 change in law, TCA 36-1-116 (f), the filing of an adoption and termination petition cuts off all of the Juvenile Court's reunification proceedings. A third party can intervene in an adoption but not a termination proceeding.

In other words, the Juvenile Court proceedings would have allowed Loren to remain a parent and Angela the protective guardian. But the foster parents' petitions set events in motion to turn Loren into a stranger to her own son and end her relationship with him forever.

Family law attorney Connie Reguli represented Angela Moyo Jr.

When DCS switched sides and signed the agreed order, DCS bifurcated the termination and adoption so that Angela Jr. could not intervene. "We were kicked out of the case," Connie Reguli explained.

Three months after the fosters filed their petition, Judge Smith had still not assigned Loren an attorney and Skyler still had no Guardian ad Litem.

Loren knows she can't raise Skyler and has always wanted him to go to his aunt. Imagine her sitting in a courtroom where she has not been consulted and cannot follow what is happening, has no lawyer to plead her case, and she's up against a whole battery of lawyers, court clerks, and adversaries, including the judge, all of whom talk faster and think quicker than she does. She is alone and without family advocates who are able to come to her defense.

"What they have done is not right. It's not fair," Loren Mitchell pleaded to the court. "We done all the things we were supposed to do as far as Skyler goes. And I don't think it's fair. I don't think it's fair. We've done all the things we were supposed to do. It's not fair," she repeated.

"I am going to allow Ms. Stark to file a brief on Ms. Mitchell's behalf," Smith said.

That was mighty big of him, considering it was a done deal after DCS, and the fosters manipulated the court system and removed the family from the case.

So, it's pretty certain Loren Mitchell will lose her parental rights, and the fosters will get to keep Skyler, permanently.

Former 4th Circuit Court Judge Phillip Smith signed a restraining order to prevent Skyler from being placed with Angela Moyo. Under state law, DCS has sole authority over foster child placements. Moyo has custody of Mitchell's older son Michael who was then six years old.

"This was in July 2021 and this thing started in April. DCS should have immediately terminated the fosters' contract and placed Skyler with his Aunt Angela. And as soon as the petition was filed the court should have appointed Loren an attorney and should have appointed a Guardian ad Litem before it did anything," Reguli said.

Update: Two years have passed since I reported this story. Loren Mitchell did get a court-appointed attorney. The parties returned to court on April 17, 2024. Davidson County Fourth Circuit Court Judge Stan Kweller terminated Mitchell's parental rights. Skyler's foster parents are pursuing his adoption, and Skyler's birth family is pursuing an appeal.

For reasons that will become clear, Connie Reguli is unlikely to enter a courtroom ever again to defend parents who have lost their children. But she had plenty to say about this case, which she had defended until she got kicked out of it by stealth and deceit.

When I told her about Loren's loss of parental rights, Reguli was disappointed; she was angry; she was disgusted, but she was not in the least bit surprised.

When she takes a case, Reguli looks for things other people ignore or don't attend to. She said Loren Mitchell's disability rights under the Americans With Disabilities Act (ADA) were probably violated. She never got a chance to argue for them in court.

In a similar Massachusetts case, the Department of Justice intervened on behalf of a disabled adult, just like Loren Mitchell, who had a child that welfare authorities had taken from the mother, Sarah Gordon. The DOJ ruled that it was a violation of her rights under the ADA.

In Tennessee, the law provides for termination when somebody is mentally incompetent to raise a child. What about someone who is paralyzed, somebody with multiple sclerosis or cerebral palsy? Reguli wonders how far will things go when we start attacking people for their disability?

"I am angry because the government is believing they can make better choices for parenting than God. In Dante's Inferno, the lowest circle of hell are the people who interfere with the relationships with others, so I think God is going to get them," she said.

•••

Child Welfare in Tennessee Can't Compare with Alabama

Alabama always has a highly ranked football team. Its child welfare system is one of the better ones, too.

James Tucker is Director of the Alabama Disabilities Advocacy Program. He has litigated class actions in state and federal courts dealing with disability, gender and race discrimination, as well as mental health, foster care, education, employment, housing, voting, corrections, and Medicaid issues.

MONTGOMERY, AL – Alabama's Department of Human Resources (DHR) was sued in federal court in 1988 over its treatment of disabled children. Twelve years later, advocates sued Tennessee over its child welfare system. Both lawsuits led to settlement agreements in 1991 and 2001, respectively.

Plaintiffs in the Alabama lawsuit, R.C. v. Fuller, had a reformist defendant they rather liked, Paul Vincent. He was the Child Welfare Director of the Alabama Department of Human Resources (DHR). Vincent's boss was Bill Fuller, DHR Commissioner, and the official defendant in the lawsuit. Child Welfare was Vincent's domain, and it was a real mess. He knew it, disability advocates knew it, family court judges knew it, and families and their children certainly knew it.

"There was about a year of discovery. The state resisted settling for quite a while, and then on the eve of trial, they settled the case," Vincent reported. He said he never spoke with the plaintiffs about Alabama's dysfunctional system until after the state agreed to a consent decree.

Instead of going to trial, both sides negotiated a settlement, and the state agreed to abide by its terms for several years before the judge dismissed the case. In Alabama's case, it took 18.

"The case ran for nearly 20 years... and we are now more than 10 years past the conclusion," said James Tucker, Director of the Alabama Disabilities Advocacy Project, one of the plaintiffs who originally brought the lawsuit.

In Alabama, caseloads were too high, caseworkers were poorly trained, children were placed too far from their families, and they didn't get to visit with them much.

"We brought kids into care that with adequate home and community-based services could have stayed with their families, but once kids got into care, they moved too often," Vincent said.

"Tennessee's child welfare system was just as bad. Tennessee is still failing to address many of the same systemic problems that Alabama faced."

"They were often put in unnecessarily restrictive placements which could be a long distance from their home, and they stayed too long. And the care they got while they were in the system was often inadequate," Vincent said. Ditto Tennessee.

"When the lawsuit was filed in Alabama in 1988, the state was so under-resourced that good social workers couldn't do good social work," Tucker said. If they were better supported, they could do the work they were trained to do.

Tucker said that after the settlement, more of an effort was made to engage families and, meet them where they were and provide services where they were needed. Vincent's insider's account is similar.

"The entire structure of the agency decided the best thing to get it implemented and exit court supervision was to enthusiastically implement it. And we did," Vincent said.

Paul Vincent spent 50 years in social work. For more than a decade, he worked in Alabama's child support office.

In 1989 he was appointed Alabama's Child Welfare Director. In 1996, Vincent founded a non-profit group that helps state child welfare agencies protect kids and strengthen families.

One main reason why Alabama has done far better than Tennessee in reforming its child welfare system is because the guiding principles adopted in their separate settlement agreements were so different.

(See Tennessee 2001, A Matter of Principles

@ https://nccpr.org/state-local-and-international-reports-and-presentations/)

Unlike Tennessee, Alabama focused on keeping families together. Returning children to their families when they were taken into foster care was the primary goal of the newly reformed system. It was etched into the agreement in a number of ways.

By contrast, Tennessee's principles contained no such language and focused more on the state's primary

114

authority to make decisions in the child's best interest. Essentially, Tennessee's principles opposed family reunification in favor of state control over children, most of whom they have continued to put in foster homes. Many studies concluded that it is a wrong-headed and very damaging approach.

Vincent said Alabama's counties were excited about the consent decree. "Because they were woefully understaffed, didn't have enough services, had a lot of turnovers because the job was impossible and unfulfilling, and now they saw it as an opportunity to make the system work. There was very little resistance to it except among some group home providers," he said.

Outside consultants helped Vincent change the department by focusing on keeping kids in their homes. They decided to implement the settlement in stages.

"We thought it was a win for us. The department didn't have much money with which to implement the settlement. We couldn't have reformed the system with any depth, so it gave the state time to experiment with some new strategies and gave us the money we did have to enrich a small group of counties to some depth instead of trying to spread it around to 77 counties."

It was a risky strategy because, at first, some counties got short shrift. A national consultant would come in once a month to coach and teach small groups of social workers how to more effectively work with families.

Vincent credited the plaintiffs with coming up with that approach. It was less expensive overall and proved to be quite successful because they could test their ideas on a smaller scale before rolling them out across the entire state.

"Counties got a lot of flexible money, which had never happened before. The state held all the purse strings, and so the state pushed a lot of money down to them so they could execute some unique contracts to do a lot of creative things that came out of these team plans that weren't present before and wrap-around services to kids, as the saying goes," Vincent reported.

"When we began with the money we had, we decided we couldn't retrain the workforce--which had to be done. There had to be a comprehensive change in the way they viewed families and the way they treated families with kids and a higher level of skill. So we decided to at least make the workforce we had competent. Creating a training curriculum to match the settlement is useless if all you do is train new hires, which is what many states do."

Tennessee is one of those states. It turns over its entire cadre of caseworkers every 5 years with dismal results. DCS is a terrible place to work, so people don't stay.

"We retrained everyone in this 4-week curriculum mainly because it was about being a social worker, not a bunch of rules. And in my opinion, our workers changed their values and improved their skills a lot, so they were good practitioners so they could make really effective use of flexible dollars. That was one big element of the reform," Vincent said.

Within four years, all DHR staffers were trained, and counties had some flexibility to tailor their operations and spend money on what was most important in their districts.

"The state had a model of practice which was consistent with that really works with families compared to what there was before," Vincent told me.

Early on, Alabama capitalized on Medicaid to finance a lot of mental health services, and that helped fund the changes until the legislature got behind the new system and supplemented its budget. Afterwards, Medicaid continued to help finance the reforms in the consent decree.

"We had a very cooperative Medicaid agency that was happy to revise the state plan, so we used Medicaid dollars to finance a number of services that helped get kids out of congregate care and foster homes and return them to their birth families," he said.

Vincent didn't know if the new strategy would work or how influential it would become. "But it proved to be effective enough and push the change deep enough so a lot of the key elements of the settlement survived the attacks on it when the foes of the reform came into power," he reported.

Reform Stalls in Alabama

Fob James was elected governor of Alabama in 1994. James was a Reagan Republican, hostile to big government, particularly the federal government, where DHS got much of its operating funds for its new approach to child welfare.

Elected into office in 2018, Tennessee Governor Bill Lee is cut from the same cloth. He has steadfastly refused to expand Medicaid, and the state remains an outlier in health policy. His approval ratings recently dropped ten points.

Vincent reported that in Alabama, Fob James "appointed a foe of the reform who operated a group home, so at that point, a number of us left the department."

James wasted no time in sabotaging the reform effort.

The state filed a petition in 1994 to exit the settlement agreement. Tucker's group, the Alabama Disabilities Advocacy Project, wanted it to continue and convinced Senior U.S. District Judge Ira DeMent to deny the petition. He did. The state tried twice more, unsuccessfully in 2005 and again in 2007, when DeMent finally dismissed the case.

In short, James couldn't get rid of the settlement agreement altogether, so instead, he did a lot of backsliding.

"There was some dismantling of the reform, which just prolonged the settlement longer than it otherwise would have been," Vincent said.

"It comes back to the classic notion that children need to be served and be consistently supported, and when children are being parented by the government, that does not happen," Tucker explained.

According to Tucker, in recent years, some positive changes have not been sustained, like reducing the number of placements in foster care, reducing multiple movements while in foster care, and keeping siblings together. "Some of those have been lost," he said.

Tucker credits that state for helping more children get adopted. "But that is different than individual plans for children and their birth families. Family engagement between a child who is at risk coming into the system and their birth family, that engagement has deteriorated," Tucker said.

"So, it's been a mixed bag since the conclusion of the case. The focus on family engagement and lack of resources that was at the heart of our consent decree is no longer the same," he said.

"We have filed a new lawsuit about a very specific piece of the foster care system," Tucker reported. The case involves several hundred disabled children who are warehoused in 19 Psychiatric Residential Treatment Facilities in Alabama. The Alabama Disabilities Advocacy Project sued in Federal U.S. District Court in May 2021.

Two of the four teenage plaintiffs are African American. They want to be placed in the community, but DHS has kept them locked up for years. The complaint alleges these children are placed in "highly restrictive facilities that isolate them from their families, friends, and communities." Plaintiffs allege this isolation, and segregation violates the Americans with Disabilities Act, not to mention the damage it causes to the child's mental health.

So, it seems a state can take great strides forward in improving the lives of children and families and then, with political meddling and interference slide right back almost to where it began.

Florida Child Agency Sued

"In a class action lawsuit similar to the Brian A case, former DCF attorneys claim Corrupt DCF officials ran a child trafficking ring to benefit insiders.

Florida Department of Children & Families

MyFLFamilies.com

SunCoast Region

Four Florida families are suing Gov. Ron DeSantis, Shevaun Harris, Secretary of the Florida Department of Children and Families (DCF), Dr. Joseph Ladapo, Executive Director of the Florida Department of Health, Patricia Armstrong, Bureau Chief of Florida Department of Health Child Protection Team, and Dennis Moore, Executive Director of Florida's Guardian ad Litem Program.

"The theme of our lawsuit is focused on all these kids who had a perfectly available and appropriate family member, and those family members were passed over or ignored in favor of people who are connected to the system," said Attorney Valentina Villalobos.

The 177-page complaint alleges that DCF, lead agencies, and contractors who operate the Florida foster care system wrongfully took children from their families without any evidence of neglect or abuse; thwarted the attempts by family members to get custody of the children; and in one case falsely accused a grandmother of abuse and instead, put the child up for adoption. In that particularly twisted and noxious bit of insider trading, a former board member of the agency handling the case adopted one of the children. The child was African American; the foster parents were Caucasian.

"The point of the lawsuit is to stop it from continuing. We can't necessarily undo the damage in the vast majority of the cases. Adoption in Florida, once it's finalized, you've got one year to try and undo it, and it's never happened," Villalobos said.

The complaint filed in the U.S. District Court in Tallahassee, is based on the right to due process, protected by the 14th Amendment of the U.S. Constitution; it does not seek punitive damages or even name any of the foster system operators who put "a thumb on the scale" and concealed their self-dealing and other misdeeds from the dependency court judge and the birth parents.

Their identities are known but not cited by name in the complaint. The plaintiffs cite numerous examples showing how foster care workers, DCF attorneys, and Guardians at Litem deliberately blocked "family placement" to steer kids into adoption by "insiders". Family reunification and placement with relatives are supposed to be the primary goals of Florida's child welfare system when kids are taken into custody. Tennessee and other states supposedly have the same priorities.

Three of the four plaintiff attorneys know a lot about DCF because they were once insiders. The lead attorney, Karen Gievers, was a dependency judge. Villalobos and another attorney who are now plaintiff attorneys in the case, used to work for DCF.

"We know this has been happening. It's just now that we're in private practice and are able to do something about it," Villalobos said. The complaint was filed last week. "We are being flooded with calls and emails and online submissions from people who are saying the same thing happened to them," she described.

When the four plaintiff families realized how their related youngsters had been essentially kidnapped, snatched, or internally diverted, they complained to the Governor and Inspectors General of various state agencies. But nobody was held to account. Big surprise. The officials charged with oversight ignored the complaints and they kicked them back to the very same bad actors who did nothing "to redress the relatives of the snatched, diverted children".

The four plaintiff attorneys decided they needed to take those complaints and file a federal lawsuit, which is exactly what they did.

"They're doing these things with the permission of the court. But then getting the permission of the court is on the basis of the court not being fully informed or not given the whole story, or evidence is being excluded," Villalobos said.

"I don't think the judge is being crooked but they're going off the information that they have," she said. Villalobos added that one judge should have known better. "The judge rubber-stamped what the department asked him to do," she informed me.

The Florida complaint alleges DCF employees, lead agencies, and their subcontractors lied, filed false reports, withheld medical records, committed fraud, and other violations of law. Those actions were widespread and long-standing. The foster system operators failed to do their job properly; they conspired with others to wrongfully take children from their families and gave them to system-connected non-relatives. In short, they corrupted the child welfare system in Florida and ran it like a large child trafficking ring.

State officials pretend such criminal behavior is not happening or that it's just a couple of bad apples—not enough to spoil the barrel. Actually, they have a financial incentive not to act in the best interests of the children. There's shame all around.

Under the 1997 Adoption and Safe Families Act (ASFA), states get federal dollars for every adoption they complete. The payments range from $4,000 to $10,000 depending on the special needs of the child. Foster parents are entitled to certain benefits, including cash payments, when they adopt a child.

Plaintiff attorneys are not asking for jail time or even for firing the people involved. They are asking for a permanent injunction to keep the DCF and its partners from playing those dirty tricks going forward and "such further relief as the Court deems appropriate". They did not call for the termination of contracts with service providers that were involved in the scheme though they had every right to.

Villalobos expects a decision from the court sometime in 2024. In the meantime, they may file for a temporary injunction and ask the court to order a corrective action plan that DCF would have to comply with. In the meantime, more children will enter the system and once again more damage will be done.

"There is no justice. Parents are like lambs led to slaughter." — Connie Reguli, Family Law Attorney.

Chapter Five: Judging the Judges

When the roosters crow Michael O'Neil gets up to feed his chickens. The 54-year-old said his two sons don't help tend the cows, sheep, and turkeys on his small farm, but I find that hard to believe.

"My 16-year-old and a bunch of his buddies came this year to help us shear the sheep. It's a lot better when you've got 16-year-old wrestlers who can hold the sheep and all I have to do is sheer them," he told me.

O'Neil is a single dad and for the last 25 years he's been a magistrate in Davidson County Juvenile Court. Before that he was a court-appointed attorney there. He commutes a half hour each way to work at the Davidson County Juvenile Detention Center located right next to the Tennessee Titans football stadium. The jail is in the basement right below the courts. It opened in 1994, has limited parking and bad plumbing. And it's overcrowded.

"This is how we do things here," O'Neil tells me. And he begins to explain that when DCS or someone files a neglect petition, he is the first judge parents see when they go to court.

O'Neil hears 800 custody cases a year. Most begin when DCS files a dependency and neglect petition against parents or caregivers.

"So, then they're served with a court date; that's like Monday mornings for what are called an "appearance hearing". It's just to make sure everybody's in court and been served with process. And if a neglect dependent petition is filed against a parent, that parent is entitled to counsel," O'Neil says.

"Generally, the Guardian ad Litem will be appointed prior to that because we have people signing up. And so, when we get the petition filed originally, then we'll appoint a Guardian ad Litem."

"I'm the one who is tasked with doing appearances and preliminary hearings for Davidson County," he told me.

"So, at that point, is there a way to dispute anything? In other words, if DCS files a neglect petition and it says, well, we got this anonymous tip, and we sent investigator Smith out to the such and such address, and this is what we found. And on the basis of that, they filed this petition. And if it's an emergency they still have to come here to get a removal order, right?"

"Not necessarily." O'Neil explains he sometimes takes an oath from a DCS attorney over the phone.

"And sometimes I'll have questions for them because they're asking for removal. And one of the things that we have to determine is whether reasonable efforts were made to prevent the removal, and reasonable efforts could include trying to find an alternate placement.

"Or maybe the child is in the physical custody of the department because the mother's not there, she's in jail. We can't leave the child standing on the side of the road," he says.

O'Neil excuses himself and comes back a few minutes later and thumps a dark red book on the table. It is bigger than your standard King's James version with small print. The *Tennessee Compilation of Selected Laws on Children, Youth, and Families* is O'Neil's bible.

If DCS files an expedited petition to take a child from their family, O'Neil will sign an emergency removal order but by law he has to hold a preliminary hearing within 72 hours.

"It may be a case where the department is just seeking to provide services. If it's a department case, somebody could be seeking to have custody."

The preliminary hearing is where DCS has to prove its case after removing a child and where a parent's attorney can dispute it, although few do which is explained below. If a child is in DCS custody O'Neil has to determine if they had probable cause, and if so, the child stays in their custody.

"There're two things. One is the appearance hearing, if the child is not in Department of Children Services custody. The other thing is a preliminary hearing if the child has been removed into Department of Children Services custody."

O'Neil told me there are a number of possible outcomes. One is the parent could say, 'I don't agree with this, and I want a hearing, and I want it today', and then O'Neil will hear it that day and the department will then present its case. Or the parents could say they want time to prepare a case, and it will be reset for some time in the future.

"If a person's having a crisis with substance abuse or something, and they say to the mother, 'look, is there someone else that can care for the child temporarily while you get care?' That's a safety plan. That's where the mother or whomever the custodian agrees that this other person will care for the child, at least for a while. That's nothing that we have any jurisdiction over," he says.

"And sometimes their attorney will talk with them and say, look, if we have the department conduct what's called a child and family team meeting.... and I will order them to conduct one," he told me.

"Then they and their counsel make the decision about how they want to defend their case. And then the department, or whoever the petitioner is, makes a decision about how they want to prosecute their case. And then it comes to me, and I'm the tabula rasa, so I sit there and

126

I'm the blank slate, so I only hear what happens in that room in front of everybody."

"Everybody" is just the people who have been summoned to appear. All juvenile courtrooms are closed to the public in Tennessee. When DCS attorneys prosecute a case, nine times out of ten, the children have already been taken from their families.

Family Law Attorney Connie Reguli is the F. Lee Bailey of family defense in Tennessee. She says ex-part orders are the weapons of mass destruction in the legal system. "Ex parte" is from the Latin meaning "from one party only".

"I call them behind-your-back orders because DCS files a petition and asks to remove your children before you even know about it. It's really a seizure warrant.

"When someone without warning knocks on your door and takes your kids, they may or may not give you a copy of the removal order. "They may just take the kids and say 'come to court on Wednesday and we'll give you a copy.' I mean that's how bad it is," Reguli told me.

Parents usually don't get a copy of the removal order, the custody petition, or meet their court-appointed attorney until the 72-hour hearing. "They're like lambs led to slaughter," she said.

On the advice of their newly appointed attorney, who they have just met, most parents waive their preliminary hearing. The judge hearing the matter would likely be the same one that signed the ex-parte order to take their kids away in the first place. Having the hearing or waiving it is a Hobson's choice for parents who aren't going to get their kids back in either case.

The bar to show probable cause is so low, attorneys usually tell their clients to waive the hearing. Although it's perverse and heart-rending to tell parents not to fight to get their kids back, it's not necessarily a bad legal strategy.

"Parents are never properly represented in preliminary hearings," Reguli says.

As a defense attorney, it's a poor strategy to let them take the stand because DCS holds all the cards at this point in the case.

"If parents take the stand, the DCS attorney is going to hammer them. If they plead the fifth and refuse to answer a question—say in a broken rib case--they look guilty."

"The best position that a parent can take is to prepare an alternative placement for the child," Reguli informed me, which means DCS might place them with a relative and then the long and protracted ordeal to get them back begins. It could take months, years, and sometimes never. Families are traumatized from the moment DCS separates children from their parents, regardless of the outcome.

Unlike a criminal case, where the defense can question state witnesses in preliminary hearings, hearsay evidence is allowed in juvenile court. DCS uses anonymous sources so you can't subpoena them to testify. Basically, the evidence is just allegations from the petition DCS has already filed with the court, Reguli says.

If the prelim happens just 72 hours after DCS takes the children, there is no time to prepare a case. You can't subpoena witnesses you know nothing about or, you don't have any records, and you have to fight DCS to get them and that takes time.

"Sometimes I ask for a delay. That's why DCS hates me," she says and laughs. Reguli had one preliminary hearing that lasted five days but took place over five months. "I just forced everything to be put on," she told me.

Reguli took over that particular case from a court-appointed attorney in Knoxville who had waived the preliminary hearing. The child was in foster care for six months before Reguli could schedule a hearing. She accepted all of the evidence the court had heard up until then and the court agreed to incorporate whatever was new in the adjudication.

"I won the case in adjudication," Reguli recalled.

"I got the parents unsupervised visitation in the middle of the preliminary hearing. After two days of the preliminary hearing, I asked for more visitation, and we got it.

By the time we got to the last day, I mean I wore the state out in that case. They didn't have anything, but it took five days over five months," she said.

As a practical matter, the preliminary hearing was the trial and Reguli managed to turn the table on DCS by forcing them to defend their flimsy case.

O'Neil stays above the fray and sticks to judging the cases on his docket.

"We don't interpret the law; we apply the law. That's what we do. We take the facts and apply the law to the facts and come out with your best guess," he said. O'Neil hears about 1,000 cases a year in his court and DCS retains custody in most of them.

In Davidson County in FY 20-21, 1,028 children were taken into DCS custody; 894 of them, 87%, were judged dependent and neglected in O'Neil's court and entered foster care. In FY 22-23, DCS filed 476 neglect and abuse petitions in O'Neil's court; Metro schools filed 370; relatives filed 350, parents filed 41; private attorneys filed 25. O'Neil held an appearance hearing for each and every one of them.

"I wouldn't see them again. It would go to one of the other, what we call divisional magistrates, that keep the case from that point until its conclusion. So generally speaking, the next thing that would happen is a plan of care and a settlement hearing to see if they might be able to resolve the case and if the child remains in care of the permanency plan in terms of what needs to happen," he said.

DCS has to complete a permanency plan within 60 days after the case leaves O'Neil's court.

"Every day I try to leave work at work because every case I have to evaluate independently of every other case. That's what I took an oath to do, and that's what all of us took an oath to do. And it's from Ground Zero every time."

Like any lawsuit, witnesses testify to polar opposite things and O'Neil has to decide who is more credible. "Isn't lying a big problem?" I asked him.

"Sometimes people are pro se and they'll stand up and object. But there's no such objection called 'he's lying'. The way you deal with that is put on another witness that rebuts it. And then again, I have to make a determination."

O'Neil does appearances hearings on Mondays and preliminary hearings on Monday, Tuesday, Thursday, and Friday.

Most days O'Neil finishes his docket before lunch, spends a couple of hours on paperwork, and then heads back to his family around 3 pm to beat the rush hour traffic. Some days he has both appearance and preliminary dockets and doesn't finish until 4 PM. He doesn't take his work home with him.

Judge Sheila Calloway: the Visionary

Judge Sheila Calloway hears cases, too. She is Nashville's elected Juvenile Court judge and manages 150 employees. Calloway is a public figure who lives and breathes to improve the lives of children in Davidson County. It's more than a job to Calloway. It's her mission. O'Neil sticks to his caseload.

Davidson County is planning to build a $94 million 14-acre campus dedicated to keeping juveniles out of jail and "on a path to success," says O'Neil's boss, Juvenile Court Judge Sheila Calloway. She wants to call it the "Nashville Youth Campus for Empowerment."

Calloway has been working with Nashville school administrators to reduce school suspensions, employ restorative justice principles there and in her courtroom. Those efforts have reduced juvenile arrests in Nashville by 72% since 2013. She believes the way to have safer streets is to prevent crimes from happening in the first place. In reformist argot, Calloway is cutting the school to prison pipeline.

The youth campus project will break ground in late 2024. The campus will have a pretrial housing wing and service agencies to help families in need. It will include a 24-hour assessment center to support youth in crisis, a safe exchange facility for custodial visitation, and meeting areas for community partners.

In contrast, nearby Williamson County is building a new county jail, courtrooms, and juvenile justice center for $281 million. The new jail will have some beds earmarked for the mentally ill. Next door in Davidson County, Sheriff Daron Hall has a new $113 million jail with an entire wing devoted to drug-addicted and mentally ill arrestees. They are treated, not just housed, until their next court date.

The new Williamson County Juvenile Justice Center will have 96 beds in the detention center. It currently has 12. It will also have a respite center and house an alternative school. Even with these amenities, at the end of the day, it's still a jail.

The neglect and abuse teenagers suffered at Wilder Youth Development Center happens when you just "lock 'em up" without worrying about how those boys got there or what to do with them once they're inside. DCS can't decide if it's supposed to rehabilitate the children in its custody or just control them. That's the age-old dilemma of the criminal justice system except the inmates in DCS's locked detention centers are teenagers.

Disability Rights Tennessee issued a 17-page report in December 2022 called "Families Not Facilities." Its primary recommendation: invest in families, not facilities.

"In order to create a youth justice system that promotes healing, growth, and safety, we must build strong families and surround them with the supports they need to love and care for their children," the report begins.

An ounce of prevention may be worth a pound of cure, but DCS is too busy snatching children to get behind that utopian idea. And Williamson County is too busy building its new jail to worry about programs that would keep people out of it.

Circuit Court Judge Joseph Woodruff, the Corrupted

Williamson County Circuit Court Judge Joseph Woodruff has been a big booster of the Triple-J project (JJJ), the largest capital improvements project in the county's history. It includes a new adult jail, remodeling of court buildings in downtown Franklin, construction of a new Juvenile Justice Center with courts, services, detention facility, alternative school, and respite center. Plus, the county sheriffs will get a bigger gun range. Total costs are expected to be at least $281 million.

Woodruff defers to DCS and its frequent practice of wrongfully taking children into custody. He helped railroad Family Law attorney Connie Reguli who appealed her felony conviction for custodial interference. She was convicted because Woodruff changed the law in his instructions to the jury and then promptly recused himself from the case. In February 2024, the Court of Appeals overturned that conviction. Had they not done so, Reguli would have made history as the only lawyer to ever be convicted under that statute in Tennessee.

Just in case Reguli was exonerated, Representative Ron Travis and State Senator Paul Bailey introduced a bill in January 2023, so she won't get away with it again.

The law makes it a felony "to harbor or hide a child pursuant to a protective custody order or emergency custody order by a court" whether or not the person harboring the child has been served with such an order. The bill passed 74-17 and was signed by Gov. Lee on April 28, 2023.

"How much worse can it get? They can take anonymous reports, and they don't have to serve you and then they can arrest you which is what they did with Wendy. That's exactly what they did," Reguli told me.

Tennessee's perverse child welfare system would not be possible without the participation and connivance of judges. The Governor, lawmakers, and DCS officials all play a part in making it the disaster that it is. We will read about some of these others in Chapter Six and Chapter Eight.

Circuit Court Judge Phil Smith, the Biased

In 2009 Gov. Phil Bredesen appointed Phil Smith to the Circuit Court in Tennessee's 20th Judicial District, Davidson County (Nashville). He was elected three times and died in office on September 3, 2022.

Smith did not live to see the Tennessee Supreme Court reverse his decision to terminate parental rights (TPR) in the case of Markus E. On May 24, 2014, Marcus was born premature at thirty-one weeks. He weighed three pounds and four ounces and spent the first three weeks of his young life in neonatal intensive care at Vanderbilt Children's Hospital. Suffice to say he also had several medical issues.

In December his mother took him to the ER at Vanderbilt Hospital at 4 a.m. on Christmas Day congested and coughing. He was diagnosed with an upper respiratory infection and discharged. On January 10, 2015, Mother took Markus to a walk-in clinic at TriStar Centennial Medical Center.

She reported he had been coughing for several days. When they x-rayed him, they found 19 fractured ribs, some were acute, and others were in various stages of healing. TriStar staff recommended that Mother take Marcus to Vanderbilt for further evaluation, which she did. Marcus remained there for several weeks.

Vanderbilt physicians looked at Marcus's x-rays taken 4 months earlier for skull abnormalities. They discovered Marcus had some broken ribs at that time and called in a child abuse specialist, Dr. Verena Brown, who could find no medical cause for Marcus's broken ribs and testified they had to be "inflicted injuries". Two lower courts and the appellate court found the parents guilty of inflicting them.

DCS did not want to release Marcus to his home, so they made an agreement with the parents to place him with relatives. Mother and her family had conflicts and so in the end DCS stepped in and placed Marcus in foster care when he was 11 months old in April 2015. He hasn't been home since then and is reportedly living in Massachusetts with his foster parents.

The complicated case that arrived in Smith's court combined DCS's TPR petition, the parent's appeal of Juvenile Court's ruling that Marcus was a "dependent and neglected child", and the Grandmother's TPR petition to get full guardianship.

In addition to the expert testimony, the trial court heard testimony from Mother, Father, and other lay witnesses. Mother and Father were both adamant they never abused Markus, and neither believed that the other parent had done so.

All of Marcus's caretakers--Mother, Father, Grandmother, and Daycare Provider—testified that they neither injured Markus nor saw any sign he had been harmed. None of them knew of any accident that could have caused the rib fractures.

Smith wasn't having any of it. From Smith's ruling: "The Court simply does not believe this testimony. This Court has no serious or substantial doubt that this was simply a cover story created to cover up the true cause or causes of the horrific injuries inflicted on this seven-month-old child. The Court finds that [Mother] and [Father] are complicit in this attempted cover up."

Smith found both parents guilty of severe abuse (saying they broke Marcus's ribs) and that DCS had proven the "severe abuse" which was grounds for termination of their parental rights.

Connie Reguli took the case to the Court of Appeals, but they affirmed Smith's decision and terminated parental rights for both parents. Reguli filed an application to the Tennessee Supreme Court. "It's rare that they accept an application," Reguli told me. She wrote a brief on behalf of the mom and the case was set for oral argument. But before that happened Reguli was convicted of a fake felony on a different case and her law license was suspended.

Reguli couldn't argue the case in front of the Supremes but by digging into the facts Reguli was able to show the mother's attention to the child. From the TN Supreme Court decision: "Mother testified that between August 2014 and January 2015, she took Markus to see various doctors on over thirty occasions."

The appellate court had affirmed Circuit Court Judge Phil Smith's decision. Generally, that's what they do. They don't knit pick the evidence to find for the parents. However, they are supposed to at least review the lower court's ruling with an open mind and no presumption that it is correct. De Novo, meaning "new", is the legal term for another look at a case with fresh eyes. Family Law Attorney Connie Reguli says it's a fresh opportunity for parents to evaluate the quality of evidence that was presented against them in a lower court.

The Supreme Court reversed on a couple of grounds. First, nobody knew about Marcus's broken ribs until an X-ray showed them. Several doctors examined Marcus, and they didn't notice he was injured and none of his caregivers did either.

Blaming the parents for not knowing and not protecting him from something they didn't know about is bad enough, but the lower courts went beyond that. They concluded the parents were guilty and were lying about it, particularly the mother. She testified that Marcus had so many medical problems, it was likely there was some unknown medical cause for his broken ribs. So, intent on laying blame somewhere, three courts dismissed that idea. They couldn't prove Mom was guilty because they had no evidence, but it was clear they didn't find her credible.

Reguli had a similar case about the same time. She represented a mom in Cumberland County who had a premature baby in 2014. He was back and forth from home to hospital for six months.

"Out of the blue he was fussy, so she brought him in, and a body scan showed 22 fractures," Reguli recalled. And like the previous case DCS filed an abuse petition in Juvenile Court. It found severe abuse in the case.

"She found me during the end of the Juvenile Court trial," Reguli told me. The judge found severe abuse against the Mom but refused to give the kid to the Dad, so Reguli appealed to the Circuit Court.

"I put on eight hours of medical testimony—video deposition of a radiologist and a pediatrician and we go through fragile bones, infantile rickets, and all these things," Reguli recalled. The new judge found there are medical conditions that mimic child abuse but there was no clear convincing evidence that the mother abused the child, so she reversed the original decision.

Reguli says that was unusual because in most fractured rib cases the courts find "severe abuse" and the baby goes into foster care. Reguli is a walking encyclopedia about fractured ribs cases. She is abreast of DCS filings around Tennessee because she has a network of informants who bring her cases. Reguli told me she has consulted with other attorneys and parents in hundreds of cases.

"We've had trouble getting good experts to talk about mimicking medical conditions and in the Marcus case the DCS attorney testified that after the child was removed from the mother, he had no other conditions," Reguli recounted.

DCS made Marcus's mother get a psych evaluation which she passed. But did she have Munchausen Syndrome by Proxy (MSbP)? It's a mental health disorder and a form of child abuse when a caregiver makes up or causes fake symptoms in a victim to seek attention. DCS never alleged the mother exhibited MSbP, so it was never an issue in the case.

However, Reguli told me Marcus's mother had a lot of medical issues herself. "She was exposed to radiation when she was a teenager and had Graves' disease. She had a stillborn baby and then after that she had twins and one of the twins died shortly after birth. Then Marcus was born two months premature and stayed in hospital for five weeks. I looked at his cat scan when he was three months old and he had holes in his skull," Reguli told me.

The mother now has a healthy little girl. But Marcus was not a healthy baby and DCS claimed he no other conditions after they took custody. Well, that's certainly gilding the lily. Marcus had plenty of medical issues.

Tennessee Supreme Court Justice Sharon Lee asked the DCS attorney if they ever took Marcus for another body scan. The attorney answered "No". The lower court judges were guilty of confirmation bias. They found the parents guilty for what they suspected but didn't know and DCS didn't follow up on Marcus's condition when he was in their custody. That admission was the reason the Supreme Court reversed the lower courts.

The ruling will make it easier for Marcus's parents to finally get him back. They will have to submit the decision to Juvenile Court and ask DCS to drop its petition. DCS could agree to do that but they could also decide to re-litigate the case.

Bad Judges

Bad judges have been a big problem in Georgia. The Judicial Qualifications Commission (JQC) investigates judges in Georgia who have had complaints. In 2008 it hired a former Atlanta police detective, Richard

Hyde, who started "traveling around the state collecting scalps", according to John Mrosek, an attorney who had twice tried to unseat a well-entrenched judge who later resigned under a dark cloud. Detective Hyde used the same method he used on criminal suspects to great effect.

He would never demand a judge's resignation outright but instead would ask, "What do you think I should do?" He never asked a question he didn't already know the answer to.

Eventually, Hyde would drop the bomb. "If you don't resign immediately, you will be prosecuted." Hyde got rid of dozens of crooked judges that way. He was very effective.

But Hyde lives in Georgia, not Tennessee, where only two sketchy judges resigned between 1971-2011. During that 40-year period, the Judicial Standards Commission and the Court of the Judiciary recommended removing five judges in all. It requires a two-third vote in the Tennessee Senate and House to remove a sitting judge. Beside the two who resigned or retired, two other judges were removed from office, one for sex crimes, another for mail fraud, and one was censured.

Between August 1991 and August 2011, 5,193 complaints were lodged, and two judges were removed, 0.000385 percent or about $3/100^{ths}$ of 1% percent. Since 2009, formal charges have been filed against judges just 11 times, less than one case per year. None were removed from the office. One resigned.

"The Board of Judicial Conduct acts as the jury when judges are accused of malfeasance. It is comprised of 16 members. Five are appointed by the four judicial conferences in the state, four are appointed by the Speaker of the House of Representatives, four are appointed by the Speaker of the Senate, two are appointed by the Governor, and one is appointed by the Tennessee Supreme Court. Eight are current or former judges, six are neither current nor former judges nor attorneys, and two are attorneys.

"The Board is divided into three-member investigative panels and five-member hearing panels. Hearing panels have the authority to rule on prehearing motions, conduct hearings on formal charges, compel witnesses and the production of evidence, make findings and conclusions, impose sanctions, and dismiss cases. The Tennessee Rules of Civil Procedure and the Tennessee Rules of Evidence apply to Board proceedings." (Quoted from BJC's website.)

Board members are supposedly independent. But the majority are current or former judges. Politicians appoint the six non-attorneys. The board does reprimand judges occasionally. It very rarely suspends them, however, and in recent years has not removed any from the office. The Board of Judicial Conduct investigates citizen complaints of corruption, malfeasance, bias, and the like, but in the vast majority of cases, all the accused ever gets is a slap on the wrist. Simply put, when it comes to Judges' misbehavior the Board of Judicial Conduct is soft on crime. More accurately, it should be called the Board of Judicial Misconduct.

You'd never know it from the board's public record, but Tennessee judges are probably just as corrupt as they are in Georgia. They are sometimes reversed but rarely held to account.

There is a great scene in the 1985 movie **Witness** that comes to mind. The villain is Philadelphia Chief of Police Paul Schaeffer. He's trying to find out the whereabouts of Detective Sergeant John Book, who is hiding out with the Amish in rural Pennsylvania because he's aware of internal police corruption. Schaeffer tells Book's partner, Sergeant Elton Carter, that cops are like the Amish. Carter is scared and plays dumb.

"We're like the Amish. We're a cult, too," Schaffer tells Carter. "Well, uh, a club with our own rules. John has broken those rules as you're breaking them now." Carter is later murdered for not giving Book up.

The judiciary is a club, too, not easily giving up its own. In juvenile courts, circuit courts, appeals courts, and all the way up to the

Tennessee Supreme Court, judges in black robes are shown great deference. When they are reversed, it's like a referee ruling the ball was caught out of bounds and the game goes on. Bad judges in Tennessee eventually retire but until they do, chances are they'll stick around long past their sell by date.

Put Everything on TV

The late Adolfo Birch Jr. was the first African American to serve as Chief Justice in Tennessee. In the late 1990s he and fellow Justice E. Riley Anderson had a great idea. They wanted to put public trials in Tennessee on cable TV.

According to Anderson, they were confident that they could find the money and they figured a lot of people would watch and learn about jurisprudence in their towns. Divorce Court, Judge Judy, and The Peoples' Court were very popular at the time, and they figured the "real thing" would draw an audience, too.

They never got a chance to find out. They polled every judge in Tennessee – more than 500 judges and magistrates– to see if they would like their trials to be recorded. Only one, Davidson County Sixth Circuit Court Judge Thomas Brothers thought it was a good idea.

All the others said "No" and so what would have been a Tennessee version of C-SPAN never got off the ground. Brothers is the only Tennessee judge who uses video as the court's official record. All the others can say whatever they like in court and then go into chambers and write completely different orders. That was Phil Smith's specialty. Litigants can't challenge orders in an appeals court using video as evidence to show the judge lied through their teeth. The appeals court won't even look at it.

As Magistrate O'Neil told me, the judiciary is supposed to apply the law but not make it. However, defendants often find that the law is what the judge says it is, especially if the judge doesn't believe them, and so they lose their case. Open courtrooms with official video as the record would go a long way to clean up judicial misconduct and poor judgments which plague jurisprudence not only in Tennessee but also in courts all over the country.

Reguli was stripped of her law license via an organized conspiracy of legal players, including three judges, none of whom were held accountable. Here is her story:

DCS Deals Dirt to Fearless Attorney

Connie Reguli and Wendy Hancock were convicted in Williamson County Circuit Court for a crime that the DA and judge made up.

Family Law Attorney Connie Reguli stands in front of the U.S. Capitol August 2020.

The trouble started in DeKalb County in August 2018. Wendy Hancock's 16-year-old son, Chantz, ran away from home when Hancock wouldn't let his girlfriend stay overnight.

Mom filed a missing person report with the Smithville Police Department on August 8, 2018. Chantz was with his estranged father, Kevin Bowling, a drug addict.

It is unclear how the Department of Children's Services (DCS) knew that but two days later, DCS caseworker Deandra Miller visited Bowling who tested positive for methamphetamine. Instead of returning Chantz to his mother, who was the custodial parent, DCS took him into custody and a week later took his 12-year-old sister, Briella.

As we have reported, punitive and perverse outcomes are common in DCS cases all over Tennessee. DCS prosecutes poor parents who rarely can afford an attorney to defend them. It is also common for DCS to use drug use as a pretext to wrongfully remove kids from their families like in *Another Child Dies in DCS Foster Care* in Chapter One.

Juvenile Court judges routinely grant a removal order to DCS after they file a dependent and neglect petition. Using that legal document, DCS removes thousands of kids every year from their families and put them into foster care, a booming industry.

The estranged Father was a drug-user, not Mom, and that should be relevant.

DCS routinely uses failed drug tests to show the children are abused or neglected even when they've tested the wrong party.

Wendy Hancock and her children.

What DCS should have done is get family services to counsel the family and work out Chantz's problem with his mother.

But this story is not about what could or should have happened but about what did. In this case, DCS ran with Chantz's allegation that his Mom, who wouldn't let him have sex with his girlfriend in her house, was a drug dealer. Rather than finding out what was true, it was those allegations that set the ball in motion.

Donkey Justice

DCS caseworker Deandra Miller visited Hancock on Wednesday August 8th, the same day she filed the missing person report about her son. Miller wanted Hancock to take a drug test. Hancock told her to talk with her attorney, Connie Reguli.

DCS Caseworker Deandra Miller got a removal order from a judge who had no jurisdiction in DeKalb County, TN.

"I don't have to talk to your attorney. I will just go and get a court order," Miller said.

And she did. But it wasn't about taking a drug test. That was just a pretext and although Hancock later passed the drug test, Miller had something more sinister in mind.

Reguli had no idea this case would be her undoing. Before it was over, at least 15 people were drawn into the conspiracy to prosecute Hancock and railroad Reguli. There were police from Smithville and Brentwood, foster parents in Jackson, a DCS foster home contractor, DCS attorneys and caseworkers, clerks, judges, and district attorneys in two counties.

Miller went to Juvenile Court Judge Michael Collins in Smith County to get a removal order but he had no jurisdiction in DeKalb County, so the order was invalid. But that didn't stop the judge from issuing the order or DCS from taking Wendy's children.

Reguli went before Judge Collins to argue he had no jurisdiction in the case and no authority to issue the removal order. He recused himself. But the damage was done, the game was afoot, and things were about to take an even nastier turn.

During that fateful week in August 2018, Reguli said that she called DCS six or seven times.

"Thursday, I call DCS. Friday, I call DCS; Friday I call the detective. Monday, I call DCS; Monday I call the detective. I made four calls to the clerk's office Monday, all trying to find out what's going on and they won't tell me. They tell me they are going to fax a petition. They don't do it.

"Tuesday comes. I call DCS again. Nobody calls me back. I call regional. I call the central office. I call the local office. I call the Smithville office. I call Deandra Miller. I call her supervisor.

All of them I leave a message: 'We will meet with you. We will cooperate. You can do a welfare check'.

Smith County Juvenile Court Judge Michael Collins issued a removal order to allow DCS to take Briella from her mother in August 2018.

Nobody calls me back and that's the critical thing because by policy DCS is supposed to have a safety meeting with the parent and they were pissed because Wendy had an attorney, and it happened to be me. And so, it was a set up. We were bamboozled," Reguli said.

"My client was denied due process every which way to Friday, right? They had my phone number; they got a removal order; they didn't call me and tell they had a removal order. They didn't call me and tell me there was a hearing. We would have been at that hearing had we known. They didn't try and serve her. A phone call would have resolved the whole thing because I told them we would come to the office and meet with them," she said.

DCS didn't want it resolved. They wanted custody of both Hancock's children.

In DCS's dependency and neglect petition, caseworker Miller wrote that "mother refused to cooperate with DCS and law enforcement."

"That was a flat lie," Reguli told me.

"Meanwhile, the mom, Wendy Hancock, was sitting at home with her daughter. She was frantic for fear that DCS would show up at her door and take away Briella, age 12. She checked into a hotel for the night, called Reguli, who told her to come stay with her while she figured out what was going on.

"They all knew she had an attorney and, instead of returning a phone call, they went behind our backs to remove the child who was perfectly innocent and safe. They pinged my phone and surrounded my house with police instead of calling me back," Reguli said.

Wendy Hancock and daughter Briella circa 2021.

A Brentwood policeman saw Briella through Reguli's rear window, and they sat outside for a couple of hours before DCS showed up to take Briella to Jackson, 200 miles away from her home in Smithville.

Chantz and Briella were in six foster homes and four schools in ten months. After eight court hearings, which Reguli described as 'aggressive and unnecessary litigation" DCS dismissed its neglect and dependency

146

petition and returned the kids to their Mom in June 2019. The case was over or so it seemed.

The Case of "Murderous Mary"

Justice was swift and uncompromising in the case of "Murderous Mary". Mary was a five-ton Asian elephant and the star of Sparks World Famous Shows. The circus was in Kingsport, Tennessee on September 12, 1916.

A newly hired and incompetent elephant keeper, Red Eldridge, led the elephant parade, riding atop Mary. He prodded her with a hook poking a badly infected tooth after she reached down to nibble on a watermelon rind.

Hundreds of onlookers watch Murderous Mary get hanged from a railroad derrick in Erwin, Tennessee on September 13, 1916.

Mary went into a rage, snatched Eldridge with her trunk, threw him against a drink stand and stepped on his head, killing him instantly.

The crowd yelled, "Kill the Elephant! Kill the Elephant!"

The circus owner, Charlie Sparks, decided that the only way to quickly resolve the situation was to lynch the elephant in public. He did so the next day.

Mary was transported by rail to Unicoi County, Tennessee, where a crowd of over 2,500 people assembled in the Clinchfield Railroad yard to witness the event. Mary was hanged from a railcar-mounted industrial derrick. She was 22 years old.

Connie Reguli stands five feet five inches tall and weighs about 135 pounds dripping wet. You wouldn't think the petite Family Law attorney would inspire the kind of blood lust that killed Mary. But she does.

"DCS wanted to get me when I fought them in Juvenile Court. The DCS attorney went to Brentwood PD to get the Brentwood police to open a case so they could later arrest us," Reguli said.

That DCS attorney was Tracy Hetzel. The DCS caseworker in Smithville who started the ball rolling was Deandra Miller.

Hetzel's malice towards Reguli was quite visceral.

Reguli was winning the match between the two in Juvenile Court while Reguli fought with DCS to return Hancock's children. During a break one day, Reguli left the courtroom but left her audio recorder and it captured Hetzel who was unaware she was being recorded.

Tracy Hetzel went to Brentwood PD and got them to open up a case against Reguli and Hancock.

"I wouldn't take pointers from you. You're seconds away from being disbarred, bitch." Hetzel said on tape. The nasty comment telegraphed the felony charges, arrests, and trials Reguli and Hancock would soon face. It is clear evidence that Hetzel was part of the conspiracy to prosecute them for custodial interference.

Indeed, she was its prime instigator. Hetzel attended Reguli's three-day trial, as did several of the other plotters, all of them like the people who came to see Murderous Mary hang from a railroad derrick.

A corrupt DA, a crooked judge, and politics

Williamson County District Attorney Kim Helper prepared the indictment for grand jury. She misstated the law pertaining to custodial interference in which a visitation order is fundamental cause for prosecution. There wasn't one.

Williamson County District Attorney Kim Helper prepared the indictments but left out the visitation language from the custodial interference statute. (Photo: The Tennessean)

The grand jury returned an indictment of custodial interference for detaining a child in violation of a court order, a class E felony. Helper charged the mom, Wendy Hancock. She charged Reguli with facilitation of a felony and with accessory after the fact of a class E felony for taking Wendy and her daughter into her home.

Custodial interference occurs when a parent refuses to return the children to the other parent as per the parenting plan. A court orders a visitation schedule both parents must follow.

Mind you, the indictments were issued after the case was closed by DCS. There was no visitation order to

149

violate. Mom had full custody of her children and dad was out of the picture. That didn't stop the conspirators from pursuing the case with these trumped-up charges.

Both Hancock and Reguli filed motions to dismiss the case because there was no visitation order. The only two precedents prosecuted under this law were about visitation orders.

During the criminal trial Judge Joseph Woodruff changed the language of the statute regarding custodial interference and wrote his own jury instructions, deleting any reference to visitation orders. In other words, the judge was interfering with the case.

The order the DA said Hancock violated was not a visitation order but a removal order from a judge who had no jurisdiction. The pair were not indicted until one year after the alleged crime took place and after DCS had returned both children to their mom.

"The judge changed the law to fit the facts so they could proceed to trial.

That's how they manufactured a crime. It's a fake felony," Reguli told me.

In addition, Judge Woodruff erred by not instructing the jury that as a matter of law, accessory after the fact does not apply when attorneys are representing their clients. They have immunity.

It was clear Judge Woodruff has a god complex. It's an occupational hazard. He thinks the law is what he says it is. But the General Assembly writes the laws and judges can't change them just to fit the facts of a case. But that's exactly what he did.

Williamson County Criminal Court Judge Joseph Woodruff made up his own definition of custodial interference and wrote jury instructions that didn't mention visitation orders.

Hancock was convicted in July 2021. Reguli's trial was inexplicably delayed—deliberately, according to Reguli--and she wasn't convicted until early voting began for Juvenile Judge in Williamson County in April 2022. Immediately after the verdict, the Tennessee Supreme Court suspended Reguli's law license.

Reguli, a Republican, was a candidate running against incumbent Sharon Guffee for Juvenile Judge in Williamson County. Because of the case and losing her license Reguli got a lot of bad press and lost to Guffee 11,909 votes to 3,959 votes. But Reguli got a five-star rating from Craig Huey, a Christian entrepreneur, who puts out a Tennessee Voter Guide. Huey gave Guffee only three stars.

"It seems she (Guffee) is more interested in going along with the system and not acting on principle," Huey wrote. He noted the race between Reguli and Guffee was "very personal" because Guffee had ruled against Reguli's daughter in a case. Huey said that the criminal charges Reguli was still facing just before the election could be a "dirty trick." It *was* a dirty trick and Reguli has since sued both Guffee and Woodruff.

Judge Woodruff contributed money to Guffee's campaign and sits on the board with her planning the $281 million Triple J project which includes a new juvenile detention center for Williamson County.

We have become a society that locks up its troubled youth in Juvenile Justice centers, that no matter how fancy, are still jails.

Hancock got two years' probation and had to testify against Reguli who was sentenced at the end of June 2022.

Reguli filed a motion for a new trial in the Circuit Court of Williamson County. She wants the court to reverse the guilty verdicts, or grant a new trial, or act as a thirteenth juror and enter an acquittal in the case. None of those things happened.

What the Case was Really About

Reguli is a staunch defender of parents' rights and always has been an advocate for reform of the child welfare system. She is also a fierce and effective DCS adversary. If the verdicts are allowed to stand, Reguli is worried about the chilling effect it will have.

"With the ability to shut me down in this way, it certainly will put other attorneys on notice not to go against DCS," she told me.

It seems on both sides there's a high price to pay when you're the fly in the ointment. The conspiracy to get rid of Reguli cost lots of money—it was a 12-month investigation–that included search warrants and electronic retrieval. It also involved a lot of respectable people—law and order types—who hate Reguli for exposing the sloppy operations and vindictive corruption that permeates DCS at every level in every county of Tennessee.

When they don't follow their own procedures or violate the law, Reguli is good at holding them to account and more often than not, wins cases for her clients.

DCS, its friends in law enforcement, and the courts like to operate with impunity. They don't like their authority challenged and because of that they've dealt Reguli a hard low blow.

If she survives and ultimately triumphs, the conspirators who tried to crush her will have to wipe the smirks off their faces and own the guilt they so richly deserve.

Whispering Judge Sentences Reguli for Custodial Interference

Judge Bill Acree decided that Reguli deserved to go to jail because she continued to proclaim her innocence on Facebook even after she was found guilty of custodial interference. The verdict was later overturned.

FRANKLIN, TENNESSEE – Judge Bill Acree, a stand-in for Judge Joseph Woodruff, who recused himself after the pre-trial proceedings, sentenced Connie Reguli to 30 days in jail and two years' probation on June 27, 2022. Woodruff was there as were other people involved in the case.

The hearing took place in Franklin's historic courthouse and lasted four hours. DCS attorney Tracy Hetzel testified for the state. She had lost a nine-month trial to Reguli who managed to get DCS to return Wendy Hancock's two children in June 2019 when DCS eventually dropped the case.

A month after that trial was over and Mom had full custody, Hancock and Reguli were charged with felonies for custodial interference. There was none. They were railroaded.

Hancock was convicted in July 2021 and Reguli in April 2022. Reguli wanted a new trial and Judge Acree decided in August she wouldn't get one.

"This whole case is legalism that pervert's justice. It means that a piece of paper, generated by a court even when it is based on lies and invalid procedures, is more important than the truth and the well-being and safety of a child," Reguli said.

Several of Reguli's clients testified in her favor and said that she fought against corruption within DCS. Dismissing their testimony, the judge said at least three times that "DCS is not on trial here." Reguli says that DCS broke the law and she's innocent.

Judge Acree is soft spoken and conducted most of the hearing almost in a whisper. The only time he could be heard clearly was at the end of the hearing when he pronounced Reguli's sentence.

Prosecutor Mary Katharine Evins made a big deal about Reguli's social media presence on Facebook and claimed she has shown no remorse and should be punished for encouraging others to disrespect the law and the courts.

"Prosecutor Evins' argument was mere speculation. There is no evidence that I told anybody to violate a court order, and no proof was presented that I did," Reguli told me.

Evins argued that Reguli should not be given diversion and Judge Acree agreed. He denied diversion. It would have allowed her to regain her law license after completing her probation and the criminal charges would be dismissed. Reguli has no criminal history and has publicly maintained her innocence throughout.

Judge Acree acknowledged Reguli has the right to speak under the First Amendment. "You can say just about anything you want to these days," he told her.

"However, after being convicted in this case, you continued to state how wrong the courts were, or how wrong DCS was. And how wrong the officers were. You're saying, basically, that you have no remorse for what you did, and you're saying in essence, in public, 'It's all right to disobey a court order, if you disagree with that order, and that's simply not an option," Acree said.

"All criminal defendants are entitled to an appeal and what Judge Acree has ruled is that maintaining your innocence is a crime in and of itself," Reguli said.

"I'm concerned that if Ms. Reguli walks away completely from this without any kind of punishment, only probation, that others will be encouraged to do the same thing," Acree said, adding, "Ms. Reguli, the Court is of the opinion that some incarceration is necessary."

And with that strange bit of logic the judge demonstrated the limits of Reguli's free speech rights. In essence, Acree was saying that if you criticize establishment figures in public you will pay a price. In other words, free speech has its limits when your criticizing the very system that can punish you.

The exercise of those rights has cost Reguli plenty already. Her law license has been suspended and if the conviction is not reversed, she will likely lose her license to practice law in Tennessee permanently. Meanwhile, her former clients are scrambling to find other attorneys to take their cases.

Courts in Kentucky and California have found that attorneys can express their opinions about judges outside the courtroom. "Who knows juvenile courts and DCS better than the attorney who is fighting them?" Reguli asked.

Reguli has been outspoken about abuses in the Child Welfare system in Tennessee and elsewhere in the U.S. She started the Family Forward Project in 2015. The project now has 17,000 members in the U.S. She went to Washington D.C. a dozen times to advocate for the end of Title IV-E funding that provides states with cash payments for taking children into custody, terminating parental rights, and arranging adoptions.

She said that federal incentives drive the wrongful taking of children all over the U.S. A class action lawsuit was filed in Florida last week alleging its Department of Children and Families (DCF) conspired to take children who had relatives willing to take them but steered adoptions to DCF insiders who were not related to the kids.

Reguli was philosophical about the sentencing hearing. "I'm just where I was yesterday. I'm out on bond pending appeal," she told me.

Williamson DA Secretly Indicts Reguli for Aggravated Perjury

Connie Reguli surrendered herself to the Williamson County sheriff August 12 and was released on her own recognizance.

FRANKLIN, TN – Williamson County District Attorney Kim Helper has escalated the prosecution of family law attorney Connie Reguli. Helper issued an arrest warrant against Reguli August 12, 2022, for aggravated perjury. Reguli surrendered herself at the Williamson County Sheriff's office Friday morning. She was booked and released on her own recognizance. She did not get a copy of the indictment when she was booked.

I had had trouble getting a copy of the charges myself. The Williamson County Sheriff's Office said they did not have a copy of the indictment; the Williamson County Criminal Court Clerk had no record of it and suggested calling the Sheriff's Department. Neither District Attorney Kim Helper nor ADA Mary Katharine Evins were in their offices when I called, and they did not return messages Friday afternoon.

By Monday morning, August 15, the criminal court clerk's office still had no record of the arrest or the indictment. Doubling-down on Reguli's conviction with an aggravated perjury charge certainly adds to her legal problems but it also brings more attention to a case that has brought sharp criticism of Williamson County judges and the Department of Children's Services (DCS) from dozens of Tribune readers after I published this story.

(See: https://tntribune.com/whispering-judge-sentences-reguli-for-custodial-interference/)

On July 22, 2022, Gov. Bill Lee announced the departure of DCS Commissioner Jennifer Nichol's and the appointment of Margie Quin who took over the troubled department in September 2021.

Politics in the Courtroom

Secret communications between judges and prosecutors, called ex parte, are illegal. Reguli has accused DCS of wrongfully taking children from their families via ex parte removal orders when parents and their attorneys are not properly notified. Reguli said that is what happened in her case.

During the sentencing hearing DCS attorney Tracy Hetzel told Judge Bill Acree that DCS frequently uses ex parte orders to take children into state custody. Family advocates like Reguli say that common practice violates due process guarantees of the 14th Amendment of the U.S. Constitution.

Connie Reguli during her sentence hearing in the historic Franklin Courthouse on June 24, 2022.

Reguli was convicted of custodial interference in April 2021. Her 30-day jail sentence and two years' probation was stayed by Judge Acree while she appeals that case. The new charge of aggravated perjury is a Class D felony. It carries possible sentences of 2 to 12 years in prison and fines up to $5,000. Examples of Class D felonies are extortion, reckless homicide, and unlawful surveillance.

According to the clerk's office, indictments are filed on Monday, Wednesdays, and Fridays and that did not happen with Reguli's indictment last Friday. The criminal court clerk's office released a copy of the two-page indictment just before noon Monday, August 15.

DA Helper could have intentionally kept the indictment under wraps, or it may have been a clerical error. However, the sheriff's office wasted no time releasing Reguli's mug shot the previous Friday.

The indictment accused Reguli of lying about a payment she said she made to CASA for $3,145.50. CASA is a non-profit organization that trains volunteers and advocates who accompany children into courtrooms. Reguli said that the payment was a fine imposed by Judge Joseph Woodruff in 2014. She said that Woodruff instigated the new charge.

"This CASA is a pet project of Judge Woodruff. He is a neighbor to Marianne Schroer who was the executive director of CASA for years.

"A CASA worker emailed confidential Juvenile Court records to a teacher which is illegal, and I brought a criminal contempt charge against the CASA worker. I subpoenaed her records, and she redacted a bunch of them. This was right when Judge Woodard got on the bench. And then as soon as he got on the bench, he sanctioned me for doing those things," Reguli told me. Williamson County Casa Executive Director Emily Layton declined to comment.

Update: In separate trials, Reguli and her client, Wendy Hancock, were each convicted of custodial interference. Both appealed their felony convictions; both convictions were reversed, and the charges were expunged. The appeals court found that no crime had been committed.

Reguli had repeatedly called it a fake felony. The two were convicted because the judge changed the law to fit the facts in his instructions to the jury. Judges can't do that. Lawmakers can but judges aren't allowed to make up the law to suit themselves, which is what Judge Joseph Woodruff did.

When Reguli won her appeal, her license should have been reinstated that very day. But it wasn't. The Board of Professional Responsibility (BPR) preemptively suspended her license again on November 20, 2023.

All the "evidence" was two sworn affidavits by attorneys with the BPR, who claimed Reguli is a threat to the general public. That's not true. But she *is* a threat to the established order and especially DCS.

Reguli claims the suspension was retaliation for her public criticism of Juvenile Court Judge Sharon Guffee and disciplinary counsel Andrew Campbell and possibly cost her an election. She decided not to appeal the BPR's suspension of her law license.

"They're all from the 'I hate Connie club' and I'd rather take the offense and sue them all in federal court," she told me.

"If you don't take care of them between zero and three years old, you're going to have them at 14." – Senator Ferrell Haile, Tennessee Speaker-Pro Tempore.

Chapter Six: Lawmakers and Public Officials

There are law-and-order types and good kind Christians in the Tennessee legislature. Some of the formers are election deniers, while the latter think God has commanded them to help widows, the poor, and the sick. The sword and the cross are as much a part of Christianity as the Holy Trinity and it's a contradiction Christians have been living with since the crusades.

Both types tend to support DCS. Yearly, its budget increases. Politicians from both sides of the aisle co-exist on the House Children and Family Affairs Subcommittee, although Republicans outnumber Democrats 6 to 3. Chairwoman Mary Littleton is the only woman on the committee.

Littleton presides over the presentation of dozens of bills related to Child Welfare. A diminutive figure with kinky salt and pepper grey hair, Littleton begins her hearings with prayer and the Pledge of Allegiance. She is very deferential towards committee members and always asks if there is any personal business they want to deal with before they take up the day's agenda.

I've never seen anybody run to the bathroom. I guess they go before the meeting starts. The hearings last about an hour. The agendas are always published but some items are subject to partisan politics instead of debate and never see the light of day.

In the 112th General Assembly session (2022) at least three reform bills never got out of the committee or were stifled before they got there, and did not make it to a floor vote. Littleton quashed a proposal by fellow

Republican Terry Lynn Weaver to provide family advocates for parents who are in the dock for abusing their kids.

Another proposal would have forced DCS to adjudicate cases in six months or give kids back to their families. Another would have stopped DCS from using anonymous tips without some sort of corroborating evidence before they took someone's children away.

That version of the bill didn't pass but it was amended, and CPS workers can still enter someone's house and then take children with an emergency removal court order.

Governor Bill Lee has plenty of fellow Republicans who carry his water in the law-making space and Lee's proposals always come to a vote. LGBTQ protections, gay marriage, and abortion rights are out in Tennessee and charter schools are in. Lee created a Public Charter School Commission to make sure regular public schools don't drain off funds from privately run ones.

After her parental advocate bill was shut down, Weaver came out publicly against Lee's school voucher program. She was primaried and beaten by Michael Hale, a cattle farmer and mortician from DeKalb County.

Politicians write the laws and judges apply them. When it comes to child welfare, Otto von Bismarck's famous quote, "Laws are like sausages, it is best not to see them being made" is apropos. The next story gives some of the nasty details.

Bi-Partisan Failure to Reform DCS

Gloria Johnson and Rep. Terri Lynn Weaver could not shake DCS control of the General Assembly.

NASHVILLE, TN – In its FY 22-23 session, the Tennessee General Assembly failed to pass any measures to reform operations at the Department of Children's Services (DCS).

A proposal to allow for a second medical assessment in cases when kids are removed from the family home based on one expert's medical opinion was not put in front of the Children & Family Affairs Subcommittee.

In Texas, parents who are suspected of physically harming their children are entitled to a second medical opinion. Prior to September 2021, doctors contracted by the Texas Department of Family and Protective Services were the only ones who decide which injuries were accidents and which were considered abuse. That practice has resulted in the wrongful taking of kids in Tennessee. (see https://tntribune.com/twas-the-night-before-christmas/)

Another proposal to have a family advocate appointed at the beginning of a DCS case was introduced by Representative Terri Lynn Weaver, a Republican from DeKalb County. Mary Littleton, Chairwoman of the Children & Family Affairs Subcommittee took it off the calendar, effectively killing it.

"Parents have every constitutional right over their kids, period," Weaver said. She said that an advocate who is present at all proceedings related to a DCS investigation can keep parents from getting mowed over by the system.

"At times the court system doesn't get it right and so it's vital that we do all that we can to keep families together. Reunification is the key," she said.

Time limits on DCS adjudications did not come to a full House vote either. Rep. Jason Powell, (D, House District 53) introduced a six-month time limit and it passed the subcommittee but didn't get out of the Civil Justice Committee. So, it died.

According to Powell, DCS objected to the bill because there is already a 30-day rule regarding time limits for hearings after a child is taken into custody. DCS routinely extends cases beyond 15 months that allows them to sue for termination of parental rights.

"There is a rule, but they never enforce the rule, so there has to be a statute," said Family Law Attorney Connie Reguli.

Representative Clay Doggett (R, Lawrenceburg) tried to get rid of anonymous reporting on the Child Abuse Hotline. He couldn't drum up enough support so he changed his bill to require some sort of corroborating evidence before DCS can enter a house to inspect the home or interview family members. That version passed in April 2022.

Representative Gloria Johnson (D, Knoxville) introduced a bill requiring the department to maintain staffing levels of case managers so that each region would not exceed an average of 12 active cases relating to initial assessments, 12 children monitored and supervised relating to ongoing in-home services, or 13 children in active cases in which the children are in out-of-home placements relating to ongoing services. The bill failed to pass in the Children & Family Affairs Subcommittee.

"Sixteen million was the fiscal note," Johnson said. "They can give $500 million to the stadium but you can't give $16 million to Tennessee's vulnerable kids," she said.

The national standard caseload for social workers is 12. Many states have passed caseload limits, including Indiana, Texas, Florida, Alabama, and Maryland.

"They have far more successes with the children. The families are very happy about what's going on. Their outcomes are great, and their employees are sane. Their employees are feeling valued, and they are able to take care of the kids on their caseload," Johnson reported.

She said it is nearly impossible for Democratic lawmakers to move legislation forward because for every Democrat on a committee or subcommittee there are two Republicans. The House Speaker determines who and how many members are assigned to various house committees. Ditto with Senate committees. Lt. Governor Randy McNally makes those calls on the Senate side.

"They stop every single one of the bills they want to stop in subcommittee," Johnson told me.

She said if there is something a Republican representative likes about a Democratic proposal, they are likely to steal it and put it in a Republican-sponsored bill. It happened to her last year with an education bill.

If there were ever a cause worth crossing the aisle for, children's welfare would be the one. But neither Democrats nor Republicans joined hands to set standards and press for changes at the troubled department. "It's not getting better. It's getting worse," Johnson warned.

For the first time, the DCS budget increased in 2021-2022 to just over a billion dollars in FY2021-22. The budget increased an additional $100 million in FY2022-23.

Update: Two months after this story was published, Governor Bill Lee replaced DCS Commissioner Jennifer Nichols with Margie Quinn. Quinn's 2023-24 budget request was $1.3 billion, the largest in its history. The legislature gave a thumbs up and the governor signed it.

•••

Governor Bill Lee

The boundaries between social welfare and personal responsibility are clearly drawn in Governor Lee's mind. He and his wife, Maria, are members of the unaffiliated evangelical Grace Chapel in rural Williamson County. It's easy to be a Christian fundamentalist when you've got more than basic fundamentals to start with.

More rich people live in Williamson County than anywhere else in Tennessee. Lee spends weekends on his family's 1000-acre cattle ranch in Franklin. Tennessee has about $1 billion in reserves, but Lee has refused to expand TennCare, the state's Medicaid program. There are eleven states like Tennessee that abandoned the working poor to fight COVID on their own dime.

So, Lee is a "no free lunch" kind of guy. Lee couldn't find it in his heart to provide health coverage to the estimated 679,000 Tennesseans who were uninsured in 2021. Adults without dependent children are not eligible for Medicaid at all in Tennessee.

According to the Center on Budget and Policy Priorities, some 119,000 uninsured adults in the coverage gap would become eligible if Tennessee expanded Medicaid.

The Medicaid coverage gap is people who are too poor to qualify for Affordable Care Act (ACA) marketplace assistance, yet ineligible for Medicaid because their state didn't enact ACA Medicaid expansion in 2020 when the pandemic hit. People of color make up 33% of the coverage gap population in Tennessee. The center estimated that 5,000 children in Tennessee would have gained coverage if Lee had expanded Medicaid.

When it comes to reforming DCS and the way it operates, the last three Governors, including Democrat Phil Bredesen, were the same in one respect. DCS has been taking more children, spending more money, and as far as reunification goes, it's been getting bad outcomes for years.

DCS Commissioner Margie Quin

And now, since it's run off so many overwhelmed caseworkers, DCS Commissioner Margie Quin has outsourced a lot of that work. She has taken one more step towards privatizing child welfare in Tennessee. She says it's only temporary, but DCS couldn't operate now without all the group homes and foster homes run by large providers that are businesses even though some are technically non-profit.

According to one NGO that works with her, Quin is a reformer who has publicly committed the agency to being more transparent, paying higher salaries to DCS caseworkers and reducing their caseloads.

All that sounds good. Quin asked for an additional $36 million in FY 23-24 for transitional housing across the state for kids to be assessed and treated before making decisions about their permanent placement. Quin has put raises into the FY 24-25 budget and Gov. Lee has not opposed them.

Quin's assessment homes are a short-term solution that all foster kids should have but most don't. The 48 additional beds for 30-day assessments are for children with mental or medical problems and DCS will pay private providers to fill those beds and treat them while DCS figures out where to place them. Quin's assessment homes are modeled somewhat like Isaiah House and Dismas House. They hold families and/or kids temporarily until they are placed somewhere else, but they are charities, not private providers.

Quin says her plan will reduce the 600 higher-needs children who spent 1,100 days and nights in offices between April and September in 2022.

"I'll know more in 6-9 months. I don't think it's going to fix the problem but it's going to move the needle," Quin told lawmakers when she asked for a supplement to the 2023-24 DCS budget.

Assessments that included transparency with birth parents about placement choices could produce better outcomes. If it doesn't, Quin's new assessment model would, at best, be more efficient than the current cruel one, which keeps moving kids into different foster homes more often than any other state. Even if that practice stopped tomorrow, it would not mean DCS would return kids more quickly to their families because it's all about making "better" initial foster placements and not reunification.

Going forward, TennCare will see a recurring $17 million increase to pay for the program. DCS's budget will increase by $3 million. Without

Medicaid expansion 125,000 people will lack health insurance in Tennessee, including 5,000 children. Funding for assessment homes allows DCS to get services for children it has taken from poor families and TennCare pays the bill. But the real cost is the trauma of family separation.

Federal funds account for 65 percent of TennCare's budget, and the state makes up 35 percent. If children stayed with their families and were provided with the services, they need at home, a certain percentage of the 1400 kids in residential facilities and the 8,000 foster kids wouldn't have to be there. Community-based services for both parent and child yield better outcomes than foster care.

State child welfare agencies are under a perverse incentive to take kids from poor families because they get Title IV-E money from the Social Security Administration if a family's income is close to the poverty line. The birth parents don't get the money, though, the foster parents do. Republicans control both houses of the Tennessee legislature. Their numbers are overrepresented on committees like Littleton's Children & Family Affairs Subcommittee.

The next story is about how party leaders block people from speaking who they don't want to listen to. The opposite is also true. People with the "right" agenda never have problems getting scheduled to speak at committee meetings.

Connie Reguli gave a list of people to Rep. Mary Littleton so they could speak at a House Children & Family Affairs Subcommittee Meeting. Littleton chairs that subcommittee. By unwritten House and Senate rules, the names of speakers must be provided 24 hours ahead of a meeting or they will not be called to the podium during the meeting's public comment period.

"I called all these families up. I told them 'I want you to come in. I want you to bring a picture of your child so we can speak after DCS speaks,'" Reguli told them.

Family members Loren Mitchell, her sister Angela and Mitchell's eldest son, Michael, went to the hearing and sat patiently in the gallery waiting for their turn. Loren's youngest son, Skyler, was given to a white foster couple. (See DCS Trolls Black Babies For Cash Chapter Four.)

DCS Families Muzzled in Children & Families Hearing

L-R, Angela Moyo, Michael, 6, holding a photo of Skyler, their mother, Loren Mitchell, holding a photo of both her sons. Michael lives with Moyo. Loren Mitchell wants both boys to live with their Aunt Angela. DCS took Skyler and helped the foster parents file for adoption.

NASHVILLE, TN – Families who came to testify before the House Children & Family Affairs Subcommittee on Wednesday February 9, 2022, were not allowed to address lawmakers. Committee Chairwoman Mary Littleton had a list of speakers two days prior to the meeting, as required, but Speaker of the House Cameron Sexton did not approve them. So, the families sat in the audience waiting for a chance to speak that never came.

DCS Commissioner Jennifer Nichols showed a video presentation to lawmakers highlighting DCS operations and she outlined future plans for the department that keeps asking for more money every year while it has been taking more children into custody every year.

Several DCS officials also briefed the committee. Among them were Sandra Wilson, Deputy Commissioner of Child Programs, Martha Shirk HR Director, and General Counsel Doug Dimond. Nine Republicans and two Democrats also attended the hearing.

The Republicans were quite solicitous to the DCS brass, told them what a hard job they had to do, and Rep. John Rick Eldridge offered Nichols some advice: recruit from 2-year colleges to find more caseworkers. DCS does hire workers with 2-year degrees, but casework requires a bachelor's degree. DCS has 554 empty positions.

"Three- or four-times Nichols told the committee to give them a call if any of their constituents was having a problem and they would find a solution. That is such baloney," Connie Reguli told me.

She said Representative Jason Hodges had called Nichol's office and met with DCS officials about a case in Montgomery County.

"They made him sign a confidentiality agreement that he would not disclose any of the meeting details with the family and he was not allowed to bring any member of the family with him. It was all one-sided," Reguli reported.

There has been progress in that case, in spite of, not because of, DCS intervention. In fact, DCS prolonged the case unnecessarily and harassed the parents by having felony arrest warrants issued against them.

The Tribune confirmed with Montgomery County District Attorney Robert Nash that DCS misled his office and when he found out, he withdrew the warrants. (See https://tntribune.com/twas-the-night-before-christmas/)

At the hearing Nichols presented a number of slides showing custody numbers, number of foster homes, and calls to the Tennessee Child Abuse Hotline.

Then DCS Commissioner Jennifer Nichols testifying at a Children & Family Affairs hearing on Wednesday, Feb. 9, 2022 at the Cordell Hull office building. She told the committee that 80% of children are returned to their parents. According to Child Trends, the most recent reunification rate in Tennessee is 47%.

She didn't tell lawmakers the number of children who entered DCS custody and the number who exited custody back to their birth families last year. DCS has not disclosed those numbers publicly since 2013-14.

"The majority of children who enter DCS custody, actually about 80%, are reunited with their families," Nichols told the committee. According to the federal Adoption and Foster Care Analysis and Reporting System (AFCARS), Tennessee's reunification rate was between 55.2%-57.8% in years 2015-2019.

The Tribune used statistics Nichols presented to the committee to verify her 80% reunification figure.

Here's the math: 8,932 children in custody, up from 8,829 last years; Nichols said the number of children in foster care was 8,211 in Feb. 2021 and 8,359 in Feb. this year; she said 1,764 kids did not go into foster care because they were placed with relatives or family friends; adoptions have been running around 1200 per year for several years. But there are more kids (1764) waiting for adoption than are actually adopted. If you keep subtracting these numbers what you get is a maximum of 2,493 children who could have been reunified with their families last year.

According to the DCS FY 13-14 annual report, 3,545 kids were reunited with their parents. Eight years later, DCS is returning at most 2,500. That is 1,000 fewer reunifications.

Nichols decried the lack of foster homes to take care of kids they take into custody. Apparently, it's a common problem in many states.

Why does DCS keep taking kids into custody when there aren't enough foster homes to take them? And why isn't DCS doing a better job of reuniting kids with their parents?

The families who came to speak at the hearing have stories about what happened to them, and they have answers to both those questions. First, if you are taking more kids into custody than you can care for, maybe you should stop taking so many children into custody. Secondly, if you stopped wrongfully taking our children in the first place, if you stopped using permanency plans and stopped delaying court hearings to block parents from getting their kids back, maybe you'd get better reunification numbers and a much better outcome at the end for everyone.

Update: A 2023 law requires all public hearings to have a public comment period. Although Republicans sponsored the bill, a majority in both parties voted for it.

•••

Katie Beckett: Not a DCS Program

In 2019 the Tennessee General Assembly voted to apply for a federal waiver of the Social Security Act to create the Katie Beckett program. Named after a five-month-old Iowa baby who became paralyzed from encephalitis, the Centers for Medicare and Medicaid Services (CMS) approved the program to provide services for children with disabilities and/or complex medical needs. TennCare and the TN Department of Intellectual and Developmental Disabilities (DIDD) launched the program in November 2020. Children in DCS custody are on Medicaid and are not eligible for the program.

Children enrolled in Part A receive full Medicaid benefits as well as a $15,000 per year for home and community-based services (HCBS) capped benefit package. Due to the complex medical needs of most children in Part A, nursing care accounts for more than 70% of medical costs.

Children enrolled in Part B receive a home and community-based services (HCBS) benefit package capped at $10,000 per child per year. In 2022, Part A expenditures of $31.2 million served 153 children.

Part B families generally use a debit card to pay directly for eligible medical expenses or have such expenses reimbursed. The card is linked to a Flexible Benefit Account of state and federal Medicaid funds. In 2022, Part B expenditures were $18.8 million and served 1,972 children.

Safe Baby Courts (SBC)

Tennessee is one of 27 states operating Baby Courts which focus on children, 0-4, whose mothers are, or have been, addicted to drugs. The

Tennessee SBC program is administered by three partner agencies, namely, the Administrative Office of the Courts (AOC), the Department of Children's Services (DCS), and the Department of Mental Health and Substance Abuse Services (DMHSAS).

DCS is statutorily charged with administering the program and reporting to the Tennessee General Assembly; the AOC is charged with SBC site selection; and DMHSAS is charged with working collaboratively with the other agencies to provide expertise in addressing mental health and substance use disorder issues.

Senator Ferrell Haile is Speaker-Pro Tempore and represents rural Sumner and Trousdale counties. He is the lawmaker who promoted the idea of Baby Court, negotiated the division of labor between juvenile courts and two state agencies with his aide, Chip McConkey, who called Haile the "Father of Tennessee Baby Courts."

"I'd rather he say that than me say that," Haile told me. But there is ample evidence he deserves the moniker.

Haile convinced Governor Bill Lee to fund a pilot program for six Baby Courts in 2017. Two counties already had Baby Courts. Now there are 14. He wants to see them in all 95 Tennessee counties.

"As a pharmacist, I saw time and again children coming through my window that shuffled around from one place to another and not in a permanent home and going from one foster family to another. It just looked like the system was broken," he said.

Haile attended a couple of conferences—one on Adverse Childhood Experiences (ACES) and another in Florida where he first heard about Safe Baby Courts. He learned 80% of a child's brain develops from 0-3. He also learned the national average to get a child to a permanent home was three years or more.

Haile is understated by nature, almost diffident, but when I asked him why Baby Courts were such a big deal, he lit up like a Baptist preacher pounding the pulpit.

"Well, you've taken three years out of that five-year development and inserted chronic ACES into that child's life. No wonder we're having so many problems going forward with children that are in foster care, and they keep in the system, and a lot of them even age-out of the system. Why are we doing this? If we keep doing the same thing we're doing, we're not going to get any better results," he told me.

Haile looks a bit like Governor Bill Lee, who is also a cattle rancher. He wears wire-rim glasses and has a soft lilt to his voice like the gentleman farmer he is.

Father of Tennessee Baby Courts Sen. Ferrell Haile at his ranch in rural Tennessee.

In the 2023-24 budget hearings, Haile got DCS to ask for $1,025,000 to start SBCs in seven more counties. Twenty-seven juvenile courts want to start their own Baby Courts.

"There's a coordinator of services in each one of these. You have got to realize that these folks, these parents, biological parents that come in, have a lot of needs, and so there's a lot of services that are available, already available, but nobody is helping them get it. So, what that person's job is, to get these services."

Tennessee's SBC are problem-solving courts, and the approach is non-adversarial.

When DCS files a neglect petition against a parent, they must go to Juvenile Court. If that county has a Baby Court, the judge can offer them a spot in the program. It's voluntary. In 2022, Tennessee's Baby Courts took 185 cases involving 336 children.

179

"We have one court in Rutherford County that deals only with children that haven't come into custody yet, but are about to come into custody," Haile reported. He said Rutherford County is the only SBC in the country exclusively prioritizing prevention cases.

On average, non-custodial (prevention) cases lasted 342 days in 2022. Custodial (foster care) cases lasted 470 days. Because there is less fighting, Haile noted that prevention cases consistently end sooner for the children.

Permanency happens faster than in typical DCS cases, too. And in some cases when the Mom decides to give up her child, the court negotiates an open adoption. The legal mechanism is called a post adoption contact agreement, so a biological parent who can't raise a child can still stay in the child's life as it grows up. The children are less traumatized by a court that moves quicker, reduces their time in foster care, and takes custody away from DCS and grants it to someone else.

For Haile, SBCs are a no-brainer.

"If you don't take care of them between zero and three years old, you're going to have them at 14," Haile told me.

The results: between 2018-2022, 352 children found permanent situations:

- 155 reunified with parents
- 134 with relatives
- 16 Guardianships
- 47 adoptions

"What we're doing is getting the child back in the home a lot quicker. And to this date, not a single child that has gone back into a biological home has come back into custody."

"The problem in the larger counties is that you don't have that community wraparound service. You don't have that community involvement. Yeah, you get Grundy County, it's almost 100% the locals putting their arms around it. In fact, I would argue that this doesn't work without that nonprofit church community involvement, because in Grundy County or Lake County, which we aren't there yet, it's not like the state has a huge presence in terms of mental health resources and things like that. So, it has to be them."

Judges like the early results. "Prior to the Safe Babies Court, it was very rare to see a parent or set of parents thank a court system which they believed placed a barrier between them and their children. It is heartwarming to see them thank us towards the end of our programming," said Judge Sheila Calloway, Davidson County Juvenile Court.

However, there's a fly in the ointment. Haile told me his vision for Safe Baby Courts was to surround his constituents with the services they need to conquer their addictions. In rural counties that implies using churches and building up the local capacity to provide services to families from people they know and trust.

But that was not the direction DCS took. In 2020, DCS outsourced services to StrongWell to help families with substance use disorders and mental health needs. Its online services were not exclusively for SBC families, but it was targeted for the counties that had established SBC sites. In 2021, StrongWell served 172 families, with 625 individual parents or caregivers receiving services such as alcohol and drug treatment, individual counseling, and mental health therapy.

That same year, Strongwell was sold to Maryland-based Mindoula, a health management company that operates in 17 states. Mindoula did not buy Strongwell because it was community-based, but because it was a good investment. Strongwell had a two-year no bid contract with Tennessee worth $2,000,000 and executive compensation was not disclosed.

•••

181

Big Fish Eat Little Fish

Community Health Systems (CHS), headquartered in Franklin, TN, announced a partnership with Mindoula in September 2023. They intend to provide mental health assessment and treatment, in person and virtual, to more than 700 primary care providers.

CHS is one of the nation's largest healthcare companies. It owns or leases 76 hospitals and owns more than 1,000 clinics in medical specialties like urgent care, surgery, and cancer treatment. CHS operates in 15 states and carries some heavy baggage

In August 2022 a securities class action suit was filed in a federal court in Tennessee against CHS based on allegations that the company misstated its financial condition in documents and statements provided to investors. Bloomberg reported CHS understated bad debts to avoid default and company officials knew about it.

Journalist and scholar Ben Bagdikian wrote a groundbreaking book in 1983 called The Media Monopoly. In it, he described the effects of corporate ownership on mass media in the U.S. Bagdikian showed how fewer and fewer companies were dominating print media like magazines, newspapers, and books as well as television, cable programming, and movies. The Media Monopoly went through several editions and by 2004, the number of major media companies had dwindled from 50 to less than 10.

Bagdikian said that when fewer large corporations' control more and more of what we read and see, especially regarding the news and public affairs, democracy suffers. Already considered ugly in much of the world, Americans were becoming dumber, too.

AT&T was broken up into seven "Baby Bells" in 1983, the same year Bagdikian published The Media Monopoly. He used that big news story to illustrate his thesis. Bagdikian said two things happen when corporations become monopolies: prices go up and customer service goes down.

The same logic applies to the healthcare industry. Mindoula bought Strongwell and then Mindoula partnered with Community Health Systems. Strongwell never had a brick-and-mortar business in Tennessee, but it had a website and still does.

Calls to Strongwell to talk to someone "now" were not answered. A free app to "get immediate access to a community of people who have been where you are" was not available for Android or iOS devices. They are apparently in the process of developing a new Mindoula app.

After looking for a while, I got a Strongwell contact in Tennessee, Anna Denino. I called her several times and left messages. Her voice mail promises she will call back within the next business day. After a week she hadn't returned my call. I also asked DCS to send me copies of contracts with its providers.

I emailed newly hired DCS Communication Director Ashley Zarach specifically asking about Strongwell. She sent me copies of the contracts. Strongwell's corporate name is 180 Health Partners. They got a second Strongwell contract with DCS for about $3 million. It began in December 2022 and expired in June 2024. Zarach said DCS will renew the contract again but didn't have details.

Ben Bagdikian was right. Monopolies aren't good for consumers because they gouge them and provide lousy service. No-bid contracts aren't good for taxpayers for the same reasons. Billed as being in the public interest, public-private partnerships aren't always a win-win situation either.

Little fish (Strongwell) is eaten by a bigger fish (Mindoula) that then becomes a partner with CHS, an even bigger fish. What does that mean for Tennessee baby court moms kicking their drug habits or coping with stress or mental illness? It means there are cheaper and better ways to get the help you need rather than relying on large private providers whose first order of business is getting a government contract.

When former DCS Commissioner Jim Henry (2013-2015) signed up local agencies to work with families who had children in foster care, things started changing for the better in Tennessee. Haile envisioned Safe Baby Courts working the same way.

How Better Things Happen

"We use a lot of our community members," Courtney Wallace told me. She is the Safe Baby Court Coordinator in rural Stewart County. She said her court has used Strongwell in the past but more often chose Health Connect America or Camelot, another DCS contractor. Both of those providers have regional offices throughout Tennessee.

"Our churches are probably some of our biggest resources. They are big supporters of our Safe Baby Court," Wallace told me.

One local church donated the labor, and a local hardware store donated the materials to fix the home of a Safe Baby Court mom, Jessica McCarty, while she was in rehab.

"The house was damaged by a tornado but even before that there was a lot of structural damage to where the children weren't safe to go back to her home," Wallace explained.

"We had funds of our own, so we tapped into our funds and paid for materials, too, got her house fixed so her kids could come back."

"Are they back in the home now?" I asked her.

"They are," she said. "This is a family of six. And all six kids returned back home."

Jessica McCarty

A single mom of six, McCarty went through rural Stewart County's Safe Baby Court in 2021.

"DCS and my probation officer told me I had to go to rehab," she told me.

McCarty's children were in foster care while she went to Freeman Recovery in Dickson about an hour away. McCarty's probation officer got her admitted quickly and Medicare paid for it because she is legally blind.

Once a week for about six months she got therapy and took parenting classes with Strongwell via Zoom. I got the distinct impression McCarty only used them because she had to in order to get her kids back. She told me she finished with Strongwell in early 2022. McCarty found her own online support group while in rehab and has continued with them since she got out.

While McCarty was in rehab, Stewart County Safe Baby Court coordinator Courtney Wallace organized volunteers to fix McCarty's house. It needed a new roof and church members even built an extra bedroom.

"Throughout that rehab stint and getting out, Safe Baby Court showed up for me in ways like paying for two months' rent at a sober living facility. Not only has Safe Baby Court been supportive of me and a huge motivator for me while I was recovering, but they have continued to stay in my life," she said.

Sometimes SBC's Courtney Wallace takes McCarty's family to church. McCarty reaches out to her when she has an issue with one of her children. She told me Safe Baby Court got Christmas presents for the children even after she was no longer with the SBC anymore.

"I went into this with a horrible thought--with resentment, really, for the criminal justice system and DCS and all that, but my perspective has changed 100%. They were not there to degrade me or damn me. They have only wanted to see me do better. And they have proven that to me time and time again.

"In recovery meetings that I do every day, I cannot express in that group my gratitude. The only way I can think of paying Baby Court back for the help they have given me and the love they have shown me, is by continuing to stay clean and to continue to do the loving thing. The only way I will ever be able to make amends to Safe Baby Court is just continuing to be a better human being than what I was when I went into the system," she told me.

Every SBC works a bit differently. Nashville is in Davidson County where Jill Overton runs the program.

"In my court we do meet monthly. Each family has a team that surrounds it. So, you may have a mom. You may have a mom and a dad. But the department is involved in all of our cases. The belly of the beast is that we have many cases of neglect and dependency within in Davidson County Juvenile Court and they also involve the Department of Children's Services. We take a small population. We only run 20 cases at a time. That's not 20 children. That's 20 family units but the child has to be under the age of four to be part of this program. So that's the entering child and then the siblings may come along.

Overton said Safe Baby Courts aren't run like DCS handles most Neglect and Dependency cases. In SBC a child's caregiver comes to court as does the birth parent(s). Another big difference is that Juvenile Court Magistrate Olen Winningham is presiding at those court reviews and hears exactly what's been going on with a case. Each family gets an hour. Winningham hears eight case reports every Monday. Overton schedules reviews at least once a month per family.

"It's a voluntary program. Both the mom and dad or whoever is involved have to be ready and willing to do the intensive work that we are going to ask of them. And really kind of meet us where we are— coming into court once a month, having family meetings once a month and getting that individualized extra support. So, I kind of glue everything together and find the missing pieces that the department can't supply," Overton explained.

If the family has insurance, it usually only pays for 28 days of drug rehab. If the family doesn't have insurance or runs out of coverage, Overton starts looking elsewhere to get families the help they need. That's a big part of her job. DCS contracts with some providers like Health Connect to do alcohol and drug assessment or intensive parenting assessments depending on what the needs are.

"One of the man reasons DCS contracted with Strongwell was to fit that missing piece. Where there may not be grant funds, there may not be insurance, so we have that contracted availability through Strongwell as well."

SBC coordinators see to it that the families get the services they need. That's a big part of their job and they hope parents take advantage of what they are offered. The context is much different than a DCS caseworker who enforces parenting plans requiring parents who have lost their children to comply and if they don't, they pay a price and eventually lose their children permanently.

"We don't run on phases," Overton explained. "We do have a family treatment court that does have a phase-specific program. That's another specialty court we have but we do not run on phases.

"Within recovery we recognize that relapse typically will come into play. We also want to make sure when we're addressing the need we're not just addressing what brought them here–not the fact that you just were just using drugs and your baby had drugs in their system.

"We're not just putting a band aid on the situation. We're not just making them do an assessment, 28 days' treatment and out the door. You did what we asked you to do, so you're done," Overton told me.

She said 90% of the cases are babies who were exposed to drugs and they come into the program straight from the hospital. Most of the parents had some trauma in their childhood that led them to use drugs, and they need therapy to get to the root of it.

"We're trying to go all the way back and look at that trauma, look at the intergenerational trauma. Sometimes we have families where the grandmother is taking care of that child. Well, that grandmother is parenting those grandchildren the same way she parented her daughter.

We need to get to the crux of where there was some breakdown and make sure we're educating the whole family, to make them all healthy because they're going to continue to be a family unit."

Not every case that goes through SBC ends in reunification but that is the goal. Overton told me every family has a specific dynamic that must change if SBC is going to be successful. Most parents whose children are in DCS custody go through what Overton called a cookie cutter program and too often it doesn't work.

"You're going to be with us for 14 months. If you don't get your baby back and you don't get clean within 14 months, you're out of luck."

The SBC family team doesn't hold the threat of termination over the parents, and it makes for better outcomes. Senator Haile told me that no child whose family went through Safe Baby Court has reentered foster care. That is remarkable.

Still, not every case ends happily ever after. Overton tells a story about a couple who stayed clean when they were by themselves but when they were together, they started using drugs again. Eventually, a great grandmother got custody of their child.

We ended up closing out that case. Sadly, shortly after that closed, the great grandmother passed away. It's a really sad situation of an elderly family member who's taking care of four little bitty children. Is that the best-case scenario? I don't know but it's also family. We really have to forward think when we're closing out these cases about what the future looks like and have those strong conversations," she told me.

At this point, Tennessee's Baby Courts are public-private partnerships resolving a serious social issue. Maybe they will continue to show good results. Maybe they won't or become too expensive. There are 22 jurisdictions with Baby Courts in Tennessee. DCS asked for funding to add five more in FY 24-25, and they got it.

SBCs are the opposite of normal DCS operations. The team approach works because family meetings not just the DCS caseworker "checking up" on the birth parents like getting detention after school except it can be much worse than that. You can lose your kids forever if those meetings don't go well.

Hearings and Floor Votes

Politicians like to hear themselves talk. They don't listen all that well, especially when it comes to reforming DCS. I sat through a dozen hearings and streamed videos of a dozen others.

Unlike Juvenile Court proceedings, you can at least see the legislative process and watch the budget hearings and see how various bills move through committees. That said, the people with speaking parts in these histrionic melodramas, are a pretty dim crowd.

They don't seem to understand the simple awful truth: DCS takes far too many children into custody, and it can't care properly for the ones it takes. A lot of lawmakers get that but nothing they do addresses that fundamental problem.

DCS Commissioner Margie Quin spoke to lawmakers April 17, 2023, updating them on a spate of new hires. Knoxville Republican Justin Lafferty deflated her spiel a bit.

"We could throw all the money in the world at this. We could hire all the people in the world to take on these roles. We could get caseloads down to five. There is still no state substitute for a loving mother and father in a home to take care of a child," Lafferty stated.

Both Lafferty and Quin spoke during a DCS sunset hearing in April 2023. They happen every four years. In this case, the department got a new lease on life until June 2024, but the bill does require quarterly reports to the Government Operations Committee. The fanfare of DCS's official parole—and all such hearings, really—features esoteric jargon and spitfire exchanges between lawmakers that amount to "kicking the can down the road."

Connie Reguli posted an article in The Tennessee Conservative in January 2023. She listed organizations that partner with DCS. Dozens of department allies, who benefit from DCS operations by their collaboration, don't face questions from lawmakers at DCS budget hearings because they don't show up. The politicians give them a pass.

"DCS works in cooperation with a vast array of resources and professionals, some funded through additional state taxpayer funds, federal grants, and private donations." The article listed 12 organizations and noted there are at least 85 private contractors who work for DCS. DCS has 574 contracts for FY24 which cost $544 million––more than one third of its total budget of $1.4 billion. Not all DCS contracts are with private providers but it's clear that Tennessee's child welfare system has been largely privatized.

The article concludes: "However, not a single commission, non-profit, or private contractor was present on December 14th to face questions from the General Assembly on how a system so surrounded with professionals, funds, and for-profit contractors could fail children so miserably."

After considering 101 bills filed under the Department of Children's Services (DCS), the Tennessee 113th General Assembly adjourned Friday, April 21, 2023. The bills fell into three general categories: administrative or bi-partisan bills which were not particularly controversial, bills sponsored by Democrats that either failed or were amended by Republicans, and lastly, bills sponsored by Republicans which either passed or were withdrawn for similar versions sponsored by fellow Republicans.

Tennessee Republicans have a super majority and some play to the extremist base within the party. There is no real competition from

Democrats so there is no need to be reasonable or even care that much about what your constituents want when you hold most of the cards. Nowhere is that more evident than in the debate over abortion rights.

There is no debate in Tennessee. It is one of 14 states that have banned abortions. You can't get an abortion even in the case of incest or rape of a child. About 80% of voters in Tennessee want exceptions to protect the life of the mother. Will Brewer is the chief Right to Life lobbyist in Tennessee. According to the Tennessee Holler he convinced Republicans not to include exceptions to the abortion law like an ectopic pregnancy.

This same Right to Life movement influenced a number of bills loosening restrictions and shortening waiting periods for adoptions in Tennessee. Getting abandoned babies into good homes sooner seems like a good policy because it cuts through red tape which delays adoptions unnecessarily. But what about parents who did not abandon their babies but had them taken away? In 2021, DCS terminated parental rights more than 1,000 times.

Sometimes parents lose their children because they didn't have a strong legal defense. According to Connie Reguli, at least two new laws facilitate child trafficking.

"All kinds of things in here are red flags to me," Reguli told me.

One bill requires DCS to file a petition for termination of parental rights within 14 days if a court finds severe child abuse in a case. I reported four stories about bogus drug charges made against parents who had their children taken away for severe abuse. Now, in such cases, it will be even harder to get them back.

Reguli told me the legislature passed other bills that allow DCS to tighten the noose around birth parents "who have no recourse" while at the same time enabling foster parents and prospective adoptive parents to enter into contracts with mothers who are willing to give up their baby and receive compensation. "This whole thing is baby trafficking waiting to happen," Reguli said.

One new law prohibits a kinship foster placement if they share a home with birth parents. One section permits foster patents to attend court hearings as a party in the case and another allows contract providers to be witnesses.

Another new law creates a cause of action for a false adoption. Someone can sue an agency or social worker but not the adoptive parents if there is a wrongful adoption like Skyler Mitchell's story in Chapter Five.

Birth parents cannot contest an adoption and have no recourse after 6 months, but adoptive parents can sue for fraud after 6 months. "If you put all these together you can see how one-sided they are," Reguli told me.

The 113th General Assembly was like the 112th except even more so. Tennessee Democrats have long chafed under the rules and procedures that make it almost impossible to move legislation through committees to a floor debate.

Frustrated with the Republicans who did nothing after six people were gunned down at a Christian school in Nashville on March 27, 2023, three Democratic representatives approached the podium in the House chamber to protest the lack of action on guns. The press dubbed them "The Tennessee Three." Two were expelled for their actions and one survived by just one vote. The two expelled members were re-appointed and back in the House in about a week.

The incident made national headlines for several days and Justin Jones, Gloria Johnson, and Justin Pearson were invited to meet with President Biden and Vice-President Harris in Washington. None of that helped Tennessee Democrats gain any traction in the law-making process back home.

Johnson talked with the press about the debilitating politics in Tennessee where there is no real bipartisanship because the process is blatantly biased in favor of the Republican super majority. Child welfare legislation is just one area, among many, where Democrats don't live to fight another day. They fight to just come back and lose another day. It's guaranteed.

It doesn't matter, for example, that a large majority of voters want reasonable gun control; they don't want an abortion ban; they want voting rights and better schools but not more charter schools, and so on. But all of this falls on deaf ears.

I asked Senator Haile, the Baby Court booster, if it wouldn't be better to change the rules to allow the same number of people from each party on legislative committees. He shook his head and recalled a time when Democrats controlled politics in Tennessee for decades and shut out the Republicans. In his mind, the Democrats have had it coming for a long time and Republicans are going to give it to them now.

Despite the veneer of legitimacy, single party politics suppresses a democratic process and tends towards an authoritarian form of government. This state of affairs infects state agencies like DCS that pretty much ignore the rule of law and its own policies when it's convenient and makes excuses when it has to but is never held to account.

Haile failed to get his fellow Republicans to pass a bill to cap the number of cases DCS workers are assigned. Some have juggled as many as 90 cases. Haile's bill would have capped the number at 20 and reduced it to 18 in a couple of years. Former DCS Communication Director Alexandra Denis said her agency was in favor of a cap but "the financial note associated with these changes kept it from passing."

Denis passed the buck to the General Assembly, which passed the largest DCS budget ever, but the caseload limit didn't make it through the budget process, according to Haile. Something is wrong with that picture. Representative Johnson and Senator Heidi Campbell said they would immediately start pushing to pass the bill in the next session.

Campbell complained that while Republicans commit to policies that would help people, they continually "let us down."

For several years running, a 20-caseload limit has been proposed for DCS workers in the General Assembly, but it has yet to pass a law that would force DCS to be more accountable and get better outcomes for everyone involved.

"Trial courts cannot ascertain what is in the child's best interests by simply deferring to a CASA's ... position. Courts must instead consider the positions of all the parties and reach their own conclusions." —Justice Mary Yu, Washington State Supreme Court.

Chapter Seven: CASA and the Role of NGOs

Isaiah 117 House and AGAPE provide temporary shelter and foster care to the needy. Several organizations including Renewal House, Thistle Farms, Catholic Charities, Dismas House, and the Metro Family Safety Center do similar work in Tennessee. However, DCS uses charities for its own purposes.

DCS uses Isaiah 117 House to shelter kids temporarily until they can be placed in foster homes. Anointed Hands is a provider who babysits kids in hospitals, so DCS doesn't have to keep them in one of its 12 regional offices overnight. In recent years, the press has hammered the department for doing that. Still, it's kind of sketchy to hire babysitters in hospitals because technically they are drop-in childcare centers and cannot provide care more than 7 hours a day or 14 hours a week. In April 2023, DCS Commissioner Margie Quin told lawmakers that DCS is no longer keeping children in offices or in hospitals overnight.

Meanwhile, foster parents get a childcare allowance from DCS. But providing childcare to working parents who can't afford it? That would be a lot cheaper than taking poor kids into custody and paying for foster parents to raise them. No, that's not in the Governor or DCS's playbook.

Court Appointed Special Advocates (CASA) is a national network of volunteers and attorneys who advocate for children in juvenile court. Founded in 1977, CASA volunteers get training by the state or local

CASA offices because states have different laws regarding foster care and their procedures vary by jurisdiction.

In 1991, the Victims of Child Abuse Act authorized CASA to train Guardians ad Litem (GAL) attorneys and volunteers. They take a 40-hour course. The goal was to ensure that by January 1, 1995, a court-appointed special advocate would be available to every victim of child abuse or neglect in the United States who needed an advocate.

The National Bar Association endorsed CASA volunteers in 1997. By 2007 CASA provided advocates to more than 2 million children in the U.S. In 2018, the number of CASA/GAL volunteers across the country grew to 93,300 who represented 271,800 children and youth in 950 programs. In 2021, Congress designated May 18 as CASA/GAL Volunteer's Day.

In Tennessee, the courts hire lawyers to be Guardians ad Litem (GAL). Judges do not automatically assign GALs to every case but CASA volunteers and some of their attorney's work with children who have been taken by DCS. Only a small percentage of CASA cases are "preventative" where children may be in state custody but live at home with their parents or relatives.

CASA has access to juvenile courts in Tennessee, which the public does not. They also have access to DCS investigations and other case files that are not disclosed. Davidson County CASA Executive Director Julieanna Huddle told me their budget of about $1 million is not nearly enough to handle every foster care case in Nashville so they have to triage and take on only the worst cases.

Richard Wexler, NCCPR's Executive Director, says there is a basic contradiction at the heart of CASA. "CASA has been passing itself off as speaking for the child. Much of the time, it does no such thing," Wexler says.

A March 2017 law review article in Social Science Research Network (SSRN) argued CASA gives voice to white supremacy because the bulk of CASA volunteers are well-intentioned middle-class whites.

They tell the judge what's best for a child and "to a frightening degree, the judges rubber-stamp the recommendations," Wexler says.

On its website, CASA brags that judges take their advice 94% of the time. But how independent are CASA volunteers when they are so cozy with judges?

CASA commissioned the largest study of its operations ever done and the results were unexpectedly poor. In its own report, CASA's only accomplishments were to prolong foster care and reduce the chance the children would be placed with relatives (instead of strangers) —while doing nothing to improve child safety.

CASA was created to be "the child's voice in court" but when CASA tells the judge it's best for the child to remain in foster care you can't be a child's voice in court if they want to go home.

A GAL's job is not always cut and dried. They must advocate for a child's best interest but also represent the child's wishes, especially if they are old enough to know their own minds. In addition, CASA attorneys are insiders who are "the eyes and ears" of judges who don't have the time but still need background and advice on specific juvenile cases. Some CASA volunteers are first and foremost advocates for children. They fight for them in court against the wishes of the child welfare agency that has them in custody.

So, CASA wears multiple hats in foster cases. Having an advocate to protect a child's best interest is a great idea. Giving judges CASA's input in a case can be a good thing. But advocating for what the child wants often gets short shrift in custody hearings which usually end up putting children in foster care. CASA, just like child welfare agencies, is fundamentally conflicted about its mission.

Juvenile courts are treacherous waters for attorneys who represent parents and families in these cases. GALS used to do their own investigations and then send for your eyes only reports to the judge. But in 2011 the Tennessee Supreme Court ruled that Guardians ad Litem could no longer file secret hearsay reports.

"So, then CASA started doing it," says family law attorney Connie Reguli.

"So, CASA goes out and does a quote-unquote 'investigation'. They talk to people, blah, blah, blah. They write stuff down, and then they file it with the court. But you are not part of that special relationship, and you don't get it. You usually don't see it until the day you walk into court and they're filing it with the judge, and the judge is reading it.

"It's trial by ambush when you walk into the courtroom and you're faced with something that you have been unable to prepare for," Reguli says.

"By statute they are appointed to investigate, which is fine, they can go do that, but they should be sharing that information with everybody equally so you can cross- examine these people," she reports.

There are two departures from the normal course of litigation that show the landmines faced by parents and their attorneys in these cases.

"Even though you're supposed to get a 72-hour hearing after DCS takes a child, the case worker can just sit up there and go 'well, we received a report that the child blah, blah, blah.' You can't even do that in criminal law. You can't do hearsay on a preliminary hearing. But they can do it in a probable cause hearing in juvenile court. They always do and they never bring the witnesses so you can't cross-examine them," she complained.

Reguli says you can't properly prepare a defense when you walk into court knowing you will be blind-sided. It's one of her pet peeves.

"DCS never provides records prior to the preliminary hearing. An attorney has to fight to get them, which could take weeks or months. And they are corrupted when you get them. They're incomplete. There are delayed entries and witnesses are not identified," Reguli says.

Juvenile Court rules state that child neglect trials should be heard within 30 days of the date of the filing of the neglect and dependency petition. But with all the obstacles DCS puts in the way, cases drag on for months.

"And all the while the parents are ordered to adhere to DCS demands like drug tests, home visits, supervised visits, and psych evaluations before they have even been found guilty of anything," she says.

How many times do judges decide the kids should go back home? Unfortunately, it's hard to know. Those statistics are not available and would be very useful to gauge how well courts are adjudicating foster child cases. Bad record-keeping is how DCS has been able to disguise— and squirm out of--the generally bad job it's been doing for 25 years investigating, prosecuting, and managing foster care cases.

CASA is no better. "We do not disaggregate our data," Lori Morris told me. She is Chief Program Strategy and Impact Office at the CASA national office in Washington.

In 2020, CASA reported 42% of case closures were the result of reunification with parents or primary caretakers and a small percentage of youth remaining with their parents throughout the case. Fewer than .5% reentered foster care.

According to CASA's own statistics, in 2021 83% of cases resulted in family reunification, legal guardianship, adoption, relative placement, or continued care at home by parents. Morris said the 2021 statistic is the combined percentages of all categories. So, about half the children were reunited with their birth families and half were either adopted or placed with a guardian. That is roughly the same percentage as the outcomes DCS gets in Tennessee.

So, what is being measured here: better outcomes or just similar results reported by both CASA and DCS? How often do they disagree on a child's placement? We don't know. While CASA toots its own horn saying children in foster care do far better, some researchers dispute that claim.

"Over 25 years that I've made observations of CASA I have seen it become incorporated into the complete power train that pushes kids into foster care. CASA volunteers may make a few home visits, but they have become nothing more than the extension of the DCS caseworker," Reguli told me.

Family & Children's Service

By way of contrast, Family & Children's Service (F&CS) is a venerable charity serving Nashville families since 1943. Only the Salvation Army, American Red Cross and Goodwill Industries have been here longer. F&CS is a social service agency.

F&CS' website says it "serves all people in crisis and transition by meeting them where they are, understanding their needs, and connecting them to the resources they need. F&CS often 'fills in the gaps' in social services, creating a safety net to ensure that all children and families can be safe and healthy."

"We work with both Tennessee Department of Human Services (DHS) and Tennessee Department of Children's Services (DCS). With DCS, we run the Relative Caregiver Program for much of middle TN and a few counties west of the Tennessee River," said Michael McSurdy, President and CEO of F&CS.

When it began, F&CS's primary mission was finding homes for WWII orphans. It handled adoptions until the 1970s when DHS became the legal guardian for children taken into custody. F&CS partnered with DHS then and later with DCS. F&CS has an array of programs and gets funding from a variety of sources, including DCS. F&CS is a DCS partner. McSurdy's outfit is like the good cop and DCS is the bad cop.

"We have what we call permanency counseling services designed to support children into permanency or in their permanent homes," McSurdy told me.

F&CS works to secure what DCS calls "forever families" for children who have special needs and are hard to place. The agency provides counseling to children whose parents are or have struggled with substance abuse or addiction. McSurdy said they counsel relative caregivers and birth, adoptive, or foster parents as requested.

"This work intersects with DCS as some of the children have been in custody, or are at risk, or live with relatives," he told me, In Safe Baby Court family reunification has always been the primary goal.

"We have found the program a real asset to supporting children and families to remain together, leveraging resources and supports to assure families remain intact," he told me.

According to Coordinator Jill Overton, the Davidson County Safe Baby Court relies primarily on F&CS to provide counseling and social services to young moms and dads who have substance abuse problems but who want to keep their babies. In 2022 and 2023, twenty-five families went through Safe Baby Court in Davidson County. That's a very small number compared with the 90,000 Tennesseans F&CS works with each year. And it's a very small number compared with the 8,000 foster cases DCS manages every year.

Jessica McCarty is so grateful because the people who were involved in her case were genuinely trying to help her out, including the DCS caseworker. F&CS helps addicted moms recover and stay clean. The gestalt is completely different from how DCS handles most cases because F&CS, the Safe Baby Court, and the family teams work towards reunification as the best result for the parents and the child. They make sure the moms get the resources they need to recover and stay clean. It is a sweet irony that F&CS lost its primary mission to Tennessee's DHS and later to DCS but now finds itself in partnership with Davidson

County's Safe Baby Court (SBC) filling a gap in social services DCS doesn't provide and couldn't hope to match.

If DCS scaled up the SBC/F&CS model by several magnitudes, the department could reunify many more families instead of tearing them apart. The next story shows how a judge, DCS, and an NGO colluded to take away a child from their parents, keep them away, and put a little boy in foster care until DCS filed to terminate the mom's parental rights.

•••

Juvenile Judge and DCS Collusion Alleged

DCS Provider Delays Reunification While Fosters Break Parental Bond.

Catrina and Chris Prokop on September 13, 2021, outside Knox County Juvenile Court.

KNOXVILLE, TN – A custody case here highlights a big problem with child welfare in Tennessee: collusion between Juvenile Court judges and the Department of Children's Services (DCS) and its foster system that takes kids from their families and abuses its power to keep them there.

The case also shows how outside contractors, who provide foster care for about half of the 8000 children DCS takes into custody every year, conspire to keep them from re-unifying with their parents. Catrina and Chris Prokop are trying to get DCS to return Catrina's 5-year-old boy, Zaylen. He has been in foster care since February 2020. The foster home provider is Childhelp, a national nonprofit that contracts with DCS for foster and adoption services in Knoxville. Childhelp operates in California, Arizona, Tennessee, and Virginia. It had state and local contracts worth $36 million in 2020.

The Backstory

Catrina grew up hard. She has been on her own since she was 16. She made some bad choices, but she has made some good ones, too, particularly where her kids are concerned.

Chris grew up in a boys' home in Oregon. "I got in trouble a little bit when I was a kid, learned 'ok', that's not the way to go and got myself corrected and kind of made a little bit of myself. I am not without means," Prokop told me.

DCS hates two things: people who have the resources to defend themselves in court and people who don't lie.

"There is so much underhanded stuff going on. There is a group who are working together to steal our baby," he said.

On November 28, 2019, Catrina gave birth to son Bentley, now 2. A drug screen showed he had methadone in his system. Mom was on methadone under doctor's order to help her kick an addiction to pills. He advised her not to withdraw from it while she was pregnant because it could harm the baby.

"There was nothing in his system but methadone," Catrina told the Tribune. Catrina had taken Percocet and Gabapentin for a blood clot in her leg and after some dental work while she was pregnant. However, she was tested, and they were out of her system three months before Bentley was born. Since then, she has slowly weaned off the methadone and stopped taking it completely in January 2022. Except for methadone, she has been clean for three years.

However, DCS has an addiction it can't seem to kick. It likes to snatch babies. They took baby Bentley into custody from the hospital on December 1, 2019. (See https://tntribune.com/twas-the-night-before-christmas/)

"I didn't even get to see him," Catrina said. She had supervised visitation every two weeks for two hours with her boy. That lasted a few months. Then DCS gave Bentley to his father, who has not let Catrina see him since June 2021. She has supervised visitation with Zaylen every week for an hour while he remains in foster care.

The Trial

DCS brought a dependency and neglect case against Catrina. According to the Prokops, the case was a travesty. It involved perjury, denial of due process, false allegations of drug abuse, and false reports filed by Childhelp that were taken as gospel by the judge.

"I feel like when I walked in there I didn't' even have a chance," Catrina said.

She said she was attacked and not listened to. "And the judge was pretty much arguing on behalf of DCS. She was biased," she told me.

"Apparently Bentley and Zaylen have a Mom who's a drug user," Magistrate Irene Joseph said.

"That's absolutely not true," Catrina said. Magistrate Joseph found her guilty anyway.

"We are appealing because the state failed to prove its case," said Brandon Potter, the Prokops' lawyer.

"We had expert testimony from a leading fetal development doctor in the country and they didn't' want to listen to his reasoning. Dr. Emanuel Vlastos said the things she did in no way, shape, or form did any harm to the child. He's not some 'joe blow' doctor we found in the corridor. He teaches in the medical school at the University of Missouri," Potter explained.

DCS has a playbook it pulls out in Juvenile Courtrooms all over Tennessee. It has many players on its team. Winning requires portraying Mom as a drug addict to get permanent legal custody of a child they have already wrongfully taken.

As previously stated, of the players in this case is Childhelp, the DCS contract provider, who placed Zaylen in a foster home.

Catrina and Zaylen on February 23, 2021, outside Childhelp visitation site in Knoxville.

Erin Law works for Childhelp. She reported that during one of Catrina's visits with Zaylen, Catrina went to the bathroom to take drugs. When she came out, Law's supervisor accused her of taking a pill while she was in there. When Catrina left, she went straight to get a drug test that came back negative.

That didn't make it into Childhelp's monthly report to DCS, so the judge never knew the test was negative. But the unfounded allegation did.

Prokop offered to pay to polygraph all three of them to find out who was lying. Childhelp declined his offer.

Foster mom, Shana Leist, reported a black truck parked outside her home that also followed her around. She said she had a photo with license plate number. The allegation was made but "the photo never showed up,'" Prokop said. He owns a black truck but said he was in Missouri on business at the time of the alleged stalking.

"But it still ended up in the report that goes to the judge and all parties in the case get copies," Prokop said.

According to Childhelp, during one of his visits, Chris peed all over the bathroom and in their opinion, he needed a psychiatric evaluation. According to Prokop, they're the crazy ones.

Zaylen's therapist, who works for Childhelp, testified against the Prokops in the trial. She didn't say much about Zaylen, except that he was anxious, had trouble sleeping, and wasn't ready for a trial home visit with the Prokops. Chris Prokop said the therapist talked a lot about what bad people they were.

Chris reached out to the foster parents, Shana and David Leist, but they were not interested in meeting them "I wanted them to see we are good people,' Chris said. For his part Zaylen calls Mrs. Leist "Mommy" now. He reported to Catrina that "Mommy" told him Trina didn't take care of him and doesn't love him. Zaylen now calls Catrina "Trina" and not 'Mommy' anymore.

DCS is required to have regular family planning meetings with the goal to either return the child to its family or seek termination of parental rights so the child can be adopted. A Childhelp caseworker was present at those meetings about Zaylen.

When DCS takes a child, it draws up a permanency plan with the goal of reunification. But the longer the case drags on, at some point DCS will put termination of parental rights on the table. That's what happened in this case.

"It was just one delay after another," Chris Prokop said. He said COVID shut down the courthouse for months and when the case finally got in front of the Magistrate, she delayed it for another 2½ months to give DCS time to refute Mom's expert medical witness.

After Magistrate Joseph found Catrina guilty anyway, it took a month to get transcripts to prepare an appeal. "When we filed a notice of appeal. It took 3½ months for them to get the case from one desk to another desk in Chancery Court,' Prokop said. It's hard to say if that was incompetence or designed inefficiency, or both. But the longer a case drags on, the more likely DCS will sue for termination of parental rights.

The Aftermath

Every year since 2015, DCS has had more than 1,000 kids waiting to be adopted. In 2019, it had 1743, according to the U.S. Department of Health & Human Services.

If you want to adopt a child, you can go through an agency or you can apply with DCS. DCS foster families sometimes adopt their foster children. But dealing with DCS can be a tricky business for everyone involved.

DCS routinely plays birth families and foster families against each other. They encourage competition between them. DCS acts like some high school kid who sets up fistfights after school. They don't care who wins. DCS takes its share of the pot and moves on to the next case. There's always another case.

When kids are about to be returned to their birth family, DCS informs the foster parents. That happened to Angela Moyo Jr. In that case, the foster parents immediately filed a termination petition in Circuit Court and stopped the placement. All this adversarial backstabbing and manipulation has a price tag. It's pricey to go through court proceedings no matter which side you are on. DCS controls the action, and kids can wind up as hostages or collateral damage. (See https://tntribune.com/dcs-trolls-black-babies-for-cash/)

The Prokops told DCS they were going to file an appeal on January 13, 2022. The fosters got wind of it, probably through Childhelp who heard it from DCS. On January 12, Shana and David Leist filed two petitions in Chancery Court to terminate parental rights (TPR) and to stop DCS from pulling Zaylen from their home and placing him elsewhere, including returning Zaylen to his birth Mother.

On Tuesday January 26, lawyers met outside court and struck a deal. Shana and David Leist withdrew their petition to restrain DCS from taking Zaylen, but the TPR petition is still pending in Knox County Chancery Court. This is an example of how DCS maintains control of child welfare cases while pretending to be acting in the child's best interest.

According to Prokop, the Leist's TPR petition copied and pasted a lot of hearsay and unsubstantiated evidence from DCS's Dependency and Neglect petition. A Chancery Court judge may insist they prove those allegations. One can always hope.

TPR cases have priority under Tennessee law. As soon as the fosters filed their TPR petition, the custody battle stopped. Even if the Chancery court denies the TPR, the foster parents can appeal, and while that plays out nothing happens. The longer the case drags on, the longer the separation, and the more alienation the child and its birth mother suffer.

"I've had termination that took 6,7,8,9,10 months, a year," Potter said. But he said three to four months would be a realistic time frame before he would expect to argue the Prokops' appeal.

At some point, however, the bond between child and Mom can be permanently severed. The Prokops think that is exactly what the opposing players are trying to do.

"During my visits with Zaylen, I could just feel their hostility. I was uncomfortable going to visit him because I didn't know what they might do," Catrina said.

As a party in the case, Childhelp not only testified falsely against the birth family, but also did everything they could to delay family therapy and trial home visits. They said Zaylen wasn't ready.

A weekend with the Prokops might well be in Zaylen's best interest but it's not in Childhelp's interest.

Zaylen and Chris December 23, 2021, at the Childhelp visitation center.

Why should they cooperate with family reunification?

Call it collusion, conspiracy, or a kangaroo court. In the Juvenile Court case, DCS, the magistrate, the Guardian ad Litem, Childhelp, and the foster parents were in cahoots.

The Prokops had an expert witness and their lawyer on the other side. The Prokops lost. The longer the case remains unresolved the biggest loser will be 5-year-old Zaylen. Nobody knows how long that will take.

Update: Two years later, Zaylen is living with the fosters and the parental bond with Catrina has been severed. "She's given up," Prokop said. The adoption has not been finalized yet, but they are no longer contesting it. "It wore me out financially," he said. Prokop lost his business in Jacksonville. "It bankrupted me," he told me. I could hear the weary resignation in his voice.

"A child is more dependent on me to figure things out." – Guardian ad Litem Jessica Ramsey.

"I find GALs to be another arm of DCS." – Connie Reguli.

Chapter Eight: Lawyers, Litigators, and How Money Flows Through the System

Guardians ad Litem are lawyers who represent children in court.

Jessica Ramsey sometimes works as a Guardian ad Litem in DCS cases in Knox County. Ramsey told me that when a parent, whose drug or alcohol addiction caused them to lose custody of their kids, the judge will typically order an alcohol and drug assessment and a mental health assessment.

"That's so the parents get plugged in with the services they need," Ramsey says.

"Most of the time when DCS files, I'm sitting in there and looking at the petition and I'm thinking 'Why did you wait so long? This child could have died!'"

Ramsey takes her role as Guardian ad Litem seriously. But she says she has seen cases when a parent goes into rehab and stays clean, they get more visitation or even trial home visits after six months.

She said regaining custody would take much longer until the family showed they had proper housing, employment to put food on the table, childcare, transportation, and meet any other conditions the judge may impose.

Her biggest beef with DCS is that they drop the case without helping the parents meet the court's conditions to regain custody at the final hearing.

"If you have a family member that can provide for them then CPS closes their case a couple weeks after the preliminary hearing is done. Then it's just me and the parents' attorney who come back for the final which is the adjudication and disposition," she said. But that could take months.

CPS workers rarely show up for final hearings. Ramsey says they don't know anything about whether the parents have completed the assessments in their permanency plan. If the CPS worker testifies, it's only about their original investigation of the case, not what has happened since.

"It's shocking, isn't it? They start these things, but they don't finish them. I would make the CPS worker stay active until the case is ended," she told me.

In the beginning when the child is placed with a relative, the CPS worker will close the case. They may do some initial referrals for mom and dad to get A&D (alcohol and drug) and mental health treatment but if they don't have insurance, it's hard for mom and dad to pay for it, Ramsey says.

She rarely sees parents do the assessments and get treatment when a child is placed with a relative. "And I believe the reason for that is they can still see the child with their family member, and they don't have to give up their addiction."

Ramsey would not talk about specific cases but gave the example of a mother who was taking drugs until two months before she gave birth. Traces showed up in the baby's drug screen and DCS took custody of the newborn. That's a slam-dunk for DCS. Fifteen months later, DCS can, and often does, sue for termination of parental rights.

In a foster case there is a permanency plan, and it stipulates things a parent must do. "Parents are more likely to do what they are supposed to do when their child is in foster care because they know that if they do not, DCS is going to be pursuing termination and adoption."

Final hearings are set about ten months after the preliminary.

"Nine times out of ten the parents are not ready for custody. And then grandma is given physical and legal custody," Ramsey told me.

"If we have a parent who has been using meth and fentanyl for years, they're going to need 6 months of sobriety before they move to unsupervised and they are going to have to continue in their sobriety probably for about a year before they re-file and ask for custody."

If the parents have been making progress the final disposition may adjust the parents' visitation schedule to allow unsupervised visits. But officially the case is closed. DCS and the juvenile court are no longer involved.

"Always in that final order we tell the parents 'This is what you need to do to regain custody'. If the parents do those things, they can file a petition to regain custody, but the parents would have to initiate that after the case is closed," Ramsey explained

The parents' petition for custody is the beginning of a new court case. And getting unsupervised visitation is like the 7th inning stretch. The home team is ahead. But the game isn't over yet for parents or their children.

If a family member takes the children, DCS takes its foot off the gas and follows a path of least resistance. If the child is in foster care, it's a whole different ballgame.

"I've seen some very grave safety concerns," Ramsey says.

Sometimes she fights a family placement that DCS is fine with. Sometimes it's a foster care placement she doesn't like.

"There have been some very inappropriate things happening in facilities—it could be a group home or could be a residential treatment facility," she told me.

A 2022 study conducted by John Hopkins University found "that children in group homes are 28 times more likely to be abused than the traditional child: in a small setting similar to a traditional foster home, the children are only four times more likely to be sexually abused than their peers. "

In a foster care case, there are more court hearings—a judicial review, foster care review board, and a permanency hearing.

"When it comes to judicial reviews, we have to litigate whether or not severe abuses occurred." If severe abuse in the family home is not on the table, Ramsey says she and DCS can agree to let parents have unsupervised visits.

If it is on the table, the judge will set a trial date. "When we come to the trial, we will litigate whether or not severe abuse has occurred," Ramsey said. This is what Magistrate O'Neil told me, too.

She laughs when I ask her if the judge likes her better than the other attorneys on the case. That's not it, she explains. Sometimes she'll pick a fight with the DCS attorney.

"A G-A-L is not constrained by federal funding. If a judge makes an inappropriate placement finding, DCS loses their federal funding and that's thousands of dollars that the federal government is sending DCS to support the placement. DCS doesn't want the placement finding because they'll be losing money."

When kids go into the system, they are assessed at one of four levels. Level 1 is "just a normal kid", she tells me. Level 4 is the neediest category and pays the highest daily rate. So, if a child "steps down" to a lower level of care, the reimbursement for that care is less.

"DCS doesn't mind if that child stays there for months because they don't want to have to look for another placement. I mind if the child is there for 2-3 months after they are technically ready to step down," Ramsey says.

After a treatment regime is finished, a child is supposed to "step down" to a lower and less restrictive level of care like moving from a residential facility to a foster home.

"When I file something, the judge knows who has what motive. When the judge is looking at my motion, knowing the child needs to step down, they are also looking at DCS, knowing if they make this finding then DCS loses money. So that's why DCS doesn't want the finding to be made."

Ramsey and DCS are not always at loggerheads. If parents have done their assessments and gotten sober, they would recommend unsupervised visitation.

Ramsey says it almost mathematical.

"If they have done the things that they have been court-ordered to do and are addressing the safety concerns, for the most part everybody is on the same page as to what's going to happen."

Sometimes Ramsey wants to see proof herself and read the assessments. If they look good, she will recommend unsupervised visitation.

Being a Litigator-Activist

Connie Reguli has been in front of more than 100 judges.

"There's probably only a handful that are overtly just mean and nasty. But there's a whole broad category who are obviously sort of just looking to do what DCS wants," she says.

Reguli has attended dozens of court hearings and DCS family planning meetings representing her clients.

"I started recording everything in 2009 because of things judges were saying in the courtroom when there was no court reporter. So, I took a tape recorder into one of these administrative family planning meetings, and they tried to block me from recording it. I'm like, why? And they stopped the meeting. They called legal counsel. I said, 'you guys are taking notes over there. I want to make sure your notes are accurate'.

"So, I would get that resolved, and they would let me record things, and then there would be a new thing. There would be the secret reports, and I'd overcome that, and then it was the faulty drug screens. So, they tried to have caseworkers testify to other caseworkers' records, and so I'd have to fight that. But most attorneys were not fighting these things."

Reguli's reputation as a gun for hire started to precede her as she travelled across the state defending parents against DCS. No matter where she went, DCS used the same bag of tricks.

The level of agency aggression did not seem to vary. The court scheduling and expectations of the juvenile court judges also seemed to be eerily consistent. And when they do one thing after another after another after another, they totally block due process, she says.

"The court is supposed to provide a full hearing within 30 days if the child was removed from its family, but the cases drag on and on and on, taking months and even years to resolve. Then, DCS staffers report to the Court that the child has spent so much time in their "new" home that to disrupt them and return them to their biological family or relatives would cause traumatic harm. And county to county, court to court, judge to judge, the patterns, the attacks and the tactics repeated themselves across venues."

Dr. Kathleen Faller from the University of Michigan is an expert on the forensic interviewing of children. Three of her nine books are about child sexual maltreatment, and she is an authority on how to talk to children about sexual abuse. Reguli had met Faller who consulted on one of Reguli's DCS cases.

In 2013, Reguli emailed the scholar with a troubling question: "Why is the state so aggressive in removing children from their homes instead of stabilizing a vulnerable family?"

217

Faller's response has changed the life of the tough litigator into a lobbyist and organizer of families across the country, each with a child welfare horror story. Faller responded with one sentence: "Because Title IV E is unlimited, and Title IV B is limited."

Title IV E and Title IV B are part of the federal Social Security Act. Title IV B funds are prevention-focused to help keep families together and states have a lot of flexibility on how to spend them. In 2018, $613 million was appropriated under Title IV B but $8 billion was appropriated under Title IV E for foster care, a ratio of 1 to 13.

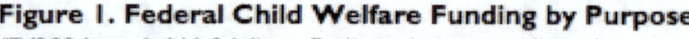

Figure 1. Federal Child Welfare Funding by Purpose
(FY2024 total: $11.0 billion. Dollars shown in millions.)

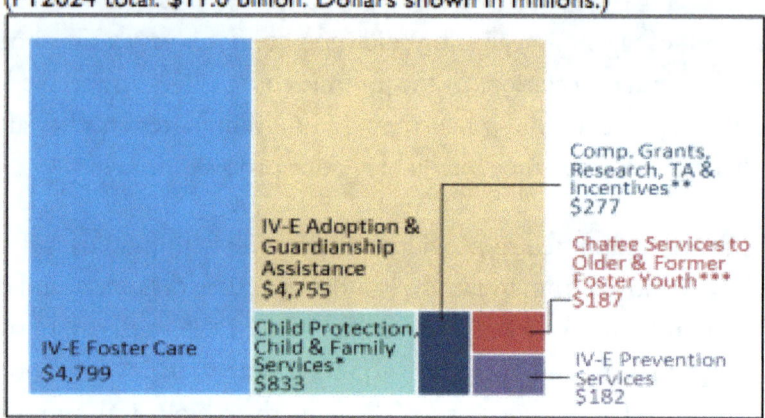

IV-E Adoption & Guardianship Assistance $4,755

Comp. Grants, Research, TA & Incentives** $277

Chafee Services to Older & Former Foster Youth*** $187

IV-E Prevention Services $182

IV-E Foster Care $4,799

Child Protection, Child & Family Services* $833

Source: Congressional Research Service Report Updated May 16, 2024, Child Welfare: Purposes, Federal Programs, and Funding, by Emilie Stoltzfus. The report is based on P.L. 118-47 and P.L. 118-42, except for Title IV-E funding, which is based on FY2024 current law budget authority as given in the President's FY2025 budget request. * Includes formula funding in IV-B and CAPTA. ** Includes competitively awarded funding and incentives in IV-E, IV-B, CAPTA, and the Victims of Child Abuse Act. *** Includes Chafee general and ETV funding.

"I discovered that federal funding was driving the ship," Reguli says. She led a dozen delegations of child welfare reformers to Washington to convince lawmakers to stop pouring money into foster care and put more into prevention services.

"When I'm in Washington I tell people IV-E funding is like sailing on the Titanic. If we can just change the course three degrees, we can avoid catastrophe.

"The trajectory of this ship was evidenced by ever increasing state budgets, an increase of children removed from their homes, and a campaign to recruit foster parents. In addition, the involvement of for-profit private contractors who ran foster care companies, privately owned juvenile detention centers, and a host of privately owned "services" were eager to cash in on the demise of a family in crisis," Reguli told me.

Turning Children into a Commodity

"There is a financial motivation behind putting kids in the system, whether it's Juvenile Justice or foster care. It's driven by private stakeholders who have created a for-profit industry by institutionalizing children," Reguli says.

From 2000-2022 Judge Donna Scott Davenport was the only juvenile court judge in Rutherford County, Tennessee. Her salary was $167,000/yr. Davenport created a "filter system" in her court like the Red Queen in Alice-in-Wonderland. As you may recall, for Alice the sentence comes before the trial.

Davenport directed local law enforcement to arrest and transport the children to the Rutherford County Detention Center for screening and then later file the charges.

Pro Publica and Meribah Knight, a reporter for NPR's Nashville station, WPLN, broke the story about how the county had illegally arrested and jailed hundreds of children for years. For example, in 2014 Davenport sentenced kids to jail in 48% of her cases when the state average was 5%.

For two decades, Davenport sentenced hundreds of children to 2-10 days in jail for minor infractions like truancy or for cursing in court. Under state law, children held for such minor acts are supposed to appear before a judge within 24 hours and be released no more than a day after that.

Davenport didn't do that. She consistently violated state law until reporters brought it to light in October 2021. She considered her method of justice "tough love", and she called herself the "Mother of the County." Lawyers who filed a class action lawsuit estimated that Davenport had improperly arrested and locked up as many as 1,500 kids. One boy from predominantly Black Hobgood Elementary School was arrested for witnessing a fight after school and Davenport found him guilty for not stopping it. He was eight.

In 2008 Rutherford County opened a new 43,000 sq. ft. juvenile detention center with 64 beds. The consultants had advised setting aside 10 shelter care beds for runaways. But the new facility did not include any.

So, Davenport set about renting out empty beds to 39 counties that would transport their young offenders to Rutherford County for $175 a day. "Just like a hotel," boasted one Public Safety Commissioner. The committee chair commented, "Hey, it's a business, generating revenue."

When the story broke, Davenport suddenly announced she would not be seeking re-election. The county settled the class action lawsuit for $11 million, $1,000 for each clam of wrongful arrest and $5000 for each claim of unlawful detention. The county paid but denied any wrongdoing as part of the settlement.

Davenport was cruel, and dafter than crooked, but two seriously corrupt Pennsylvania judges went to prison in the infamous "Kids for Cash" scandal. Luzerne County Judge Mark Ciavarella closed down a county-run juvenile detention center and then took bribes for sending juveniles to privately-owned ones.

In 2011, Ciavarella was sentenced to 28 years in federal prison for taking $1 million in bribes from a builder and the co-owner of two private juvenile detention centers in western Pennsylvania. In return, Ciavarella imposed harsh sentences on juveniles who were then sent to those facilities.

Ciavarella had a reputation for having a harsh and autocratic courtroom demeanor, just like Davenport in Tennessee. While Davenport filled up Rutherford County's detention center with local and out-of-county kids, Ciavarella filled the beds of the private jails with children as young as 10, many of them first-time offenders convicted of petty theft and other minor crimes—just like Judge Davenport except she put children in jail for things that weren't even crimes. Perhaps this is a distinction without much difference because both were cases of children harvested for profit.

During the "Kids for Cash" trial, prosecutor Gordon Zubrod said Ciavarella had "verbally abused and cruelly mocked children he sent away after violating their rights." He called the ex-judge "vicious and mean-spirited" and asked for a life sentence.

Another crooked judge, Michael Conahan, pleaded guilty for taking bribes and extorting hundreds of thousands from the facilities' co-owner, Robert Powell.

Powell pleaded guilty for failing to report a felony and being an accessory to tax evasion conspiracy for the $770,000 in kickbacks he gave to the two judges in connection to the 2,400 juveniles they sent to his detention centers.

The co-owner and developer who built the private lockups, Robert Mericle, pleaded guilty for failure to disclose a felony. He tried to cover up the $2.1 million "finder's fee" he paid in kickbacks to the two judges. Mericle paid a $2.15 million fine and served one year in prison. He paid $25 million to settle victims' lawsuits.

In the aftermath of the scandal, Pennsylvania's Supreme Court overturned hundreds of delinquency verdicts in Luzerne County. In addition to their prison sentences, Conahan and Ciavarella were ordered to pay more than $200 million in damages.

These culprits got caught but there are hundreds of businesses that provide services and operate foster homes or residential facilities for juveniles whose cases have been adjudicated by juvenile court judges.

In 2021, WNEP news anchor Chelsea Strub reported on the "Kids For Cash" trial. She described the crowd of 300 who told their stories about being wrongfully jailed and how it affected them.

Mark Aguilar testified about Judge Ciaverella and the impact he had on his young life.

"He took all my childhood," Aguilar said. "I didn't come home until I was almost 18. I was 13, and I didn't come home until I was 18.... I only knew jail... I thought that was normal here. Know what I'm saying?"

Aguilar talked about how his single mother was affected. "My whole time she didn't have me, she couldn't, she couldn't do nothing. She couldn't even visit me," he told the court.

Private providers with government contracts make millions from their captive clients who are child welfare agencies. The public officials who pay providers rarely scrutinize them very much. In Tennessee, they just keep passing bigger budgets so DCS can keep paying its bills.

Can For-Profit Companies Deliver the Goods?

According to a 2022 report by the Private Equity Stakeholder Project private equity firms have gotten fat by investing "in behavioral services for children and adolescents, including services for youth with intellectual and developmental disabilities, services for youth in foster care, services for youth in the juvenile justice system, troubled teen programs, and autism services."

This was a key finding by Eileen O'Grady who authored the 31-page report, *The Kids Are Not Alright.* O'Grady describes how private equity firms are profiting off the behavioral health services they provide to vulnerable and at-risk youth but, in many cases, they deliver substandard services.

Here is the gist of her argument: public-private partnerships are often not a win-win situation but rather a "kids lose, and companies win" rip-off of public funds.

"Behavioral health services for youth are largely privatized. Non-profit organizations operate most facilities, but increasingly for-profit companies, including companies owned by private equity firms, make up a significant share of providers," O'Grady wrote.

"For-profit youth behavioral health facilities and for-profit foster care have garnered criticism from youth justice and disability rights advocates. In residential facilities, criticism has included:

- Inadequate counseling or education services;
- Physical, sexual, and emotional abuse;
- Forced isolation
- Use of physical and chemical restraints;
- Squalid living conditions.

In privatized foster care companies, concerns include:

- Inadequate screening of foster parents,
- Increasing workloads for social workers and high social worker turnover
- Filling beds using a quota system, and
- Relying on unlicensed workers.

"The private equity business model may exacerbate these problems. Private equity firms often aim to double or triple their investment over 4-7 years. The pursuit of these outsized return expectations over relatively short time horizons can lead to cost-cutting that hurts care. In addition, use of high levels of debt can divert cash from operations to interest payments and dividends paid out to private equity owners."

The report cites cost cutting to increase profits and a tangled web of county, state, and federal agencies that can't ensure safety or get accountability from providers. The report examines how private equity investment in several key areas of youth behavioral services negatively impact quality of care.

And the report goes on to give examples of failures by companies like Sequel Youth & Family Service in foster care, troubled teen programs, residential behavioral health, and juvenile detention facilities. Between 2010-2021 eighteen Sequel facilities were shut down but twenty-one new ones were opened.

Similarly, the report critiques live-in residential facilities for people with intellectual and developmental disabilities. And it cites the increase in private-equity-backed autism deals from 2012-2021 but makes no conclusions about the business model because it is relatively new.

The report concludes: "Private equity's track record for investing in youth behavioral services is troubling. A pattern of harmful conditions, often related to insufficient staffing and other cuts to expenses, suggests that private equity firms' focus on maximizing profit over short periods of time may come at the cost of children's and teen's safety and well-being."

"Despite horrific conditions at some youth behavioral health companies, their private equity owners have in some cases reaped massive profits."

So, can private companies deliver the goods? Maybe they can, but they often don't. Can they make a profit? The short answer is "Yes" until they shut down, move on, and set up operations in some other town.

How Juvenile Courts Operate

Unlike private equity firms, juvenile courts have to stay within their jurisdiction.

The lawyers who work in juvenile courts wear different hats. A GAL and a court-appointed defense attorney have different roles, but some lawyers do both. Especially in rural communities, a lot of attorneys will take juvenile or criminal court appointments. It's their bread and butter.

"A lot of these court appointed attorneys literally work out of the trunk of their car. They don't have offices; they don't have insurance. They work with their cell phone. That's it. They don't meet with the clients. They just talk to them over the phone," Reguli says.

"And they're totally dependent on appointments from the judges. They don't want to bill too many hours because there is a cap. At the same time, they want to get more appointments from the same judge, and they want to keep the judge happy."

"So, they would rather convince their clients to take the DCS deal and just say they're guilty of something. And it's the same thing with criminal attorneys. Generally, they don't want to do trials."

"My experience had shown me that court appointed attorneys rarely challenged the system. They just seemed to roll in the same direction as DCS. DCS wants to keep kids in the state's care for a year because they could maximize the Title IV E federal funds if they did so. So, court delays, confusion over services, challenges with parent-child visitation, and secretly filed reports were the order of the day. Justice was never swift, the 30-day rule was ignored, and parents became exhausted in the process."

"Court-appointed attorneys cap out the amount of money they can make, and each one wants to make sure they make the cap, but don't want to expend any time or effort once the cap is reached. They don't want to fight a case tooth and nail with evidence and cross-examination and all that. So, they convince their clients to take a deal even if it means they lose their kids," Reguli told me.

Once a prosecutor, Reguli has seen her share of criminal defendants.

"Most of the people who end up getting arrested and end up in General Sessions Court are guilty, okay? I mean, they just are. It's either a shoplifting or a DUI. Honestly, most of them are guilty. It's totally different with parents in juvenile court. In those cases, the majority of the parents are not guilty," she says.

"By 2015, I decided to use social media to search out and collect families from across the United States who were going through similar circumstances. I created the Family Forward Project and Innocent Families on Facebook. It did not take long for families across the country to post stories of family tragedies that mimicked those I found in Tennessee.

Families in Texas, Montana, Oregon, Florida, New York, Arizona, and Indiana were reporting similar aggressive tactics of child protective services (CPS). I learned of other cases in other states—Oklahoma, Arkansas, and Texas."

Squeaky Wheels Get Greased

Child welfare has a well-oiled political machine in every state, and they are financially driven. Reguli claims people who expose it have been killed.

Reguli told me about Georgia State Senator Nancy Schaefer and her husband, who were found dead in their home from gunshot wounds in March 2010. The press tried to spin it as a murder-suicide by her husband but failed to describe the gripping report she had made about child trafficking through child protective services.

On November 16, 2007, Schaefer published an eleven-page report, The Corrupt Business of Child Protective Services. Schaefer had been making waves in the Georgia senate by sponsoring bills to reign in CPS. She was ousted by Georgia's Republican Party leaders who replaced her with Jim Butterworth in 2008. Schaefer was working on a book and video when she and her husband were found shot dead in their home.

Family and friends think they were murdered and reject the official version that the Schaefer's were in financial straits and noted that the couple had gotten death threats, and those threats had increased shortly before they died.

The following is taken from a speech Schafer gave at the Eagle Forum Conference in Washington D.C. on September 26, 2008.

"The department of child protective services has become a protected empire built on taking children and separating families. This is not to say that there are not those children who do need to be removed from wretched situations and need protection, however, my report is concerned with the children and parents caught up in legal kidnapping. Having worked with probably 300 cases statewide and hundreds and hundreds across the country and in nearly every state, I'm convinced there is no accountability in Child Protective Services."

Schaefer in Georgia, came to the same conclusions Reguli has in Tennessee. Both claim caseworkers and social workers are very often guilty of fraud, they withhold and destroy evidence, they fabricate evidence, and they seek to terminate parental rights unnecessarily.

"That the separation of families and the snatching of children is growing as the business grows, because state and local governments have grown accustomed to having these taxpayer dollars to balance their ever-growing budgets," Schaefer said.

In that regard, Tennessee and several other states are just like Georgia.

"The tax dollars are being used to keep this gigantic system afloat. Many grandparents have called me to get custody of their grandchildren, before being lost in the system. Grandparents who lose their grandchildren to strangers have lost their own flesh and blood. The children lose their family heritage, and grandparents and parents too, lose the connection of their heirs."

According to Schaefer, federal and state incentives have turned child protective services into a business that separates families for money.

"The system cannot be trusted, it does not serve the people, it obliterates families and children, simply because it has the power to do so," she reasoned in her speech.

"What is happening in America regarding child protective services is a criminal political phenomenon, and it must be brought to an end," Schaffer concluded.

In Neighboring Tennessee and Across the Pond

"When I decided to run for judge in Williamson County one of my complaints was that the county was launching a $180 million project to build a new juvenile justice center," Reguli told me.

She feared they would take on a partner like Davidson County did with the running of its facility on Woodland St. next to the Titans football stadium. That arrangement did not end well, and Youth Opportunity Investments left in 2022 four years before its $28 million contract was up. The company has more than 1,000 employees and operates in several states.

"If they're using private equity funds, they have to make a profit," Reguli explained. Williamson County officials said they are building their new facilities without private partners. They plan to use grants and issue bonds to be paid back with future tax revenues. Williamson County has a strong property tax base, and they may succeed. But many states are using a different funding formula.

"The current popular model of juvenile justice and child welfare adopts more for-profit funding. It's a whole entire industrial sector in which the children have to be institutionalized for it to work," Reguli told me.

She is not the only one raging against the machine that keeps money flowing to a corrupt and dysfunctional child welfare system.

"Reaching across the Atlantic Ocean, there is Attorney Marius Reikeras in Norway and Attorney Ruby Harrold-Claesson in Sweden who took on the challenge of protecting families in these Scandinavian countries only to be persecuted, silenced, and shut down," Reguli told me.

Reikeras sued the Norwegian government in a European Court of Human Rights seventeen times for human rights violations and won. Despite those victories, he eventually lost his law license," Reguli reported. The same exact thing happened to her in Tennessee.

"And then there's me, Connie Reguli, trudging my way through the system for three decades calling out government abuses, restoring families, and then stripped of my law license over a fake felony created by a system that could not tolerate change."

But nothing will deter Reguli. When she wants to speak about child welfare bills, she stalks legislators into meeting rooms. When they won't let her talk, she writes up flyers and tries to pass them out. When they won't let her do that, she follows the politicians back to their offices to make an appointment. Sometimes, not often, that works.

Reguli's tailing of politicians in the Cordell Hull legislative office building bore bitter fruit on April 13, 2023. Senate Bill 1319 passed 74-17. It makes it a felony if you don't surrender your child after a judge issue an emergency removal order even if DCS doesn't bother to notify you.

"It's got your name written all over it. Let's call it the Connie Reguli Law," I tell her, and she laughs. "Nobody wants to fight them. They're scared and part of it is what they did to me," she explained.

Reguli's three grown children don't say much when I've seen them with their mother. But they are well aware of everything that has happened to her, and they worry. She adopted them from a Russian orphanage when they were five.

"Don't forget who I am. I'm the single mom who flew 9,000 miles twice to pick up kids I didn't know," she laughingly told me.

"In their heart they know that I rescued them. They were really scared when I got cancer. They were really scared when I was threatened with incarceration. They depend on me still for help and to guide them. I'm sort of Jewish mom. I hover a little bit."

Reguli was diagnosed with breast cancer in 2012. Her kids thought she was going to die. "I lost all my hair, and I was still working. I got diagnosed in January. I started chemo in February. By March I had no hair. None. I was wearing rags around my head, and I was still going to court. I was pitiful looking," she told me.

"Then I get this letter from the Board of Professional Responsibility (BPR) basically saying 'we've received information that you are suffering from a serious illness, and we recommend that you put your license in inactive status.'

"They thought it would kill me. And I wrote back a letter and asked "How do you know that? I would like to know how you know that." And they refused to tell me. So, they just continued to pursue me in the middle of cancer. They filed another petition just to be stupid."

Connie Reguli is a tough cookie—one that child welfare authorities can't stomach. She doesn't care if the BPR keeps her law license. She doesn't care if good child welfare bills get killed in legislative committees.

"I don't care what kind of state law you have; I'm going to one-up you with a federal law. We're going to call that the 'Connie law', too," she told me.

"The first thing we do, let's kill all the lawyers." — *Henry VI, Part 2, Act 4, Scene 2 by William Shakespeare.*

Chapter Nine: Family Defense and Parental Advocates

We don't have these things in Tennessee. Parents are guilty until proven innocent. That's just the way it is here.

New York, Washington, Colorado, and a dozen other states get better outcomes with a multidisciplinary approach that uses "high quality" attorneys working with social workers and parent mentors or advocates. This collaborative method reduces the need for foster care at the beginning of a case, and for kids already in foster care, it shortens their time in state custody.

So, while the legal system is still adversarial, the best solutions are often fashioned through collaboration, not confrontation. Some states have changed the nature of child welfare by giving all parties fair access to the courts and, secondly, by focusing on positive outcomes instead of punishment and blame.

Better outcomes are possible in Washington, Colorado, and New York because new organizations have formed and pioneered ways to finance their work on behalf of families and children. Judges do not pay attorneys in those states; they are not controlled by the child welfare agency; they are independent and able to sustain strong family defense where they practice.

Poor outcomes in Tennessee are due to a number of factors. Some of it is politics, some of it is law, some of it is prejudice, some of it is rank corruption---but all of it together makes for a dysfunctional child welfare system and the numbers don't lie. Taking a proven approach that works well suggests that states like Tennessee should adopt it. Child welfare in Tennessee could have a more hopeful future than the dreadful picture I have painted in this book. A brighter future for child welfare in Tennessee is possible but a lot of things would have to change before that happens.

Child Welfare in Washington

Washington State Office of Public Defense (WOPD)

In 2000 Washington began a pilot program with attorneys, social workers, and experts to help indigent parents when they were facing charges of dependency and neglect. In the "good old days" indigent defense was a crapshoot. Lawyers could have 300 cases and often met their clients for the first time in court after their children had already been taken into custody. To sum up: poor legal defense yielded poor outcomes from bad beginnings. In many states, it still does.

Michael Heard remembers when the public defense program was first rolled out in a handful of Washington state's 39 counties. "I feel like I'm up on the national landscape as much as anybody. I've been in child welfare for 33 years. I'm one of the early passers-by. I kind of figured it out by now," Heard told me.

Back in 2006, Heard was a social worker but now he runs the social work part of Washington's multidisciplinary group. The Washington State Office of Public Defense (WOPD) is a big piece of the group and part of a national movement. Twenty states have family legal defense programs. They vary by state and jurisdiction. Some have parent advocates—other parents who have been through court—and some provide expert testimony when medical issues are involved in a case. In Washington, WOPD attorneys work under contract. They are not state employees.

"We're all passionate and on fire about making sure parents' rights are given back," Heard told me. "Our goal is to get parents the very best representation possible, and position parents in the best place possible to get the best outcome. And that generally is going to be to return home. But it might not be."

WOPD lawyers intervene at the very beginning of a dependency trial after children have been taken into custody and sometimes represent parents beforehand. One thing they all have in common—the judges and child welfare departments do not control trial outcomes as much as they used to because now there are trained opponents for the defense who are not assigned to a case by the judge from a list of volunteer lawyers.

"Here's what I would say after being involved in child welfare for all these years. It is that parents have much, much better representation that holds the department to their statute, to federal expectations, and their original best practice expectations."

"You've got the courtrooms, you've got working with the department, you've got working with the legislators. And we're trying to improve families' outcomes in all of those areas. So, I think we're very effective, particularly relative to other states."

When the Washington State Department of Children, Youth & Families (DCYF) wants to terminate parental rights a judge makes the call. "There are some contested hearings where we're arguing that it's safe for a child to go home. More and more the court will decide with our attorneys."

ADA Lawsuits

Heard has been co-chair of the American Bar Association's National Interdisciplinary Committee. Heard told me his office collaborates and consults with Disabilities Rights of Washington on complex cases. This is not coincidental or accidental. WOPD is all about providing the best legal advocacy regarding parental statutory rights.

ADA lawsuits have been brought against a number of states—twice against Washington in 2021 and 2022. One lawsuit was settled for deaf children in DCYF custody who now have the right to interpreters to sign what is being said about them and to them in DCFY hearings.

Another lawsuit filed on behalf of hundreds of youth in the state's foster care system was settled in June 2022. That does not mean the problems went away. You may recall from the Introduction that at any given time in the U.S. there are dozens of class action lawsuits pending, or agreements are being negotiated, or have been settled but remain under federal supervision, sometimes for years before they are dismissed. Even then there can be back-sliding like in Tennessee and Alabama.

Disability Rights Washington brought the lawsuit on behalf of three young people and other similarly situated foster children. The Plaintiffs, all of whom identified as having behavioral health conditions, described their experiences of being separated from their families, being sent to out-of-state institutions, and spending time in single night placements or hotels over significant periods of time instead of licensed foster or group homes.

"DCYF's practices are re-traumatizing children, destroying their ability to bond with and trust adults, interrupting delivery of mental health care, disrupting educational attainment, and extinguishing any hope that children and their families will have the long-term stability they need and deserve," the complaint said.

Eleven months of negotiation ended with a groundbreaking settlement and high hopes to transform Washington's foster care system. DCYF promised to implement new statewide models for supporting youth in foster care and their families and to collaborate in additional ways with child welfare clients, alumni, and stakeholders to improve its policies and practices.

Washington does not have enough foster homes for children with special needs. And DCYF does not have a facility specifically designed to house and treat children with unique psychiatric needs, or who have a history of physical aggression, or who have acted out sexually with other children. Washington's Children's Long-term Inpatient Program (CLIP) has 109 beds. There are four facilities in the state but they are psychiatric hospitals, not long-term housing where foster kids can grow up and get the services they need.

Eleven ADA lawsuits were filed in U.S. District Courts in Washington from 2016-2017. In August 2022, news broke that DCYF couldn't account for $293 million in federal funds paid out to low-income families. DCYF spokesman, Jason Wettstein, claimed the funds were spent properly even though a state audit couldn't account for them. Ironically, he suggested a bigger budget would help them track their finances better.

Getting into the Child Welfare system happens pretty much the same wherever you are. A child is removed from their family home in Washington with a protective custody order signed by a judge based on an anonymous report or one filed by a CPS worker from the Department of Children, Youth, and Families (DCYF).

A law enforcement officer takes the child deemed at risk and immediately hands him or her over to a DCYF caseworker. Then, within 72 hours a judge holds a sheltered care hearing. In Tennessee it's called a preliminary hearing.

Getting released from state custody, however, is very much affected by where you live and the length of time spent in custody varies widely. Numbers of placements while in foster care also vary widely by state. If you are placed in several foster homes, you will change schools a lot, your life will become less stable and being uprooted continuously can create further emotional damage. If you stay in foster care too long, you will age out at 18 pretty much traumatized.

The state of Washington places about half the kids in state custody with family members and about half in foster homes. In 2018, DCYF had 5,109 licensed foster homes; 45% of the 9,200 foster children were living with relatives. Washington has the fourth highest reunification rate at 65.6%.

Most states have reunification rates around 50%. In 2021, 13 states had adoption rates higher than 30%. In 2021, Washington's adoption rate was 23%. In most states it's around 25%.

Family Defense

When people claim that states with robust family defense and parent advocates have better outcomes, they usually mean that higher numbers of children exit state custody quicker, returning to their families and relatives (aka kinship care); fewer months spent in foster care prior to adoption; more children with fewer placements; fewer children entering foster care overall and fewer children remaining in foster care over time. By all these standards, Washington is getting better outcomes than states like Tennessee.

The new approach to parent representation grew out of a conference in October 1999 sponsored by the Annie E. Casey Foundation. With the foundation's support, the American Bar Association (ABA) began a program to improve representation for parents in 2001-2002. Then, as now, the key to "high-quality legal representation" for parents is adequate funding.

By 2006, a dozen states had applied for a waiver of Title IV-E rules so they could use federal dollars to experiment with foster care programs. A handful of states concentrated on high quality legal defense and high-quality social programs for poor parents to find work, get over an addiction, and stabilize their lives. The goal then, as now, was protecting "all parties' legal rights" and family reunification.

"When I started this work, there was almost never a parent or another parent's attorney, or in fact anybody speaking for parents in meetings. Now it would be unthinkable not to have parents participating. We have seen so many positive changes in the understanding and attitudes of judges and the department," said Joanne Moore, Washington State Office of Public Defense Founder and former Director of the Parents Representation Program.

WOPD started in two Washington counties as a pilot program. Moore said it got good results and over the next decade legislators expanded it to other counties. Moore remembers how terrible things were when she first started.

"It was a passion that I had," she told me. She hated seeing decisions being made by state actors about families when parents were not even invited to meetings.

"In the first study we did, I described what it was like to see frightened parents all by themselves in court except for their incompetent attorney with a lot of people on the other side going after them."

That's how Connie Reguli described parents in Tennessee Juvenile Courts trying to keep DCS from taking custody of their children.

Minnesota Supreme Court Justice Helen Meyer was an early defender of family defense and a critic of Minnesota's child welfare system. "We need to elevate this work and help people understand how quality representation for parents helps achieve reunification. Better funding of parent representation will result in cost-savings," she said.

A corollary: adequate funding for preventive and other services is critical to the long-term well-being of families. Children who get services at home avoid a number of pitfalls and bad outcomes foster children experience. Those include: almost three times more likely to be involved in juvenile justice systems, more likely to become teen mothers, less likely to hold a job for at least three months, and 2-3 times higher arrest, conviction and incarceration rates.

Welfare officials, even with "the best of intentions", put too many kids into foster care and prolonged stays in foster care, as studies have repeatedly shown, can have devastating and permanent effects. Foster care doesn't tend to save kids as much as it's likely to ruin them. By investing in children and their families early, much of these heartaches can be avoided. Some of the studies that came to that conclusion are summarized at the end of Chapter Three: How Children Welfare Agencies Operate. Details are in the story with the headline: DCS Needs a Major Overhaul.

A 2019 study of the interdisciplinary approach to parent representation compared outcomes in Washington and New York Family Courts after children entered foster care. The study assessed safety outcomes of 9582 families and their 18,288 children. Foster care entry was not affected and did not show any difference in the likelihood of a child experiencing repeated maltreatment regardless of whether they had a "standard panel attorney" or "interdisciplinary law office representation (ILO)".

However, when children's parents received the interdisciplinary representation, children spent 118 fewer days on average in foster care during the four years following the abuse or neglect case filing. Subsequent competing risk models show that children whose parents received the ILO model achieved overall permanency, reunification, and guardianship more quickly. These results provide evidence that interdisciplinary law office parental representation is an effective intervention to promote permanency for children in foster care.

Interdisciplinary law office representation (ILO) is not a silver bullet but it's a lot better than SOP with overworked lawyers who don't generally—almost never – mount a stiff defense. After all, they have to be back in front of the same judge tomorrow or next week and for them, making waves does not make for smooth sailing in the long run.

Behavioral Rehabilitative Services

A 2016 report by the Washington Department of Social & Health Services (DSHS) found Behavioral Rehabilitation Services (BRS) accounted for 41% of out-of-home care spending. In other words, almost half the children in foster care had special needs.

Washington state's Children's Administration contracts with community agencies to provide BRS for children and youth with serious emotional, behavioral or medical challenges who cannot be served in regular family foster homes. Services are offered in three different placement settings including the child's home, a treatment foster care (TFC) home, or a facility-based setting providing for special needs.

BRS provides a high level of structured care and treatment for children and youth with the most severe and intensive needs. The bulk of the children in BRS are at the highest reimbursement rates but for several years there has been less money to pay for those services.

Cutbacks in Washington from 2009-2012

In 2010, the Behavioral Rehabilitation Services (BRS) budget was removed from the forecasted adjustable funding model and allotted a much-reduced fixed budget. In 2012 the out-of-home care budget was reduced by $50 million.

While budget cuts across government were necessary as a result of the economic downturn, an increasingly healthy economy has not resulted in a restoration of pre-recession rates. The elimination of forecasting BRS, a service intended to meet the needs of behaviorally challenged children and youth with mental health needs, has resulted "in a compression and reduction of resources".

One of the most significant impacts of the BRS budget reductions is the loss of Interim Care and Residential Assessment Beds that Children's Administration (CA) relied on during these transitional periods. As children present more problems eventually their caregivers can't handle them, and they need a higher level of intervention. Waiting for beds to open up has put a lot of stress on everybody.

When you look at annual expenditures by type of care, you find disproportionately higher costs at higher care levels of care. While BRS represented 5.9% of the population in 2016, it was 41% of the total expenditures and out-of-state placements represented just 1.2% of the population but 8% of the expenditures.

Informed Dissent

Dee Wilson, a former Washington child welfare caseworker, doesn't have much good to say about DCYF. He says the department has fewer residential care facilities and group homes than it needs. According to Mark Fullington, Executive Director of Community & Family Services

Foundation, a dozen BRS facilities have closed in the last decade. Wilson claims providers don't trust DCYF Secretary Ross Hunter who cut back on their contracts. Wilson is not a big fan of Washington's public defender program either.

He is uneasy with recent changes. After years of thinking and acting differently, judges, caseworkers, and welfare agencies now think that too many kids are being placed in foster care. "They have bought into the idea that foster care most of the time does more harm than good so there's a desire to reduce the number of kids in care," Wilson says.

Wilson says caseworkers are unwilling to remove kids from unsafe situations because of a new state law that requires evidence of abuse or imminent harm in order to get a removal order. Lawmakers in Tennessee have not gone that far and caseworkers here are still using emergency removal orders to tear families apart, often without justification. Wilson is a reformer, not an abolitionist.

"There's been a big reduction in foster care and nothing in the services that are being offered by the agencies would account for that," he says. It's the effect of changes at the Annie E. Casey Foundation and its programs to provide services and engage families better so fewer kids wind up in foster care.

Wilson worked with Casey Family Programs (CFP) in Seattle for six years. "The goal of Casey Family Programs around the country was to reduce foster care by 50%. So, when Ross Hunter came here in 2017, he made that his goal," Wilson says.

That's a very dangerous way to manage and the new milieu accounts for the reduction in care, he says. In his view, family legal defense and social services are just two among many reasons why foster care numbers have been dropping.

Wilson noted a 2022 report by the Washington Office of the Family and Children's Ombuds. The report said there are 14 fewer licensed group homes in Washington since 2020 and about 1,000 foster homes have stopped accepting placements. That finding is probably COVID-19 related. DCYF records confirm there are fewer active foster homes today than in 2016 but there are also fewer foster kids. DCYF says they had 150 group homes in January 2023, up from 137 group homes in 2016.

However, Hunter has made no bones about his goal to cut Washington's foster care numbers in half. Wilson says Hunter is throwing the baby out with the bath water. Reducing foster care overall is fine but doing that by fiat is pretty dumb. Special needs kids—and special needs adults, although they are not DCYF's responsibility—require well-supported and well-run group homes. It takes a village to raise a child, and it takes one to provide for disabled people, too.

That means not only a decent budget but also good managers, well paid staff, family involvement, and input from stakeholders. Just bringing down numbers to reach a set goal may not be the best solution especially at the same time budgets are being cut for much needed support.

●●●

Child Welfare in Colorado

Colorado Office of Respondent Parents' Counsel (ORPC)

The Office of Respondent Parents' Counsel (ORPC) is an independent governmental agency within the State of Colorado Judicial Branch and is vested with the oversight and administration of Respondent Parents' Counsel (RPC) representation in Colorado. The agency opened on January 1, 2016, and the agency assumed oversight for RPC attorneys on July 1, 2016. ORPC also trains social workers whose clients have ORPC attorneys. The WOPD is like this, too. So are the Bronx Defenders in New York

The Colorado Department of Human Services' Office of Children, Youth and Families (OCYF)

In 2022, Colorado's rate of child and youth out-of-home placements was the lowest in the state's history, but the child welfare system remains heavily invested in out-of-home care, foster and adoption services, and investigations of alleged child abuse and neglect.

CDHS has created an advisory council for people who have firsthand experience of the child welfare system. It is asking them what positive supports and services they need to thrive, to prevent child maltreatment, and to avoid unnecessary out-of-home placement. Meeting monthly, the goal is to re-imagine Colorado's child welfare system and affect positive changes by mid-2024.

Colorado Office of the Child's Representative (COCR)

OCR is an independent state agency within the judicial branch charged with providing competent and effective legal representation to children and youth involved in judicial proceedings in Colorado. OCR establishes attorney practice standards and provides litigation support, accessible high-quality statewide training, and oversight of the practice.

Hundreds of lawyers litigate child welfare cases in Colorado. Colorado child welfare gives all parties fair access to the courts and focuses on positive outcomes instead of punishment and blame. So, while the legal system is still adversarial, the best solutions are often fashioned through collaboration, not confrontation.

These three agencies make up Colorado's child welfare system and each plays a role in child dependency cases. By federal measures Colorado's child welfare system is one of the best in the country.

Joe Homlar, Director of Child Welfare

Homlar traces the beginning of better child welfare in Colorado to the 1996 Contract with America when things actually got worse for people living on the margins. For example, Aid to Families with Dependent Children (AFDC) stopped after five years, it required women to work, and denied them benefits if they got pregnant again.

Republicans flipped both chambers of Congress in 1994 and conservatives proposed a contract that included a balanced budget, tax cuts, changes to social security, welfare reform, and term limits for elected officials. Then President Bill Clinton referred to it as the "Contract on America". Most of the eight major reforms Republicans proposed on their first day of their majority in the House, failed in the Senate.

Since then, several states have applied for federal waivers of Medicaid, Title IV-E of the Social Security Act (foster care funding). Waivers cap federal spending for a certain amount of time and give states greater flexibility to run their own versions of federal entitlement programs. It's a way to let states experiment with different things and make permanent the ones that work well. But it can also allow for misuse of funds and make things worse. It's different from state to state. Colorado continues to be a model for the nation.

"Our system is not punitive. Our system is rehabilitative. Over 97% of the time when folks get that knock on the door from child protection services... there is no out of home placement. And we're proud of that because we're able to level with families, to work with families, to make sure they have what they need," Homlar told me.

243

Colorado's system has more reunifications and fewer terminations of parental rights. "I would point out that there's less placement to begin with. And in fact, we've reduced our out of home care by about 45% in the last 15 years. And that's, I think, a large part because of the family engagement practices that we've taken on. I think we've actually doubled the number of kids in kinship placement and reduced our congregate care numbers by over 85%," he said. In short, Colorado has fewer kids in foster care and helped more families stay together.

Parent Representative Melanie Jordan

Colorado's child welfare system is organized a lot like Washington's.

"We're a state run, county administered system. So, what that means is that each of our 64 counties have their own county attorney's office that represents the county Department of Human Services. So, we face off against the county attorney and a county department," says Melanie Jordan.

Jordan manages a cadre of parents' attorneys as Case Strategy Director for the Office of Respondent Parents' Counsel (ORPC). Jordan is also ORPC's in house policy wonk. From her desk in Denver, she weighs in on proposed legislation and follows what is going on with child welfare in other states.

"I used to be a county attorney. I was a county attorney before we had our office. So, I went to law school. I had always wanted to be a parents' attorney. There wasn't really a path to do that prior to 2016."

Since the ORPC started in 2016, we've have had an increase in contested hearings, evidentiary hearings, time and support, she says.

Prior to 2016, it was all flat fee, just over $1,000, and starting July 1, 2023, ORPC started paying its contract attorneys $100/hr. Federal authorities made a change to Title IV-E funding five or six years ago that reimbursed lawyers who represented parents and children. Prior to that federal funding only covered caseworkers.

"How we're paying for pre-filing representation is through the federal Title IV-E," she says. When "interdisciplinary law office representation (ILO)" goes beyond the 4-5 counties where it is currently offered, the child welfare system will really change because interventions will occur before children are removed from their birth families. Right now, it's generally the other way around.

"A lot of times people are scared and so they're not really figuring out how to navigate an investigation. If you have an attorney and a social worker–because we have CASA or an attorney and a parent advocate come in there when the investigation is happening, they can see, 'oh, this is a custody issue or this is a DV case (domestic violence),' and we can help mom get custody or protection or get this mom into inpatient treatment.

She has a plan for her grandma to watch the child while she's an inpatient, and so we can help create a safety plan and a power of attorney. Places with robust representation I think that you see a decrease in removals and court involvement because a lot of families have those solutions to their own problems. They just maybe need some help navigating that system to really get it in place formally or to have something that feels safe enough that Social Services is like, 'okay, we won't file, right?' The role of pre-filing is to help people communicate that and navigate all that. It's called pre-filing."

ORPC lawyers spend more time in court and they don't have to close a case before they get paid. You can imagine the perverse incentives that there are, she says.

"I'm not saying there weren't people doing good work, but we have people that are fairly paid now, who are fairly compensated, and they're doing great jobs for their clients," Jordan says.

"The other two biggest changes are that we now have social workers and parent advocates available if people want them on their case. So the parent advocates are parents who have lived through the system, gotten their kids back, and they're getting paid by our agency to go out and help other parents who are going through the same things.

"Social workers really are a game changer because no longer do you have to rely on the caseworker to help find services for your client, help figure out what your client needs. Now they have somebody on their defense team who's able to help the client navigate a really complex system," Jordan says.

"An OCYF caseworker might have just a few hours because they've got a ton of cases. They don't have time to sit down with a parent and call up apartments and try to get into housing or try to navigate getting their child benefits, things like that, that our social workers can do," she says.

Jordan is one of 15 ORPC staffers who defend families, advocate for change, and promote equity in the child welfare system. ORPC's record is very good: 32,076 parents represented since 2016; 22% increase in reunification with ORPC's interdisciplinary representation model and an average of 31 fewer days in foster care when parents have an interdisciplinary legal team.

ORPC's Director of Family Justice Programming Maleeka Jihad

Maleeka Jihad, aka MJ, finds it hard to sit still. She runs her own consulting firm and a non-profit and she teaches part-time at the University of Denver Graduate School of Social Work.

"So, I teach social work students how not to be white colonizers, essentially," she told me.

In addition to all those hats, MJ ended up with a state job she never really wanted but it suits her. "I was in the child welfare system in Oklahoma. I was an ICWA kid," she told me. ICWA stands for Indian Child Welfare Act.

"So, being in foster care, we had a terrible experience, and we were removed from our father who was a single black man raising five kids on

246

his own because he worked in the evenings and there was no childcare in the evenings when he worked as an overnight janitor.

"That's when we got involved in foster care. So we were all removed. I never wanted to be in this field," she told me.

Jihad ended up doing her undergrad in Durango, Colorado at Fort Lewis. "And then I got my Masters of Social Work in Tulane in New Orleans and ended up moving back to Colorado because I had a lot of connections in Denver, but I could not get a job at all because I was not connected to the social work field."

MJ had a mentor who worked at an agency that supported families involved in dependency and neglect cases. She worked as an in-home therapeutic service provider alongside caseworkers and Guardians ad Litem to decrease family separations.

"So, my job was to be in the homes, to do in-home therapy to keep the families together. I realized very quickly how much power Guardians ad Litem have in the state of Colorado and how much influence they have representing children.

"I said, well, I got to get over there to where the power is. So, I became a clinical consultant who is a social worker working alongside attorneys at Rocky Mountain Children's Law Center. At the time it was the largest multidisciplinary office in the state of Colorado," she told me.

But then she says politics happened and the Rocky Mountain Children's Law Center lost its state contract. "So all of us dispersed as independent contractors. Some of us created our own firms. I created my own LLC. I went out on my own in 2017 as a consultant working with Guardians ad Litem."

One day a consultant friend asked her if she ever considered working with parents.

"And I said, I don't know what that would look like. I've only worked with children of the system who then are juvenile delinquents of the system and so forth. And she said, well, it's exactly the same. It's the same population of people."

Children in the system later become adults of the system. "We know of all dependency and neglect cases nationwide, that 45% of those parents were in foster care themselves. So we know that we create generational trauma. So I said, okay, I'll see how that works."

MJ worked as a social worker at the Office of Respondent Parent Counsel alongside attorneys to help parents in a multidisciplinary approach. "I realized very quickly how awful parents are treated. I realized very quickly how the foster care system has been used as a private adoption agency for people that cannot afford to actually adopt."

She did that for a couple of years and despite personal misgivings, she became an adoption expert. ORPC and CDHS started hiring her as a consultant to fight for kinship placements to keep kids in the family.

"I was the only expert in the state of Colorado who testified about the racism in child welfare, the negative impacts of transracial adoption, and how it's important to keep families together—to do that cultural piece." During all these changes, MJ was getting her PhD in international psychology.

"So, I did some work in the Philippines. I did some work in Germany. I realized very quickly how psychology is weaponized against people of color and that with my degree, I was becoming that colonizer. So, I left my PhD program with a year and a half to go and transferred to Fielding Graduate School to obtain my PhD in leadership development and social justice change."

MJ does a lot of teaching and consulting with DHS. She has a government contract to do in-home work but also trains caseworkers to be more aware of the racism within the agencies they work for.

"No one understands the system unless you've been a professional of the system or you are a product of the system and I'm both," she said.

I asked Jihad to rate ORPC lawyers' job performance. "Has that been a good thing?"

"An amazing thing. Now my job is to make them better," she says.

ORPC hired her to teach attorneys how to see child welfare through a different lens.

"People don't like to think of child welfare as a civil rights fight, but families of color have been fighting to keep our children within our community from day one since we were dragged over here and enslaved. So, it's a civil rights fight, and that's what I have to help them understand. We hired a civil rights attorney who came from Georgia, one of the best in the nation, and then we hired a specialist in ADA accommodations for anyone that has a disability, so they can fight for the rights of our parents who are of color."

The Bronx Defenders

Emma Ketteringham joined the novel Public Defender nonprofit in New York in the late 1990s.

"We began as a criminal defense organization that wanted to practice a new way, which we called Holistic Defense," Ketteringham told me.

The model takes a team approach to defending indigent clients. It was a really cheeky idea: give poor people the same kind of legal representation only rich people can usually afford. The idea took off and spread to other boroughs that got city contracts as public defenders in Harlem, Brooklyn, and Queens.

Today, the Bronx Defenders are a full-service legal firm with a staff of 75. Each year, the firm represents 27,000 low-income Bronx residents in criminal, civil, child welfare, and immigration cases, and reaches thousands more through our community intake and outreach programs. The Bronx

Defenders operate a charitable bail fund called The Bronx Freedom Fund, the first of its kind in New York.

A traditional public defender represents an indigent client in court. But the Bronx Defenders operate differently. "You didn't just represent the person in the case to which you were assigned. But you also made efforts to address embedded consequences to that arrest, including housing, including loss of citizenship, including all the immigration consequences, loss of income," she explains.

"And we worked hand in hand with social workers who addressed what might have led to this person having contact with the criminal legal system. What we realized very quickly that what the community cared a lot about was--what at the time was called Bureau of Child Welfare BCW) now is called Administration of Children's Services (ACS). But the fact that they were losing their kids to the foster system.

"We work in teams, not just of attorneys, but with social workers who are part of the defense team, who get paid the same as lawyers, as well as parent advocates who have often survived this system themselves, to make sure that no parent is ever in a room alone with an ACS official.

"So much of what happens, happens outside of the courtroom. By the time you show up in court, you've probably had two months since the last court appearance where visits might not have taken place, or the service referrals that the agency promised to make were never made. Or there are such barriers to a parent doing their service plan that they can't move forward in their case. Or they've met with CPS officials and said things that hurt their case because no one has advised them how the information will be used. So, what we make sure of is that anytime our client is meeting with ACS, they're not alone.

"They have a social worker and a parent advocate by their side to help them advocate, and we have the information. We know what's happening between court dates. So, when ACS walks into court with their report and says, oh, we sent the parent to three drug tests and they never went. We know it's because the parent told them they were at work that day, or the parent told them they objected to the test or whatever it might be, and we're not catching up in the court appearance. They don't have all of the control of the narrative."

At any one time, Ketteringham says the Defenders have 3000 cases pending.

"New York City by far is like the gold standard. There was also a study done by NYU which compares the outcomes over the first ten years of us operating. It compares the outcomes in our cases with the outcomes in the solo practitioners' cases. And it just shows that children spend many, many fewer months in the system, and that we prevent children ever getting into the system by providing quality and robust and very aggressive representation from day one."

"We also do an extraordinary amount of advocacy with ACS and the city about this system. And so, case filings have dropped dramatically. The number of children in the foster system dropped dramatically since parents have had robust and funded legal representation.

They've had different ACS commissioners over time, she says. "We are sort of the office they kind of hate to love, but that's better than being the one that they love to hate.

"They recognize that in order for parents to really (succeed)...they're supposed to do reasonable efforts. We have good laws in New York State. I don't know the law as well in Tennessee, but the state is required to make reasonable efforts to keep families together before they separate them. And we hold them accountable to those laws.

"And I think they recognize that when parents have strong advocates, that's as important, if not more important, than the children having strong advocates, because we make sure that parents have a chance to stay out of the system altogether, keep their kids out of the system altogether or not, or get them home as quickly as possible."

In the next chapter, we look at how scholars and community activists are challenging child welfare's first principle —that it is beneficial because it keeps children safe. But disproportionality and disparities are baked into the system that is impervious to reform. When child welfare agencies rely on state surveillance to separate children from their families, it's no wonder why parents don't trust them.

"Never let your head hang down. Never give up and sit down and grieve. Find another way." — Satchel Paige.

Chapter Ten: Abolitionist Scholars and Community Activists

A small but growing number of academics are calling for an end to the child welfare system all together because it does more harm than good, especially to Black families. Many people think about child welfare intervention as a "helpful service" provided to vulnerable families. But that is a widespread misconception about the nature of child welfare, according to one prominent researcher.

Dorothy Roberts published Killing The Black Body in 1997, and Shattered Bonds, The Color of Child Welfare in 2002. Her most recent book, Torn Apart: How the Child Welfare System Destroys Black Families—and How Abolition Can Build a Safer World was published in 2022. After every book she wrote, Roberts became more of an abolitionist.

Roberts has her critics. The Child Welfare Monitor posted a negative review of Torn Apart in April 2022 by Marie Cohen. She called Torn Apart "a skewed portrait of child welfare in America."

"But when she talks of dismantling child protection, she is proposing the abandonment of abused and neglected Black children in homes that are toxic to them, an abandonment that will perpetuate an intergenerational cycle of abuse and neglect," Cohen wrote.

Roberts responded to such criticism in a Time magazine interview. "We have a child-policing system today that investigates a large number of Black families and removes so many—one out of 10 Black children—from their home to be placed in foster care."

For Roberts the question is not why are so many Black children raised in toxic homes but why are Black communities in America so toxic and so poor?

"You can't fix a system that is doing what it was designed to do: oppress Black, Indigenous, and impoverished communities. The only way to stop that is to build a completely different approach, one that isn't based on threats to families, doesn't confuse poverty and child neglect, and doesn't blame parents for structural injuries to their children."

Roberts has been a lone wolf for 20 years, but her thinking got boosted in 2020 by an article in the Journal of Public Child Welfare. "It is not a broken system; it is a system that needs to be broken: the upEND movement to abolish the child welfare system."

This radical paper was written by Alan J. Dettlaff, then Dean at the Graduate College of Social Work, University of Houston, and four co-authors from the Center for the Study of Social Policy in Washington D.C. In the introduction the authors threw down the gauntlet.

"This paper will discuss the history and consequences of racial disproportionality and disparities, why they exist, and why, after decades of attempts to reform the child welfare system, it is time to acknowledge that reforms cannot right a fundamental wrong. The harm perpetrated on Black children and families by the child welfare system will only end when we can envision a society where families are strengthened and supported, rather than surveilled and separated," they wrote.

The paper has had 25,237 views. It remains to be seen whether it will jump start a reformation in child welfare like Martin Luther's 95 theses, which led not only to the Protestant Reformation but also to Luther's excommunication by Pope Leo X in 1521.

Dettlaff was punished in the kerfuffle that followed the article's publication and his call for an abolitionist movement. He didn't lose tenure but he was removed as dean of the Graduate College of Social

Work at the University of Houston. He had served in that position for seven years.

The paper's main thesis is that "the child welfare system disproportionately harms Black children and families through systemic over-surveillance, over-involvement, and the resulting adverse outcomes associated with foster care."

The paper announced the upEND movement, an anti-racist framework that aims "to end the current child welfare system as we know it, and collectively reimagine new, anti-racist means of keeping children, families, and communities safe and thriving...that seeks to partner with the many organizers and activists who have laid the groundwork to reimagine a future where families are strengthened and maintained rather than surveilled and separated."

Dettlaff and his colleagues stood on the shoulders of many others. Roberts tells a story about parent activist, Joyce McMillan, who founded and directs JMACForFamilies in New York City. New York's Administration for Children's Services (ACS) took her baby girl in 1991. The taking was instigated by an anonymous call to their Child Abuse hotline. It took her two years to get her daughter back with the help of Brooklyn Defender Services.

"I love Ms. McMillan's forthright condemnation of family policing and creative strategizing to undo it," Roberts said. "Under her direction JMACForFamilies has led influential grassroots campaigns to call attention to and dismantle ACS. She created the Parent Legislative Action Network (PLAN), a coalition of family defenders, professors, and parent activists, to promote laws to protect families from ACS."

She has also held rallies and posted billboards with bold messages like "Some Cops Are Called Caseworkers" and "They Separate Children at the Border of Harlem, Too." I feel honored to work with activists like Ms. McMillan in the struggle to abolish family policing and build a safer, more humane, and caring world," Roberts said.

McMillan worked hard to pass New York's Family Miranda Rights Act in 2023. Under the new law, CPS Investigators have to advise parents of certain rights at first contact, or risk all collected evidence from being automatically excluded. Two other JMAC campaigns are underway in New York. One requires people who report child abuse to leave their name and contact information but would prohibit the Office of Children and Family Services from releasing that information. An Informed Consent bill would require patient consent before drug testing a delivering mother or her newborn.

Big successes are measured in legislative victories, and they don't come easily in New York or Tennessee. There are other Black activists, like BeKura Shabazz, who got Tennessee's DCS to stop persecuting her daughter's family. It took three years. That story is in Chapter One. Shabazz is President of the Criminal Injustice Reform Network in Virginia.

The child welfare reform movement is made up of like-minded people who are trying to reform the Child Welfare system. These change agents see criminal justice and child welfare as carceral systems of oppression.

The Bronx Defenders and sister organizations in other boroughs engage the legal system as lawyer/advocates on behalf of mostly poor clients, many of whom are immigrants or people of color.

And then you have people like Maleeka Jihad (MJ) in Colorado and Michael Heard in Washington who are working inside the child welfare system trying to educate and get the best outcomes for their clients. You have people like retired caseworker Dee Wilson, who thinks Washington's DCYF Secretary Ross Hunter has skimped on funding for kids who need higher levels of care in congregate settings and there aren't enough beds to accommodate them all.

Some good news on that front. DCYF opened a new therapeutic facility in July 2024 to help youth, ages 13-18, with intellectual and developmental disabilities, autism spectrum disorder and behavioral health needs including substance use disorder.

The current state of child welfare reform is best described as a convergence of many players both inside and outside the child welfare system. Some 600,000 children who are separated from their families each year in the U.S. and about 400,000 of them go into foster care. Those staggering and shocking numbers are the elephant in the room everybody sees but nobody knows what to do about it.

Connie Reguli fights one case at a time and she's in touch with other hardened litigants like herself around the country. They share information and sometimes resources with each other when they are caught in the middle of a particularly difficult case. The system is more or less a monolith, and you can't change it one case at a time. You can only survive it, like the clients they help.

For 25 years Reguli has put her heart and soul into fighting "those horrible people" at DCS and she is under no illusions about it. She told me that in all that time she has "maybe managed to move things a couple of inches."

However, different people are becoming aware of how bad child welfare is –– academics, ministers, politicians, parents, and others. Reguli says that more and more of them are speaking out. Once a critical mass is reached, it will only take one little shove to push it all over the cliff.

Reguli started going to visit politicians in 2008. She soon realized you need either money, which lobbyists have plenty of, or you need votes, which she decided to find. Otherwise, working the hill where the Tennessee General Assembly does its business, would be fruitless.

The Family Forward Project

"That's why I decided to start the Families Forward Project. When I was able to create a social media platform and have 19,000 followers, then I could say 'we have 19,000 families.' And to them that converts to 19,000 votes." Reguli is a player but even so, she rarely has a winning hand. She told me that's why she started organizing trips to Washington

257

to lobby federal officeholders to rethink how child welfare is funded under the Social Security Act.

Indefatigable, Reguli is used to crisis and it started early in her life. Reguli's father died of cancer in 1953 when she was one. In 1964, her 16-year-old brother died of leukemia. She was 12. Her mother remarried in 1960 when Reguli was in first grade.

She tells a story about one night when one night her stepfather attacked her mother.

"My drunken stepfather tried to murder my mother in the kitchen when I was 12 years old and instead of running away, I jumped right in the middle of it." Her only thought was 'We're not going to be defeated.'

"There was a butcher knife. And there was my stepfather, and he was drunk. And there was my mother and my baby brother was in a high chair. I reached and grabbed for his hand on the knife.

"All I can remember is grabbing at the knife and then the knife broke in two and the pieces went flying across the room and the night went on.

"I was in the middle of a life-threatening event. These events that happen in our childhood, these are the things that make us who we are.

"When events put a person in the middle of a conflict, you gotta have the strength and the power to proceed," she told me.

Never attempt to teach a pig to sing; it wastes your time and annoys the pig." — Robert Heinlein.

Chapter Eleven: Treating People Like Criminals and Keeping them in the Dark

Tennessee is one of 26 states that close juvenile courts to the public and the press. They are closed to protect children from wearing a scarlet letter for the rest of their lives for something they did when they were young. Juvenile courts are also closed when child welfare agencies want to take custody away from parents accused of neglecting and abusing their children.

Juvenile Courts don't have jury trials although the U.S. Supreme Court has ruled they can, provided defendants are tried as adults. This can happen automatically if the alleged offender is over the age of 16 and the charges are serious, like rape or murder.

Georgia, Texas, and Wisconsin have lowered the age to 16 when juveniles can be tried as adults and sentenced in open court. The most common method is through judicial waiver. Forty-six states and the District of Columbia give juvenile court judges the discretion to waive jurisdiction in individual cases involving minors, so they can be prosecuted in adult criminal courts.

When child welfare officials say they are protecting neglected and abused children they don't say that juvenile court proceedings are essentially the same as in criminal courts except that parents don't have the due process rights criminal defendants have. They like it that way.

Reporter Amelia Vorpahl wrote a piece for the Council of State Governments in May 2022. In it, she listed five reforms that would make juvenile courts better. The last one is particularly relevant.

"Identify statewide performance measures for juvenile court judges and collect and use data to strengthen decision-making and accountability. Few states have established the infrastructure required to evaluate whether court decisions are aligned with research and best practice. States must define what juvenile court effectiveness looks like as well as establish a transparent and collaborative performance measurement system."

Accountability

Some of the stories told in this book are examples of how DCS uses safety plans, family planning meetings, and permanency plans to run roughshod over parents. Some of them are about judges who let them get away with that. Some of them are about how parents suffer through all that and the interminable delays of the entire ordeal. The process is traumatic for both parents and children, regardless of the outcome.

By discounting birth parents in its case management, DCS is getting poor outcomes. By any rational standard, DCS is the main cause of its own failures. And except for DCS top officials, most DCS workers are just middle class. Until 2023, DCS didn't provide a decent life for the bulk of its staff much less poor parents who fall victim to its excesses, incompetence, and hostility.

In the course of researching this book, I queried DCS many times for statistics to better understand how well its policies are working. I wanted to see if those figures reflected what the families I have been writing about are going through. Those queries never got any meaningful response.

I also requested interviews with every person in DCS leadership and many of its second-tier officials who deal with the nitty-gritty problems of everyday DCS operations. All requests were denied. Regarding Quinn's supposed openness and commitment to transparency, I haven't seen it yet. She, too, like Commissioner Nichols before her, has declined to be interviewed.

DCS operates in secrecy and its poor reputation for lack of accountability is well-deserved. I've reprinted a DCS response to one of many requests I made for information.

January 7, 2022, Peter White

pwhite545@gmail.com

PUBLIC RECORD REQUEST RESPONSE FORM Department of Children's Services, 7th Floor, UBS Building, 315 Deaderick Street, Nashville, Tennessee 37243, Via Electronic Transmission.

Mr. White,

The Department received the following request from you on December 16, 2021:

"How many children in DCS custody, including delinquent children, were served by private providers in 2018, 2019, and 2020?"

The Department received an additional request from you on December 19, 2021, as follows: "Can you tell me how many children were reunited with their families between 2018-2021?"

The Department does not keep data in the format you have requested, and the requests would require the Department to compile data. Tenn. Code Ann. § 10-7-503(a)(4). As such, your requests are denied.

In response to your records requests received on December 16 and 19, 2021, our office is taking the action(s)1 indicated below:

(X) No such record(s) exists, or this office does not maintain record(s) responsive to your request, as it would require the agency to compile information and sort through files to provide the requested information.

Sincerely,
Douglas Earl Dimond General Counsel

DCS spends millions every year tracking foster kids and the ones who were reunited with their families. It's basic information but apparently DCS can't or won't provide it. DCS operates in secret, and it tightly controls information released to the public. They say it's to protect the privacy rights of juveniles in DCS custody but oftentimes it's to protect themselves.

• • •

DCS Computers Stuffed with Data Public Can't See

Why is DCS hiding Data in its multi-million computer system?

In 2019-2020 DCS had 3,589 Black children in custody.

NASHVILLE, TN – We can't prove it. Between 2010-2014 the Department of Children's Services (DCS) installed a new computer system called TFACTS. The Tennessee Tribune has asked DCS for information TFACTS could provide. But DCS's General Counsel, Douglas Dimond, has repeatedly said they do not have or do not track that data. They have it. They just don't want to share it.

How many kids get returned to their parents? How many permanent placements get how much in federal bounty under the Adoption and Safe Families Act of 1997? How much in monthly payments do adoptive parents get when DCS gives them custody? How many kids, once taken by DCS, never get out until they turn 18? What is the case manager workload across all 12 regions in the state? How many monthly visits with the families and children in DCS custody do they miss?

The answers to these questions would show what DCS is actually doing with its $1.4 billion budget. It has been playing a musical chairs game since at least 2016 when DCS stopped including performance and real outcome data in its annual reports to the Governor.

In those reports DCS gilds the lily and hides the truth by stressing process over actual outcomes. "Suppose they can show in 2017 there were fewer cases per worker. That doesn't mean the kids are doing better," said Richard Wexler, a prominent critic of Child Welfare systems in the U.S.

Richard Wexler is a noted child welfare advocate and executive director of the National Coalition for Child Protection Reform.

Child welfare has become a profitable industry at public expense.

In the business world, DCS's lack of accountability and transparency would prompt a major housecleaning. But this is social welfare for children and DCS plays the role as their champion and defender.

Critics like Wexler say what they are really all about is taking poor kids from their families to feed a network of foster homes that collect money for strangers to parent the children DCS has wrongfully removed from their families.

The Tribune has reported a number of those cases. But to really know how badly DCS is serving Tennessee's neediest children, somebody has to lift up the curtain DCS officials have dropped around its TFACTS computer tracking system.

It will take elected officials to demand access to TFACTS to get information DCS is hiding, or it will take some brave soul who works there to leak it. There are 6200 DCS workers with access to TFACTS. One whistleblower leaked documents to Channel 5's Ben Hall in October 2021.

"She voiced her concerns about high caseloads, high turnover and children falling through the cracks to supervisors... but nothing was done," Hall reported. The whistleblower sounded the alarm but lost her job in the process. Ultimately, it may take another lawsuit like the 2001 Brian A. v Sundquist case to force DCS to be more transparent and open about its operations.

In the meantime, the Tribune can report Tennessee is spending a lot more money than the national average on child welfare but not getting the results Alabama gets getting kids adopted or returning them to their parents while spending much less money.

In 2014 DCS spent $271,421,700 on custody services. In 2019-20, DCS spent $384,251,000 on custody services. The department is taking more kids into custody every year and that costs more money but children are not exiting at the same rate, so room and board costs have skyrocketed in 7 years.

According to the federal Adoption and Foster Care Analysis and Reporting System (AFCARS) Alabama does a better job returning kids home. From 2015-2019, 70% of children taken into custody were returned to their parents. In comparison, from 2015-2019 in Tennessee only 56% of children taken into custody were reunited with their families.

One third of children who entered the system in Tennessee between 2015-2019 were taken back into custody after leaving it. In Alabama between 2015-2019, only 18% of kids returned to the foster system.

Between 2015-2019, 78% percent of children in Alabama had two or fewer placements in their first year in foster care. In Tennessee, that number was 68%.

Rates of Removal

The National Coalition for Child Protection Reform (NCCPR) created indices of spending, removals, and placements for all 50 states to create a national overview. The data come from the Census Bureau, Department of Health and Human Services Administration for Children and Families (ACF), AFCARS, surveys, and state data.

With all those sources, it's not all guesswork but NCCPR notes a number of caveats they considered before ranking states by how much they spend per child, how many kids they take into custody in a year, how many poor kids they take, how many kinship placements are not reported, which skews the foster care numbers in some states like Texas and Kansas.

"There are three kinds of lies: lies, damned lies, and statistics," Mark Twain wrote in his 1907 autobiography. Richard Wexler, Executive Director of NCCPR, is well aware that numbers are often used to persuade people to a point of view. When they aren't accurate or they're missing, they distort reality and that's not good.

You can read about NCCPR's analysis, methodology, and find the tables for 2019 and 2020 here:

The rate of removal index ranks states by the number of children taken from their homes for every 1,000 impoverished children in that state. The purpose is to "compare the propensity of states to adopt a 'take-the-child-and-run' approach to child welfare."

NCCPR's rationale for using children's poverty rates rather than the total child population in a state is because child protective services agencies almost never take children from affluent families, and using the total child population would allow affluent states that still take large numbers of children from impoverished neighborhoods to camouflage this fact.

"Remember the parable about blind men describing an elephant? Each touched a different part of the elephant, so they came to different conclusions about what it looked like. But what if there were more people involved – and they had to compare notes? The picture still wouldn't be precise, but it would come closer," Wexler said.

The removal index does not use a "snapshot" at the end of the fiscal year to rank states but rather custody numbers over the course of a year and it compares them to the number of children living in poverty in each state using the Census Bureau's last three population surveys.

Wexler argues that using poverty statistics is a more accurate way to assess child welfare in the U.S. But he notes that ACF is not enforcing regulations that require states to report "hidden foster care" placements with relatives, and states like Texas and Virginia simply do not report them.

2020 NCCPR Rate-of-Removal Index

State	Average number of children living in poverty, 2018-2020	Entries into foster care, 2020	Rate-of-Removal per thousand impoverished children	Rank
Alabama	220,667,	3,504	15.9	36
Tennessee	281,000	5,860	20.9	31

Note: The higher the rank the better by comparison. The national average rate of removal of poor kids is 19.1. For all kids it is 3.0

2020 NCCPR Rate-of-Placement Index

State	Average Number of children living in poverty 2018-2020	Children in Foster Care, Sept. 30, 2020	Rate-of-Placement per thousand impoverished children	Rank
Alabama	220,667	5,573	25.3	39
Tennessee	281,000	8,839	31.5	33

Note: The national average rate-of-placement for poor children is 35.8. By comparison, the national average rate of placement per thousands of total child population is 5.5.

In 2019, the rate of removal in Tennessee was more than 20% above the national average. In 2020 it was about 10% above the national average but because of COVID, 2020 data may not be as reliable as 2019 numbers, which are worse than 2020.

"The point is, Tennessee is an outlier – it takes away far too many children and that problem drives everything else. Such widespread kidnapping by the state--when it's not justified––drives practice, drives financial incentives, drives foster care recruitment, drives contract provider contracts––the Full Monty," Wexler told me.

"For 50 years we've responded to tragedies that are needles in a haystack by making the haystack bigger. The result has been more tragedies. Isn't it time to start shrinking the haystack to make it easier to find the needles?" Wexler asked.

Rates of Spending

NCCPR compared 2018 child welfare spending among the states and like the other indices, they divided spending both by the total child population and the number of impoverished children in each state.

"Because poverty both contributes to actual child abuse and neglect and is so often confused with child neglect, we believe this is the fairer measure," said the May 2021 press release.

The report notes some caveats: it does not factor in cost of living among states, it does combine all federal, state, and local child welfare expenditures but not figures where counties run their own welfare systems. The data comes from voluntary surveys.

"Despite these limitations, we believe that the comparison is useful for determining "outliers" – that is, states which spend far more, or far less, than average. And we believe it is useful for noting significant differences among states," the report said.

NCCPR 2018 Rate-of-Spending Index, Impoverished Children

(See https://bit.ly/2018spending)

State	Impoverished child population	Child Welfare Spending	Spending per Impoverished child	Rank
Alabama	252,000	$328,862,115	$1,305	45
Tennessee	262,000	$840,484,149	$3,208	21

The average spending on impoverished children was $2,779.

NCCPR 2018 Rate-of-Spending Index, Total Child Population

State	Child population, 2018	Child Welfare Spending, 2018	Spending per child	Rank
Alabama	1,085,000	$328,862,115	$303	38
Tennessee	1,473,000	$840,484,149	$571	13

The average spending for all children was $450.

"It turns out Tennessee spends at a rate above the national average, Alabama is below the national average, but Alabama gets better results. Part of the reason: foster care costs more than keeping families together. In child welfare the worse the option, the more it costs," Wexler said.

No wonder DCS is hiding the TFACTS data. It spends more money but gets worse outcomes than neighboring Alabama.

•••

As he has argued before, Wexler says it's easy to take the years you want to prove whatever you want. He noted between 2018 and 2020 entries into foster care in Tennessee declined by 15%. He also noted there was an increase in child fatalities between 2018 and 2020. But it does not follow that DCS should take away more children to reduce overall child fatalities because kids die from crib death, car accidents, drowning, among other causes.

Cherry-picking a statistic is not evidence of the need to take away more children. "Why did fatalities drop dramatically in Texas after they passed new laws that reduce foster care?" he asked.

Wexler concludes, "There is no evidence for the claim that Tennessee is bending over backwards to keep families together. On the contrary, even when rates of child poverty are factored in, Tennessee takes children from their families at a rate nearly 50% above the national average."

Garbage In Garbage Out

In 2010 DCS spent $100 million on a new computer system that was supposed to track foster placements, manage cases, pay vendors, and do payroll. A March 2012 Audit by the Tennessee State Comptroller concluded TFACTS couldn't walk and chew gum at the same time.

Case managers found it clumsy to use and the permanency plans it produced were too long and complex. Entering data was so painstakingly slow that calls to the Child Abuse Hotline were not investigated quickly but put on hold indefinitely.

In 2012, DCS awarded a $2 million no-bid contract to Compuware Corporation to fix TFACTS glitches and deploy the software on 2400 tablets issued to DCS caseworkers. In other words, they threw good money after bad to put software that didn't work well in the hands of overworked case managers.

Ten years later, TFACTS can pay vendors or find a placement for a special needs child but still can't do both at the same time. DCS

Commissioner Margie Quinn asked Gov. Lee for $56 million to strip parts off TFACTS like an old Ford and put them on a better chassis or maybe just start from scratch and buy a new Prius.

TFACTS does have its boosters. Dr. Fred Wulczyn at the University of Chicago did some studies using TFACTS data and he told me it's one of the best systems ever designed for social science research. Maybe so, but for everyday users, not so much.

I wrote about DCS regularly, including TFACTS, for more than a year. Dozens of queries for information and stats were answered long after my deadline with standardized forms and a checked box that said, "We don't track that information" but if you want to pay for it, maybe we could work something out. I'd rather sue them for violating the Public Records Act.

The stories printed in this book are anecdotes, not data. And that's a problem that goes beyond TFACTS and DCS hiding behind HIPAA privacy protections. For instance, I went to Davidson County Juvenile Court to get data on how many emergency removal orders Magistrate O'Neil had signed in the last three years.

Court Clerk Lonnell Mathews could provide the information because Metro's IT department built a database for his office. For statewide data, Mathews suggested I contact the Administrative Office of the Courts where he reports his data. They didn't have it or wouldn't release it. The Tennessee Commission on Children and Youth said they didn't have it. I felt like a dog chasing its own tail.

I have relied on federal resources like NICANDS and AFCARS to critique DCS. I've compared those records with DCS annual reports. Sometimes, the feds report things DCS tries to hide or obscure. DCS is not responsive to press queries seeking information or clarification or even simple requests like copies of PowerPoint slides from budget presentations it makes to the Governor and legislative committees.

To be accountable, child welfare agencies must keep good records. To be transparent, they have to make them readably available. Recognizing that need, in 2023, Davidson County Juvenile Court advertised for a full-time strategic data coordinator. It's a civil service job and pays $63,608.96 per year.

As then Senator Nancy Schaefer warned, "I have witnessed such injustice and harm brought to so many families that I am not sure if I even believe reform of the system is possible! The system cannot be trusted. It does not serve the people. It obliterates families and children simply because it has the power to do so."

Why Doesn't Somebody Just Sue the Bastards?

In Great Britain, hundreds of subpostmasters were accused of theft and fraud after the government-owned central Post Office computerized the postal service. In little towns and hamlets throughout the country, small post offices, run by local families, had always used ledgers to keep their books. Seniors came weekly to cash their pensions.

Many small post offices were located inside a shop that sold bakery goods or general merchandise. They were the heart of social life in rural Britain where everybody knows everybody else.

Mr. Bates vs The Post Office is not a typical English comedy with much hullabaloo over trifling and silly conflicts roiling the British heartland. The program dramatizes what is one of the greatest miscarriages of justice in the country's history. ITV produced the 4-part series and PBS Masterpiece Theatre picked it up. A documentary featuring some of the people whose lives were ruined was also produced.

Hundreds of subpostmasters lost their contracts, lost their shops, and many were even sent to prison––"leaving lives, marriages, and reputations in ruins" according to a story in Deadline.

One subpostmistress from Walsall, Jess Kaur, had a nervous breakdown because she was accused of stealing 11,000 British pounds and couldn't prove she didn't do it. Kaur attempted suicide and only stopped trying to kill herself after fourteen electroshock treatments.

Deadline reported that the issue was actually caused by errors in the Post Office's own computer system. They denied it for years and kept telling subpostmasters they were the only one who had a problem. But they used faulty data from the Horizon computer system to convict more than 700 subpostmasters of theft and fraud; they forced people to give up their life savings or mortgage their homes to repay the shortfalls in their accounts.

The Horizon computer system used proprietary software and hardware made by Fujitsu. While faulty computers were the source of the problem, the company did not prosecute innocent people. Posts Office officials did that. They maliciously prosecuted their own people and deceitfully tried to cover it up.

So far, none of them have gone to jail but the British Parliament voted to compensate the victims in January 2024.

For years' communities all over England raised money to support the postmasters. The scandal broke only after the victims found Members of Parliament to press their case and only after they organized 500+ plaintiffs to file a lawsuit.

Class action lawsuits in the U.S. have not had permanent impact or led to major reform of child welfare in the U.S. Child welfare officials in Tennessee continue to use their computer system to cover up what they are doing. By controlling information DCS can keep operating with impunity and avoid being held to account.

Advocates, parents, officials, and activists have not yet reached a critical mass in the U.S. to do what sub postmasters and their allies have done in Great Britain.

Connie Reguli Did Sue

On May 1, 2024, Reguli filed a lawsuit in the Middle District of Tennessee U.S. District Court against the conspirators that took her license. The complaint describes how DCS attorney Tracy Hetzel and District Attorney Mary Katherine Evins went to the Brentwood Police Department to open a criminal investigation on Reguli and Hancock.

Three of the four people in that meeting were lawyers, including Police Capt. David O'Neil. They could have reviewed the language of the statute and realized that no crime had occurred.

Instead, they concocted a scheme to rewrite the law in order to get a search warrant on Reguli's social media and indict her for a fake felony. They almost got away with it. She was convicted in a jury trial, but the state appeals court reversed the conviction, ruling that no crime had been committed. She expects the conspirators will try and claim immunity, but she doesn't think they will succeed.

Connie Reguli was convicted on trumped up charges, exonerated on appeal, and now she's suing her tormenters. Meanwhile, she went to Washington D.C. to lobby for a parent's advocacy bill.

"Where there is fabricated evidence, there is no immunity for that," she told me.

Reguli is suing them for malicious prosecution and asking for $200 million in damages for stealing her life, credibility, and reputation.

She hopes they lose and appeal to the federal appeals court in Cincinnati. It will give her more ammunition to take to Washington to drum up support for a parents' advocacy bill.

On June 4, 2024, the diminutive litigator filed a second lawsuit against Williamson County Circuit Court Judge Joseph Woodruff, Williamson County District Attorney Kimberley Helper, and Emily Layton, a

CASA worker, and her attorney, Dana McLendon, for filing a false affidavit in a case involving a fine Woodruff had levied against Reguli in 2014.

"Woodruff used the cloak of the judiciary, but he wasn't acting as a judge. He did it all in secret and he did it through a third party and after the case was over. He did it to try to get me charged with something criminally. But this case was dismissed before it got to trial," Reguli explained.

Reguli's faith in the law may not triumph against corrupt state actors. Remember, this is Tennessee where the infamous Scopes Monkey Trial took place in 1925. William Jennings Bryan argued for the prosecution and Clarence Darrow argued for the defense. Darrow lost the case. The Tennessee Supreme Court overturned Scopes' conviction on a technicality. Things aren't that much different in Tennessee a hundred years later, but I wouldn't count Connie Reguli out, not by a long shot.

Chapter Twelve: Drug Wars

One cannot talk about juvenile justice or the foster care system without talking about race. Racial disparities are baked into criminal justice and social welfare like cinnamon in apple pie. Racial injustice in the U.S. is rooted in policies that discriminate against Black people and people of color.

Overt racism and bigotry have always been behind efforts to deny voting rights, but the unconscious bias of policymakers and decision-makers are also to blame. They perpetuate what scholar and litigator Michelle Alexander named her 2010 book, The New Jim Crow.

A number of studies have backed up Alexander's main thesis: namely, the new Jim Crow looks an awful lot like the old Jim Crow. A paper by Heather D. Evens and Steven Herbert looked at juveniles sentenced as adults in Washington State, 2009-2019. In their introduction the authors summarized prior research on the topic.

"A Black youthful offender is six times more likely to be detained at arrest than a White youthful offender, and a Latinx juvenile offender is three times more likely to be detained than a White counterpart."

"Black youthful offenders are also more than five times as likely to be incarcerated in state juvenile facilities as White youthful offenders; American Indian youthful offenders are more than three times as likely; and Hispanic youthful offenders more than twice as likely, though there are distinct differences across the states," they wrote.

Even counting those differences, the authors noted that "the pattern of disproportionate minority contact is a persistent one across time, and one that has resisted overt attempts to reduce its size."

Criminologist Myrna Cintron reached similar conclusions in her study of Latino juveniles.

"Latino juveniles are disproportionately arrested, detained and tried in adult criminal courts. Their sentences are harsher, and their commitments are longer than those for White youths who have committed the same offenses," she wrote.

In short, juvenile judges throw the book at black and brown youth and put them in jail at higher rates than whites. Similarly, child welfare agencies take children into custody and put them into foster care. Child welfare agencies disproportionately affect Black children, and racial disparities continue to exist throughout the U.S. According to Richard Wexler, child welfare is a carceral system, too.

Two Sides of the Same Coin

I wrote hundreds of stories for The Tennessee Tribune including a handful of drug-related articles. As you know, the legal process in criminal court and juvenile court are different. For instance, there are no jury trials in Juvenile Court. But criminal courts and juvenile courts have at least two things in common: they are both likely to involve people who are poor, and hearsay evidence can have devastating effects on defendants in either court.

Sometimes parents who lose their children in juvenile court wind up in criminal court, too. For those who do, they face the prospect of jail time and asset forfeiture in addition to having their kids put in foster care. Even if you got caught with a small amount of a controlled substance, law enforcement agencies can take your car, your RV, your boat—maybe even your house. Without a good lawyer your goose is cooked. It starts the minute you get arrested.

Parental substance abuse was at least one reason DCS took children in 42% percent of its 4966 new cases in 2019. The Children's Bureau says neglect accounts for 63% of all removals and drug abuse is in second place at 36%. Four stories in this book are about DCS falsely accusing parents of drug abuse in order to take their children. It turns out false reporting happens more often than we realize.

DCS uses the stigma of drug addiction to show a child is without proper care and judges are inclined to let DCS take children into custody "for their own good" when they accuse parents of drug abuse.

In order to take a child, DCS must file a dependency and neglect petition in juvenile court. Dependency is defined as a child without proper care, not a parent who uses drugs, but DCS has convinced itself and too many judges that they are the same thing. In fact, research shows that babies develop motor skills better when their drug-addicted Moms keep them instead of when they are put in foster care.

University of Florida researchers looked at two groups of mothers who abused drugs during pregnancy. One group kept their babies, the other had them taken away. After six months, they tested the babies using the usual measures of development like rolling over, sitting up, and reaching out.

"Typically, the children left with their birth mothers did better. For the foster children, the separation from their mothers was more toxic than the cocaine," says Richard Wexler, Executive Director of the National Coalition for Child Protection Reform.

While some addicts are so strung out, they can't take care of their kids properly, most parents can. Whatever the real facts are, DCS routinely exaggerates them to make things seem much worse than they are. As pointed out earlier, when DCS says children are in danger from "exposure to drugs", they could be talking about a doctor's prescription.

As for neglect, it can mean anything from unwashed dishes in the kitchen sink to children left unattended while Mom goes grocery shopping. When DCS alleges neglect because the children are chronically truant, it doesn't matter that they are home-schooled. Accusations are enough to be pulled into the system and lose your children. Too often juvenile court judges let DCS get away with

279

allegations instead of insisting they do proper investigations. And too often, court-appointed attorneys don't mount a stout defense because they are overworked or don't want to rock the boat.

In the war that DCS wages against families, truth is the first casualty and fear mongering about drugs is a useful weapon. Winning that war means taking children as prisoners and putting them in foster homes. The next story from rural Obion County in northwestern Tennessee is about a vulnerable family who lost their kids while they were being evicted from a rental home.

•••

Lives Interrupted: Illegal Eviction Led to Wrongful Taking

Local police stop dad walking with his two children and DCS takes them away.

DCS kidnapped my kids." Claudia Gheorghe-Nery

SOUTH FULTON, TN—One of the town's six police officers was waiting at a stop sign in a squad car as Joe Nery and his two kids walked by. The officer made Nery wait for an hour and a half in a church parking lot before two women who drove a black pickup truck with big wheels and tinted windows showed up. They wore T-shirts and jeans.

"One was wearing flip flops and the other was wearing tennis shoes. It would be very difficult to believe that someone who works for the state to handle an important matter like this to be dressed so totally inappropriately. They looked just raggedy, you know? I had to take their word because I had three officers in front me ready to tackle me if I put up a fuss or if I wanted to fight for my kids," Nery said.

He does not know their names because the two women did not show any identification before taking the kids. One of the women flashed a photo on her cell phone of what she said was a court order, but she pulled it back before Nery could read it.

They trundled the two kids into their big black truck and left Dad alone in the parking lot. He said they had no booster seat and didn't give him any paperwork, although he asked for it.

The kids, Izabella, 10, and Franky, 6, have been in foster care since July 20, 2022.

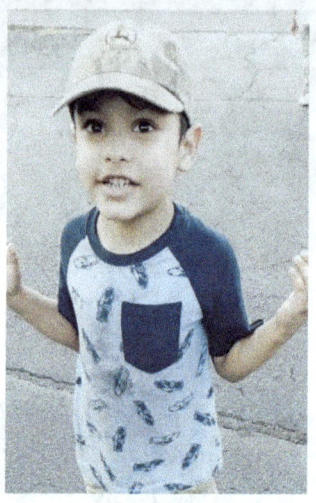

On July 21, DCS attorney Marlene Simpson told Obion County Juvenile Court Judge Sam C. Nailling Jr. that there was probable cause for the removal of the children. DCS had gotten an emergency removal order to take the kids because someone had reported the parents to DCS.

Franky Nery, age 6, was taken July 20th and remains in foster care. He has seen his parents twice.

In its court petition, DCS said the children were removed for "educational concerns, environmental neglect, and drug exposure concerns." The parents said those were just excuses and they denied all the allegations.

The Sleazy Landlord

The unnamed witness who reported them was probably their landlord, Joseph Mathews. He was in the process of evicting the family from a rental on 325 Forestdale Ave in South Fulton.

On Wednesday, July 13, Mathews sent Deborah Turnbo to the house. She gave Claudia Gheorghe-Nery, the mother, an ultimatum. "I begged her basically to please let me do what I can until Saturday. She said 'yes, you have until Saturday but if you're not out by then I will call child protective services on you'." She wasn't out by then and so they did. Turnbo admitted it in a text to Claudia.

A legal eviction can take 1-3 weeks. If the landlord wins in General Sessions court, the judge will grant a writ of restitution. Tenants usually have 10 days to vacate. The parents said that they didn't go to the hearing on June 29th and don't think their landlord showed up either. In any case they didn't receive a notice to vacate the property because county sheriffs usually remove you within 48-72 hours and that did not happen.

(See https://tntribune.com/250000-tennessee-households-face-eviction/)

DCS Gets Involved

On July 19, DCS case manager Jesse Cochran showed up at the house around 10 am with two other DCS workers.

"It was clear that I was in the middle of moving due to all the boxes that I had already packed and carried out on the porch," said Claudia Gheorghe-Nery.

Cochran and his two colleagues invited themselves into the house that was, understandably, in disarray. Gheorghe-Nery explained her situation to them.

Her husband was serving an 18-day sentence for an unpaid parking ticket. Mom had to do all the packing herself. Nery got out of jail on July 19 but was not home when DCS interviewed Claudia earlier that day.

Izabella Nery, age 10, won't wash off the polish on her fingernail and toes. It reminds her of happier times.

"During the entire meeting at my home, my children played, interacted with your employees, laughed, introduced pets," Gheorghe-Nery later wrote in a letter to DCS Commissioner Jennifer Nichols.

That is in sharp contrast to what Cochran wrote in his report.

"The children were observed to be dressed in dirty clothing and covered in dirt. Both children had several bug bites on their arms, legs, and backs," Cochran said.

Gheorghe-Nery called Cochran's investigation "a pack of lies."

"As the meeting went on, I was advised to leave and find a place that's cleaner; without a car it was rather difficult to find a rapid solution to my problem," she said.

Cochran promised a second interview but that never happened because DCS seized the kids the next day.

"There was no investigation done before KIDNAPPING my kids," she wrote Nichols.

"I still have no hard copies of the charges and investigation of my case," Gheorghe-Nery said.

In its report to the judge, DCS claimed they didn't get a full urine specimen from Mom on July 19, but it showed positive for amphetamines and THC. Gheorghe-Nery said she told Cochran that she was taking prescription phentermine and pulled the bottle from her purse and showed him. Cochran did not include that information in his report to the judge

The report and it is full of innuendo and "concerns"; it is long on conjecture but short on facts; Given the circumstances, no reasonable person would conclude the children were in serious danger without further investigation. But in hindsight it seems DCS came to that conclusion before they even knocked on the door.

The Child Abuse Hotline collects reports of child abuse from anonymous callers. DCS investigators follow up on those tips to find evidence of serious child abuse. Too often they deliver false or misleading evidence to justify an emergency removal when their "investigation" is actually part of a personal vendetta, as it was in this case.

Gheorghe-Nery wrote then DCS Commissioner Jennifer Nichols that her children were never in imminent danger. She said there was no evidence of physical, emotional, neglect, or sexual abuse. In short, DCS had no grounds to take them, and she wanted her kids returned immediately.

Later, DCS caseworker Brian Hill wanted the parents to sign "a neglect and dependency" petition. They refused. It would have given DCS another legal weapon to keep Izabella and Franky instead of returning them to their parents. They did agree to a drug test that both parents passed.

Mom never heard back from Nichols but did get a note from the Customer Relations Unit (complaint department). It was under Nichols' watch an employee leaked a survey exposing disgruntled "workers quitting, rising caseloads and a toxic work environment." The final straw was a video showing kids sleeping on the floor "of an office building, many without blankets." Following a yearlong investigation into DCS by the Tennessee Tribune, Margie Quin replaced DCS Commissioner Jennifer Nichols in September 2022.

"They told us personally that our daughter wanted to come home and she wanted to be with her mom and dad because we're good parents to them. And my son said the same thing to them," Gheorghe-Nery said.

Life in Foster Care While Parents Fight DCS in Court

Regarding their custody conditions, the foster home is set up with triple-tier bunk beds. "Basically, they eat a lot of hot dogs and pizza," Gheorghe-Nery said. She said they have seen the children twice since they were taken.

"For the first time in my son's life, who is 6 years old, we found scabs on his head, his skin is dry as dry can be; he had bites all over his legs and his arms visible to the naked eye. Both children were emotional, crying, asking us not to leave them. My daughter won't remove the nail polish off her toes, because she said that it reminded her of me, and she was happiest with me. I did her nails before she was taken from me," Gheorghe-Nery said

Judge Nailling held a show cause hearing on July 21st. DCS attorney Simpson objected during Nery's testimony. The judge overruled Simpson and let Nery continue but said that he didn't want to pull the case out from under the feet of DCS. He set a disposition hearing "to decide what the consequences will be" for August 17th. At that hearing the parents asked for a court-appointed lawyer and the judge scheduled the next court date for September 29th.

"He should have pulled the case out from under her feet. They take kids from a happy environment and for the first time in their lives they are traumatized emotionally, psychologically, and now I see that there is also physical (abuse)," Mom told me.

Unfortunately, Juvenile Court judges, DCS attorneys, and court-appointed lawyers often fail to reunify the families with the children DCS has wrongfully taken. The parents are not in the courtroom for very long and then they go home with or without their kids. DCS is like a bad case of poison ivy that never seems to go away and the more you scratch the more it spreads.

An ever-present litigant, DCS is always in court and a force to be reckoned with. DCS usually brings multiple staffers to a trial, and they often get their way because judges and court personnel simply don't want to confront them. DCS takes into custody about 6,000 kids a year. Many are snatched on the flimsiest of grounds with no actual investigation like Izabella and Franky were.

Rural Obion County has a population of 30,466. According to its official website, Obion County courts provide "fair, courteous, and timely service to every individual and agency having business with Chancery,

Circuit, General Sessions & Juvenile Court." So, we know they are big on nice and tooting their own PR horn, but the jury is still out on whether they will dispense justice in "Case NO. 6675 In the Matter of Izabella Nery, age 10, and Franky Nery, age 6." There is a dark underside to the picture of friendly corn-growing in Obion County. Three local policemen, a landlord, his flunky, and several DCS employees worked in concert to seize Izabella and Franky and take them from their parents because being evicted is apparently a serious case of environmental neglect.

"Those kids have gone through an immense amount of distress just so that DCS can make some money on my children. I know exactly what they get paid. I've been doing my homework. I know what they get paid and why they take them so quickly," mom said.

As previously stated, foster care is a booming business in Tennessee. It's not the boon to the local economy that a prison would be, but it's a good little racket they have going up there in northwestern Tennessee.

DCS paid out $14,33,900 last year to foster parents and other contract service providers like the child collectors who snatched those kids from a church parking lot and the foster parents DCS is paying to feed them hotdogs and pizza. Claudia Gheorghe-Nery didn't tell me any details, but she emailed me on February 7, 2024, to say the family had been reunited after the children were in foster care for seven months.

•••

The next five articles are about how law enforcement in the U.S. targets the poor and African Americans.

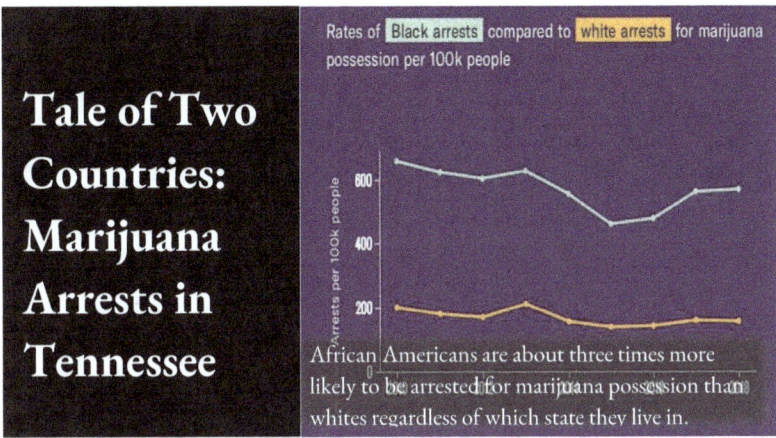

As of April 2024, recreational marijuana is legal in 24 states, comprising almost half the country. Still, nine out of ten marijuana arrests in the U.S. are for possession. Since 2010 pot busts have decreased nationally but the rate of decline has stalled, and in some states, has reversed upward.

According to a new ACLU report, *A Tale of Two Countries*, African Americans are 3.6 times more likely than white people to be arrested for marijuana possession, despite similar usage rates. In the last decade, this disparity has actually worsened in most states despite marijuana decriminalization in places like Minnesota and North Dakota and legalization in states like Vermont and Illinois.

Racial profiling and bias in enforcement in Tennessee mean Blacks are 3.2 times more likely to be arrested than whites for marijuana, slightly less than the national average. Per 100 thousand people, Tennessee ranks 7th among states for highest marijuana possession arrest rates. Between 2010 and 2018, Tennessee's arrest rate for possession increased 21%. Marshall County (349%) and Robertson County (331%) were among the top 20 counties in the U.S. for the biggest increases in arrest rates between 2010-2018.

The Black arrest rate for marijuana possession in Tennessee ranks 13th in the nation. The Black arrest rate is 820 per 100 thousand vs. 255 per 100 thousand for whites in Tennessee. Carter County in East Tennessee is the worst place in the country to get busted for pot if you are Black. Between 2010 and 2018, the percent increase in racial disparity in marijuana arrests was 976.7%.

"For decades, marijuana laws have been used to criminalize Black and Brown people, waste taxpayer money, and fuel the mass incarceration crisis," the report states.

In states where pot is either legal or decriminalized, there are lower average arrest rates for possession and sales, as you might expect.

The ACLU notes that states are taking strides toward reforming these outdated and harmful drug laws. Eleven states and the District of Columbia have legalized marijuana, and 18 states have decriminalized, which means they've removed some of the criminal penalties for possession of small amounts. Furthermore, these reforms are driven in large part by the will of the people. Two out of three Americans — more than ever before — now support marijuana legalization.

The report findings reveal an uncomfortable truth: While there has been some progress in scaling back the war on people who use marijuana, it is still wreaking havoc in much of the U.S. Despite decades of failure, prohibition and punitiveness generally remain the centerpiece of governments' approach to drug use. Law enforcement continues to make hundreds of thousands of marijuana possession arrests every year, accounting for almost half of all drug arrests nationwide.

According to the **Vera Institute of Justice**, Tennessee is the second highest of six nearby states in incarceration in local jails and state prisons. In 1983, there were about 14,000 people locked up in Tennessee. In 2015, there were 48,000 people in jail or prison, an increase of 242%. Disparities exist for incarcerated Black people. In Tennessee, Blacks make up 18% of the population but 36% of people in jail and 42% of people in prison.

Since 1978, the Black incarceration rate has increased 136 percent in Tennessee. In 2017, Black people were incarcerated at 3.1 times the rate of white people. In a seven-state region including Kentucky, West Virginia, Virginia, North Carolina, South Carolina, and Georgia, Tennessee has the second highest rate of jail admissions and the third highest prison incarceration rate per 100 thousand populations.

It's Time for a War on the Drug War

Kassandra Frederique is Drug Policy Alliance executive director.

NASHVILLE, TN – Lauren Johnson lives in Texas with her husband and her three children. After her husband lost his job in 2008, the family received less federal food aid because both parents had felony drug convictions and couldn't get food stamps (SNAP).

"There's no end to the collateral consequences of a criminal conviction," Johnson said. "Here in Texas, 55,207 total individuals in the fiscal year 2014 were disqualified for SNAP, Supplemental Nutrition Assistance Program for federal drug convictions. That doesn't include all of the individuals that didn't even apply because this had been the law for so long that all your friends had told you, you don't qualify. And a lot of people just didn't even bother trying," she said.

Every year since 1996, following the passage of Clinton's infamous crime and welfare bills, there has been a Texas bill to opt out of the federal law. It never passed until Johnson, who works for the ACLU, started working to overturn the punitive law. "In 2015, we changed that law. Many, many people who have now come home from prison or used to be disqualified, are now accessing the food stamp assistance," she said.

Although that particular law was changed in Texas, the effects of the War on Drugs still impact millions and "goes far beyond the criminal legal system in its heinous impacts", according to the Drug Policy Alliance (DPA).

The DPA said the drug war is "insidiously waged inside public policies across the board" and has contaminated six critical areas: child welfare, education, employment, housing, immigration, and public benefits. It's time to end it.

"Only through creating awareness of the drug war's insidious impacts across sectors can we begin to disentangle it and the culture of criminalization it promulgates from our lives," said Kassandra Frederique, DPA executive director.

As we reported last week, despite decades of failure, prohibition and punitiveness generally remain the centerpiece of governments' approach to drug use. (see Tale of Two Countries: Marijuana Arrests in TN, Tennessee Tribune, February 18-24, 2021, page A10).

In the hysterical language of the War on Drugs, marijuana was often called "a gateway" drug. That is hyperbole but it is absolutely true that conviction for marijuana possession can ruin your whole life. The consequences can be severe and devastating because of the culture of punishment for drug use that has little to do with matters of personal and public health.

According to the DPA, the war on drugs has fueled mass incarceration and has also produced profound employment discrimination.

The very presence of a drug arrest or charge can keep you from getting a job and can be an automatically keep you

293

from getting a professional license for a trade like trucking, barbering, or nursing.

The drug war against kids started in 1973 with the passage of the Child Abuse Prevention and Treatment Act (CAPTA). Since that time, real and perceived drug use has been used as an excuse to remove children, primarily children of color, from their homes and communities.

The DPA website provides details of a system featuring "relentless attacks on parents" by lawmakers and pundits; "constant surveillance" and increased child maltreatment investigations; and forced participation in abstinence-based drug treatment programs, even for parents who don't have substance use disorders.

Regarding education, drug use has been used as an excuse to search lockers, drug-testing, harsh discipline–all of which leads to higher dropout rates and limits on assistance to higher education.

Discriminatory policies have unjustly criminalized communities of color.

The DPA education report notes that that Black, Indigenous, and Latinx students "receive the highest percentages of federal financial aid and are also targeted by drug war enforcement at higher rates."

While there is little evidence that drug testing improves job performance, mandatory testing and discrimination have robbed people from access to stable employment.

In housing, the Anti-Drug Abuse Act of 1988 had a section on "Preventing Drug Abuse in Public Housing." It has been used for decades to disqualify or evict poor families from public housing. According to the DPA, the Drug war is a war on families because it puts people "in the impossible position of choosing between giving up housing or turning their backs on family members who would make the entire family ineligible for assistance by using (or even being suspected of using) drugs."

Photo by Sonya Yruel/Drug Policy Alliance

Drug hysteria has been tied to immigration since the Chinese Exclusion Act of 1875.

Asians and Latinos are generally not drug addicts but have been treated as if they all are.

"Drug war thinking has led us to "surveilling immigrants, turning anything related to drugs into a severe crime, deporting people in record numbers, and enacting harsher punishments on noncitizens," the DPA report says.

Furthermore, the War on Drugs brands "all people who use drugs and people suspected of using drugs as lazy, irresponsible, and not deserving of any public assistance." The report said that people of color are disproportionately targeted with racist names like "drug-addicted welfare queens." The DPA report notes "over 25% of states require welfare applicants to submit to the invasive and humiliating procedure of peeing in a cup to be drug tested" and "over half of states have instituted modified bans to limit welfare and food stamp eligibility for people with felony drug convictions."

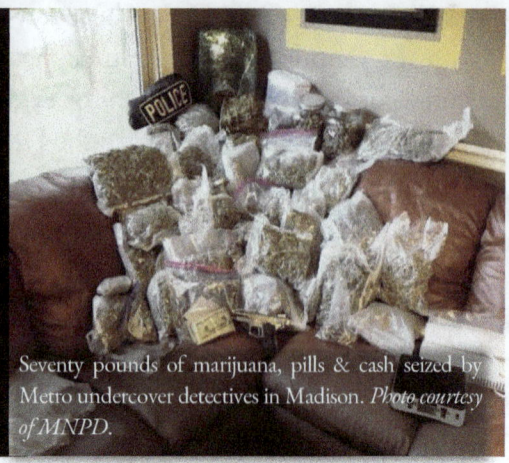

Will the New War on Drugs Target Crime Bosses or the Poor?

Seventy pounds of marijuana, pills & cash seized by Metro undercover detectives in Madison. *Photo courtesy of MNPD.*

NASHVILLE, TN – Civil Asset Forfeiture is when the police take your stuff, and you have to pay to get it back even though you did no wrong. It's big business.

According to the Department of Justice, cops took $407 million from people they were sworn to protect and serve in 2001. By 2012, the seizures increased to $4.3 billion. Law enforcement agencies are addicted to taking people's cash, cars, boats, houses, and business property. They know they should stop but can't.

Police started taking things in 1984 to help fight the War on Drugs and soon every cop in the land was hooked. After 30 years, many police departments, including MNPD, still haven't kicked the habit.

Seized drug profits and expensive homes, airplanes, and boats have paid for the DEA's anti-drug efforts for decades. And they share the cash with local police agencies. But really big drug busts are rare. In the vast majority of cases the seized assets do not belong to Pablo Escobar, El Chapo, or Joe "Peg Leg" Morgan.

In small towns, local governments rely on confiscated cash and property to pay for parks or water lines or garbage services. In bigger towns they pay for new jails, SWAT teams, and DARE programs.

Sometimes, they pay for salaries (but not in TN), sports cars, wild parties, and week-long junkets in Hawaii. By the way, it's all legal.

Attorney David Ridings cuts a deal in the case of the giant Teddy Bear. Photo by Peter White

"Civil asset forfeiture is a key tool that helps law enforcement defund organized crime. It takes back ill-gotten gains from them and prevents new crimes from being committed and weakens the criminals and their cartels," former Attorney General Jeff Sessions explained.

Sessions returned to the Wild West days of the 1980s and wanted to get tough on crime and restart the War on Drugs. He got President Trump's approval. Sessions announced stiff minimum sentences for drug convictions.

Then President Trump called the opioid crisis a national emergency. "It's a serious problem the likes of which we have never had," he said. Trump said that he was drafting a response to the opioid crisis that is killing 91 people every day. The President is expected to rely on a report by the drug commission headed by former New Jersey Governor Chris Christie.

Meanwhile, Sessions started going hell bent for leather after drug dealers. They would be pharmaceutical companies like Purdue Pharma, Janssen Pharmaceuticals, and Allergen.

Prescription drugs killed many, if not most, of the 30,000 opioid drug users who overdosed in 2015. Doctors wrote the scripts that hooked patients with a single 30-day prescription. Women overdose almost twice as often as men. When it comes to drugs, Sessions is a man from the last century.

"Criminal enforcement is crucial to stopping the violent transnational cartels that smuggle drugs across our borders, and the thugs and gangs who bring this poison into our communities," Sessions told the DEA summit on Heroin and Opioids in West Virginia on May 11, 2017.

Going after violent criminals who are international drug traffickers does not describe what's happening now and Sessions ignores the behavior of law enforcement agents who are addicted to the power and money that comes their way from acting like Nazi storm-troopers.

"The War on Drugs has never produced a victor in the African-American community," stated Representative Harold Love (D-Nashville).

Two dozen witnesses, some from law enforcement, state legislators, attorneys, civil rights advocates, and social workers testified to the U.S. Commission on Civil Rights July 24 at the Main Library. Love said the War on Drugs has decimated black communities, allowed gangs to sell drugs with impunity in poor neighborhoods, and filled prisons with addicts and low-level drug dealers.

"I think we need to address the fact that everybody who's driving around with cash in a car is not selling drugs. Everybody who is driving around in a particular neighborhood is not engaged in those activities," he said.

See more testimony by Representatives Love, Hardaway, and Clemmons here:

https://www.youtube.com/watch?v=bRZqO_8ELxA

Love cited a 2015 ACLU report that found African Americans make up 9 percent of Philadelphia's residents but 53 percent of the population whose assets were seized. Groups like NAACP have long held that drug enforcement is higher in black and immigrant neighborhoods. For a criminal charge to be filed there has to be probable cause. But cops can seize your car using the lesser standard of a "preponderance of evidence" and that means you will have two legal cases: one for yourself and one for your car. It turns out your car's freedom will probably cost you more than your own

Rep G.A. Hardaway testified that the risk of driving while black increases the risk of having your car or money being seized by police when they stop you. Attorneys who represent claimants at Department of Safety administrative court hearings deal with the arcane

299

policies and outsized costs associated with trying to recoup seized civil assets.

The main burden is proving your car, or money was not part of a crime. Cops may not have probable cause to arrest you, but they can arrest your car and impound it on the suspicion that it was involved in a crime you may or may not have committed. This Orwellian state of affairs violates the presumption of innocence upon which the American justice system is based. It also sidesteps habeas corpus.

By law, you can't hold a person in jail indefinitely without showing cause, but you can impound someone's car and hold it for months. If you're poor and need your car to get to work, it amounts to the same thing.

"This is the slowest process in the entire criminal justice system, hands down," says Attorney David Ridings. Ridings was a Metro cop for a decade and also worked for the Davidson County District Attorney before becoming a defense attorney.

Last week Ridings faced Dept. of Safety prosecutor Jennifer Crim in the case of the giant stuffed Teddy Bear. Riding's client, who requested his name not be used, was carrying a five-foot stuffed bear to his friend's house in May to hide it until Mother's Day. It was a gift for his wife. Coincidently, Metro police were serving a warrant upon the friend at the same time. Assuming the giant bear was filled with drugs, the police ripped it to shreds.

The bear wasn't holding. Police were so embarrassed they arrested everybody, including Ridings' client and impounded both his cars. In order to do that, they had to get another search warrant to enter the man's home, where they found cash but no drugs. They took the cash and charged Ridings' client with felony drug possession. His bail was more than $100,000, higher than the bail set for his friend who actually had drugs in his possession.

The criminal case never went to trial. The arrest was in May. Four months and several thousand dollars later, the forfeiture hearing took place last week and lasted about five minutes. Ridings was smiling when he emerged from the courtroom. Ridings considered the result a win. The DA agreed to release both cars and half the money that the drug squad had seized from a man they had clearly arrested without probable cause.

"He agreed to take half the money rather than fight for a year and a half to get it all back," said Ridings. People rarely take their fight to chancery court to recoup all they have lost. It's almost impossible to do that. In the Teddy Bear case, Ridings' client did not get reimbursed for the stuffed bear and he was out thousands of dollars the drug task force gets to keep.

"Most people get weary and agree to settle because they drag it out so long," says Ridings. Ridings said that if a case is not settled at the first appearance, it could be months before a second one can be held.

It costs $350 just to file a petition in the forfeiture court. You don't get that money back even if you committed no crime, as in the Teddy Bear case. There were towing and storage fees on the two cars that amounted to $690. Riding's fee was several thousand, he said.

Here's the best advice Ridings can give: don't buy a five-foot teddy bear for your wife if Metro's drug task force is hanging around or it could cost you about ten grand.

Statistics and Hearsay Plague Hearing on Civil Asset Forfeitures

Martin Daniel (R-Chattanooga) cited Department of Safety figures showing that 45% of seizures made in Tennessee in 2016 were made without any criminal charges being filed.

NASHVILLE, TN – One thing became clear in last month's Civil Rights Hearing about civil asset forfeiture. How many seizures are happening depends upon where you live. But there is a lot of dispute about how many seizures arise from drug investigations and testimony about the average amount of cash or assets seized in Tennessee varied widely.

According to District Attorney General Stephen Crump (10th Judicial District), the average amount of civil forfeiture in Tennessee is about $10,000. Representative Martin Daniels (R-Knoxville) said the amount was closer to $2,200. Both men cited Department of Safety figures.

Hedy Weinberg, Executive Director, ACLU of Tennessee, suggested the number was probably closer to $500. And homeless advocate Samuel Lester said if you're talking about people living on the street who have their backpacks and IDs taken by police, the amount is probably closer to $100 or less.

Changes in the forfeiture law in 2015 now require better record keeping but still don't track demographic information, have a minimum seizure threshold, or require a criminal conviction before assets can be seized. Tennessee law enforcement seized $19 million in cash in FY 15/16 and the Department of Safety got another $13 million from the federal drug task force sharing program last year. But where it actually came from and where it actually goes is not clear. There is no legislative oversight of asset forfeitures in Tennessee.

According to Carlos Lara, a Metro narcotics detective, between 2014 and 2016 only 2.7 percent of seizures were made in Nashville without a criminal arrest. That is 32 out of 1170 seizures. Lara also said 95 percent of seizures in Davidson County are done by detectives, five percent by regular police officers. He also said MNPD keeps detailed records about what happens to seized cash and property in Davidson County. But Representative Martin Daniel (R-Chattanooga) told the panel that Department of Safety figures show 45% of seizures made in Tennessee in 2016 were made without any criminal charges being filed. The total number of property seizures in TN was 11,122 in FY15/16. Of those 5,858 were forfeited, and about half were returned to claimants who petitioned to get their stuff back.

The Department of Safety kept all of the $19 million in cash seized last year. Sales of confiscated vehicles totaled $2.5 million for a grand total of $20,376,200. In 2016, 44 bank accounts were seized, 442 cell phones, 247 wallets, furs, and purses, 405 computers, 43 personal documents, 98 lawnmowers, 362 firearms, 3.054 cars, 1987 trucks, 139 motorcycles, and 181 jewels. A total of 7840 items were seized and 1635, or about 20 percent, were returned.

"I submit to you that the current state of Tennessee's forfeiture laws provides a perverse incentive to maximize property for law enforcement agencies," Daniel said. Contradicting Daniel's statement, District Attorney Mike Dunavant (25th Judicial District) said that in his rural district of five west Tennessee counties, the vast majority of asset forfeiture cases have criminal charges filed with them.

Lee McGrath, Senior Legislative Counsel for the Institute for Justice, says it's time to delink asset forfeiture cases. Drug cases should be pursued vigorously as they are now, says McGrath. That's about ten percent of the total but represents about 70 percent of the money seized by law enforcement. The other 90 percent of cases should be tried in criminal courts and asset forfeiture should be part of that process which has more protections for defendants. He says cases with less than $100,000 are 90 percent of all forfeiture cases and have just 30 percent of the money.

He suggested during his testimony that law enforcement should be fine with that. They aren't. Neither is the Tennessee District Attorney's General Conference. Speaking on behalf of all 31 judicial districts, Conference President Mike Dunavant said, "I agree with my colleague that a conviction-only standard would not be workable in the sense of providing true justice for people who are committing crimes for financial gain and reaping the benefits of that."

There is that. However, police and prosecutors like the certainty of having seized assets in their possession before they try a drug case. It allows them to make deals and persuade low-level criminals to snitch on their bosses.

Local Attorney Calls Civil Asset Forfeiture A Huge Scam

Lannom-Williams: Attorney Frank Lannom says that in forfeiture cases judicial independence is a legal fiction because the prosecutor's boss writes the law that is binding on the one independent person involved in the process, the administrative law judge.

Frank Lannom is a rubber meets the road kind of guy. "If you want to know how to get your stuff back and the problems that are so unfair about this process, I'm the guy to talk to, okay?" he told the Commission on Civil Rights last month.

Here is an excerpt of his testimony:

"So, they show up at your house and they've gone to the trouble of getting a search warrant. They've had to convince a judge somewhere that they had some reason to come into your home. That makes sense, right? To get a search warrant. But when they get to your home, they are allowed to take everything you own without a search warrant.

"The last case I had when they took all of the electronics and all of the little Game Boys, you know, that the children play, the PS4s and things. They take all of those, they take all of the cars, they take all of the money, and they busted -- is that a word? -- the piggy bank and took $147 out of the piggy bank.

305

"There were two children in the home - without a warrant. So, they take all of your stuff. They take all of the cars. You have no car, you have no money, and they attached a seizure to the bank accounts that the individuals had. No rent money, no electric-bill money, no anything. That's where the process starts. But they do hand you a green piece of paper that says, "Here is why we're taking your property."

Check, "Narcotics." That's it. You don't get 'You sold narcotics last week, you sold narcotics today, we think you're moving heroin.'

You get a green piece of paper. That's how I always know my clients have had their property taken, they have a green piece of paper in their hand, and it has a box checked that says "Narcotics." So they come to me and I tell them they have a right to petition to get their stuff back."

But it is a tortured lengthy process and one that Lannom says is unfair from start to finish. For example, in a criminal case, there is a court clerk who is an impartial keeper of records. In forfeiture cases, the prosecutor is the court clerk.

"They decide if my filing is on time. They also get to pass the rules that say how many $350s you have to pay. 'We took three cars from your client, Mr. Lannom, and we took them on three different days, so you have to pay three times $350.'"

"Now, this isn't a judge making this decision or a clerk of the court, this is my opponent who decides how much money I must pay to ask my clients to ask the government why they took my client's money."

"If we ask for a deposition and the judge says I get to take it, my opponent, the Department of Homeland Security, can appeal to the administrative -- the appellate position of Homeland Security, their co-workers, and they can stop the deposition from happening by rule. Guess who wrote the rule? The Department of Homeland Security. My opponent writes the rules that stops the process that prevents me from taking the deposition.

But eventually I may get through that part of the process, and we got a statute that says we get a hearing within 30 days. Well, you don't really get a hearing within 30 days, you get told when your hearing will be within 30 days, and it may be six months. So, we go to the hearing and occasionally I put on the proof and this administrative judge says, "You're correct, Mr. Lannom. your two clients, who are Jehovah's Witnesses, who have never seen a drug in their life, whose son worked for them and got caught with drugs after nine months, should get their cars back."

"Thank you, Judge.

"My opponent in this case can then appeal. Would you – can anyone speculate who they appeal to? Anyone, please guess? Her boss, the Commissioner of the Homeland Security. And he can override the administrative judge. She literally appeals to her superior. That is an unfair process for anyone to labor under. And what happens is the boss then can make a ruling of whether or not the administrative judge was correct or incorrect."

Lannom says in forfeiture cases judicial independence is a legal fiction because the prosecutor's boss writes the law that is binding on the one independent person involved in the process, the administrative law judge.

A National Drug Crisis

Interstate 880 in East Oakland is elevated, and the dismal space underneath is where homeless people used to gather to get out of the rain. Like similar encampments all over the U.S. the inhabitants are mentally ill, some are just down on their luck, and some are addicts. On July 25, 2024, California Gov. Gavin Newsom ordered homeless encampments to be shut down.

Law enforcement agencies pursue drug offenders. Interdiction, arrests, and criminal prosecutions have filled prisons mostly with users, not big-time traffickers.

First, it was all about marijuana and heroin, then cocaine and crack, then opiates and methamphetamines. Today, synthetic drugs containing fentanyl are pouring across the border from Mexico.

The Center for Disease Control and Prevention (CDC) says 56,000 people died from fentanyl in 2020. In 2021, fentanyl was involved in 71,238 overdose deaths. Methamphetamine was implicated in 32,856 deaths, cocaine in 24,538 deaths, and prescription pain medications in 13,503 deaths.

Synthetic drugs come in different colors and teenagers are eating them like candy. So, it's a really big problem and getting worse. The next story is about these deadly new imports.

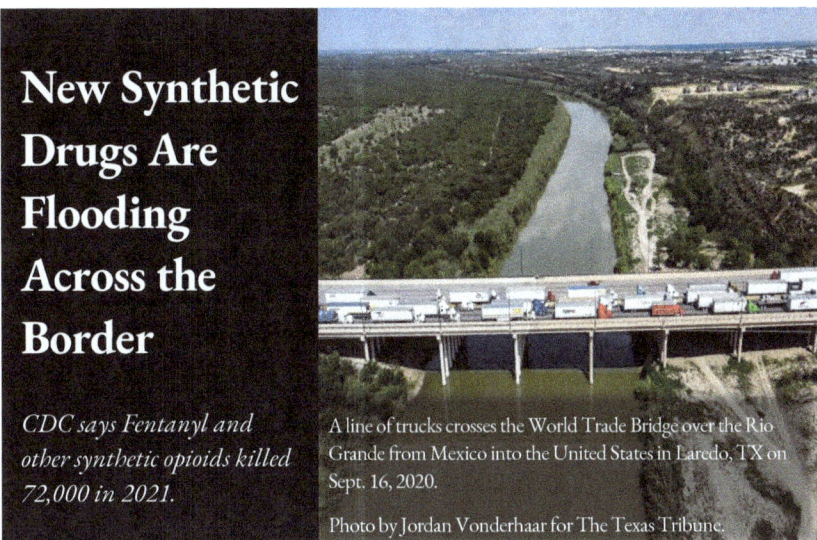

New Synthetic Drugs Are Flooding Across the Border

CDC says Fentanyl and other synthetic opioids killed 72,000 in 2021.

A line of trucks crosses the World Trade Bridge over the Rio Grande from Mexico into the United States in Laredo, TX on Sept. 16, 2020.

Photo by Jordan Vonderhaar for The Texas Tribune.

December 11, 2022

There is a border crisis but it's not what you think. And the homeless crisis is not just about the lack of affordable housing, according to one award-winning reporter.

It's about synthetic drugs made in Mexico and sold in the U.S. that are killing tens of thousands; many of the victims are young, many are homeless, many are people of color and that's something new.

"I never saw a black person ever know, ever buy, sell, use, or even know much about methamphetamine," says Sam Quinones, author of four acclaimed books dealing with synthetic drug production in Mexico and the effect those drugs are having in the U.S.

"Cocaine was the drug of choice. And now the drug is so vast, you go down skid row, largely black, due to crack for many, many, many years, and now it's all black people on methamphetamines," Quinones says.

He noted that the cocaine people are buying in the black community has fentanyl in it. Quinones cited the case of actor Michael K. Williams, who played Omar in the HBO hit crime series, The Wire. "He died about a year ago from cocaine. He had a cocaine problem, but the cocaine he bought was laced with fentanyl, and he died."

With these new drugs, you don't have the luxury of time, says Quinones. Unlike heroin addicts who can use for 40 years, these new drugs drive a person mad or kill them, sometimes with a single dose.

Sam Quinones is the author of *Dreamland* (2015) and *The Least of Us (2021)*.

"There's no such thing as a long-term fentanyl addict. They all die. And meth will drive you psychotic long before you ever express a sincere desire for treatment and getting off the street," he says.

Quinones talked about a drug-treatment program in Kentucky————a jail, actually—where addicts get clean. The new jail in Nashville, Tennessee, has an entire wing where addicts are housed and treated. Locking addicts up is the most compassionate thing you can do for them, he says.

He says a new class of synth drugs is being produced by Mexican drug cartels in staggering quantities. They are mixed into toxic cocktail pills with other drugs like heroin and cocaine, and smuggled into the U.S.

"We are now in the synthetic drug era," he says. Remember Walter White, the high school chemistry teacher and meth-maker in *Breaking Bad*? Well, the chicken restaurateur and drug lord, Gus Fring, dies from a bomb White made in the Season Four finale of the popular crime TV series. Jesse Pinkman and Walter White are still alive in *Breaking Bad's* final season.

But in the real world of Mexican drug traffickers, small-time meth cooks like White and Pinkman have all but disappeared to the likes of Fring and associates.

"Those have been run out of business by this very cheap, very potent stuff coming out of Mexico," says Quinones. The little meth labs of yesteryear are all gone. He says all the meth and fentanyl are produced in Mexico. "All of that is trafficked north by the many groups that are down there," he says.

Quinones spoke to reporters during an Ethnic Media Services briefing last week. There's some corruption, he says, but you cannot explain the quantities coming through by corruption. It's more a Free Trade story, Quinones says.

"It's far more about the simply massive quantities of trade between the two countries and that so much is coming through and we just simply do not have the capacity to check even a moderate percentage of all the trucks coming through."

Two milligrams of pure fentanyl can kill you. Barring extraordinary intervention like multiple doses of Narcan, the drug is so addictive, and dosage/pill vary so wildly, that it eventually kills everyone who gets hooked on it, says one ER doctor who has a front row seat to this crisis.

Pilar Marrero, EMS Associate Editor, interviewed Dr. John from a major Western city who spoke on the condition of anonymity. She asked him to describe the drugs and their effect on people.

"It's important to know that heroin and morphine, oxycodone, your typical opiates before fentanyl, are dosed in milligrams, right? Whereas fentanyl is dosed in micrograms," Dr. John said.

He said it's a quick on, quick off drug used in the ER for patients who are bleeding and have low blood pressure. So, people will get fentanyl, they'll be high for a very short amount of time, or their pain will be treated for a very short amount of time, and then they'll have pain again," he says.

So, you can give repeated small doses on top of one another. "But on the street, it's very hard for people to use it in a way that is safe," he says.

Another big problem is the extremely pure meth people are using. It induces psychosis in many patients who arrive in the ER stark raving mad.

"The methamphetamine psychosis does not go away when the high of the drug goes away. It takes weeks to months to even years to go away," Dr. John says. Bottom line is that it's really, really difficult to affect change in the methamphetamine user because they will swear "it's not the drugs, man".

Dr. John says ER staff share that bit of gallows humor with each other, knowing full well it is the drug talking despite the mortal fear it induces in their patients. Heroin addicts are reasonable by comparison. They know they are addicted. Meth users are usually in complete denial.

These cocktail drugs have replaced the opioids that were over-prescribed from the late 1990s to 2016 and were responsible for so many deaths during those years. A new health crisis of synthetic meth and fentanyl, marketed in colorful counterfeit pills, is killing thousands.

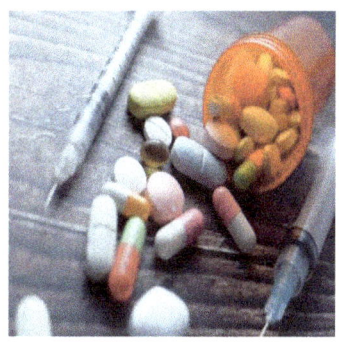

New synthetic drugs come in different styles and colors. Young people are eating them like candy, and they can be deadly.

In about 2017 Mexican traffickers started packaging fentanyl as counterfeit phony pills that look very much like legitimate pharmaceuticals, says Quinones. But that was just a passing phase. Now, it comes in different colors.

"That fentanyl, if it comes in a yellow pill or a green pill or a blue pill, they do not care.

They need the pill, and that's all that matters to them," says Quinones.

The pills are being sold frequently on social media apps like Snapchat or Craigslist.

"This took place during COVID because the kids couldn't leave the house. The only way they connected to the world was through their phones. And now people went on anonymously selling drugs with kind of very colorful menus, that look like an ice cream truck menu, almost. That's what I thought when I saw one of them."

"And so, you're seeing the social media app become kind of like the new street corner in a sense," he says.

Dr. John noted that the police have backed off arresting people for drug-related issues.

"We don't have the capacity in most ERs to put every person who comes in with methamphetamine intoxication on the 72 hours hold because we need those beds for heart attacks, for strokes, for everything else. There's not enough capacity in health care to address this issue," he says.

Quinones says an international drug collaboration between Mexico and the United States absolutely has to happen. Current interdiction programs are inadequate. "I think this has reached beyond simply a drug issue, and it now resembles to me like a poisoning, like a national poisoning," he says.

Quinones says the new synth drugs are killing so many people we can't just look at it as "the drug problem." "It really has to be taken up by the State Department," he said.

The U.S. Congress passed a bill, signed into law in April 2024, declaring the fentanyl crisis a national emergency, created new powers to disrupt money-laundering and distribution networks and imposed new sanctions on criminal organizations and drug cartels.

Like opioids, the fentanyl crisis eventually hits home. According to research published in JAMA Pediatrics, the number of cases of children entering the foster care system due to parental drug use has more than doubled since 2000. The data came from the Adoption and Foster Care Analysis and Reporting System (AFCARS).

"Researchers analyzed AFCARS data about children in foster care in the United States. They looked at nearly 5 million instances of children entering foster care between 2000 and 2017 and analyzed how many times foster children were removed from their homes due to their parents' drug use each year."

A ten percent increase in overdose death rates corresponds to a 4.4 percent increase in the foster care entry rate and a ten percent increase in the hospitalization rate due to drug use. Hard drugs containing fentanyl are driving an increase in the number of foster kids. Until we as a society get a handle on this growing epidemic it will continue to destroy too many lives, especially young lives caught in the crosshairs.

"The road to hell is paved with good intentions." —Anonymous.

Chapter Thirteen: Solutions

The federal government has financed state child welfare agencies in the U.S. since 1974 when Congress first passed The Child Abuse Prevention and Treatment Act (CAPTA). It has been amended several times, but federal dollars still flow largely to foster care and adoption services. States like Tennessee have privatized much of their operations. Child welfare now costs more than it ever did, and we have been failing to do it well for 50 years.

"When we started to go to Washington seven years ago, we really went to attack the Title IV E funding scheme about how it was financially re-homing children and social engineering, basically, by removing children from poor homes and paying people to raise them," Reguli told me.

"The Families First Prevention Act was an attempt to redirect some funds toward rehabilitation, but it's been unsuccessful because it's in competition with the removal funds."

"If you give a family domestic violence classes and leave the children in the home you only get 75% reimbursement of the cost for that domestic violence class. But if you take three kids, you get funding for all three kids and 100% reimbursement. So, the competition between the financial incentives is irreconcilable."

Insanity is doing the same thing over and over again and expecting different results. By that definition child welfare in the U.S. is crazy. More and more people, many different kinds of people, are calling for an end to it. But right now, there is little appetite to cut off Title IV E funds and redirect them.

If ever so slightly, the winds of change are beginning to blow in Washington D.C.

Congressman Barry Moore (R, Ala) and Susan Wild (D, PA) are sponsoring the Advocates for Families Act of 2024. It would give parents an ally in juvenile courts. In about half the states they don't have one. A draft version of the bill can be found in Chapter Fourteen.

"The reason we have to have a federal bill is because under federal law everything is confidential and so it closes off and they won't let us participate. So, all this bill does is open the door and says that if you take Title IV B funds, which is the companion to Title IV E, you have to permit family advocate so participate with families and have access to their documents, the courtroom whatever, as long as the family agrees," she explained.

"So, it' s by permission of the families only."

In Tennessee, DCS is a failed agency, akin to a failed state, where social institutions and rule of law do not help people but make their lives worse, even unlivable.

Even agents with the best of intentions can't be trusted when protocols are ignored, when caseworkers and their supervisors lie to parents and their children, and when due process rights are routinely denied or ignored in juvenile courts. Any one of those things is like a terminal case of cancer and DCS has *all of them*.

I asked Reguli what she would do, if by some twist of fate, she suddenly became Commissioner of the Department of Children's Services.

"The first thing I would do is make regional visits in the state of Tennessee and invite all the families who have children in custody along with their case files to express to them that we do not want to keep children in state custody unnecessarily and give them an avenue if they believe their child is not appropriately in state custody."

Reguli said it could be that there was no finding that they hurt their kids, they completed their plans and DCS refused to return them, or because

DCS refused kinship care. She said that would reduce the number of kids out of foster care by one third.

"For those that are remaining in foster care. We know 40% of kids in custody are there because of substance abuse. Is there a gap in services in that poverty area––which is employment, housing, food, and substance abuse––that would put these families back together and get that feedback directly form the families."

If Reguli was in charge, she would split the department in two.

"As I tell lawmakers in Tennessee, you have got to split this agency up. You cannot call it children's services and be a prosecutorial agency. You have to divide the support services and be a support agency like the Department of Development all Disabilities and then you have to have a separate department for the protection of children. It needs to be quasi-law enforcement. They need to work directly with law enforcement."

What would have to change?

Better child welfare means reducing the number of children taken into custody in the first place. At the back end, it means increasing the number of kids who are returned to their families instead of languishing in foster care or being put up for adoption.

Having less of another common practice—holding children in higher-level residential care when it's no longer recommended---is something DCS should stop doing. Sure, it keeps bringing more dollars to the provider and it's easier to keep them there than find a better placement but it's cruel and unjust punishment.

We know that when parents are accused of neglect, it is likely the effects of poverty that authorities are punishing them for. This is well known. Less well known is that neglect accounts for between 25% to more than 75% of children taken into custody, depending on who is counting. Sexual abuse does happen but not that often, about 4%. According to the Children's Bureau, just over 1,000 children were trafficked for sex in the U.S. in 2021, less than two percent of all cases.

Drugs, especially fentanyl, are a serious problem. But punishing the user is the wrong approach. Criminal courts get that. Juvenile Courts don't. I reported on several children taken into custody based on fabricated drug charges made against good parents.

If parents were given support to raise their kids better, they would, but as long as they aren't, many will be found wanting, and the child welfare system will continue to run on self-fulfilling prophecies and there will be no end to it.

I began investigating DCS wrongfully taking children in July 2021. The department should stop doing that. Sadly, DCS is still snatching kids with the flimsiest of excuses. In February 2023, DCS took five young Black children into custody after a traffic stop for driving too slow in the passing lane. The family was en route from Georgia to a funeral in Chicago. Dad had five grams of marijuana, a misdemeanor. Mom had a registered gun in her purse. Their names were not Bonnie and Clyde.

DCS should stop overreacting and respond better to queries, whether from families, their attorneys, or the press. When people with every right to know ask questions, DCS is duty bound to answer but too often, doesn't. Essentially, DCS operates in secret. Meaningful oversight is impossible, especially given Tennessee's lopsided politics and the demented well-meaning smiles of the politicians who keeping throwing money at DCS.

Tennessee's DCS budget has increased every year for a decade. Much of its budget has been spent providing support payments to foster parents and fees to group home operators. DCS is also paying for services for foster children like dentists, tutors, therapists, and medical specialists. And it's paying for things like childcare for foster parents, too.

DCS should spend less time trying to terminate parental rights and more time helping parents *enroll* in TennCare to pay their kids' medical and dental bills until they turn 18.

Not only health insurance but also affordable housing, a good job with childcare, and food security are the basics of a decent life. All these things are ultimately political issues and DCS is certainly not the only player in that space.

However, DCS is spending more of its budget on foster care families and adoptive families to subsidize decent lifestyles for them. DCS could, but does not, provide those benefits to parents trying to regain custody of the kids DCS has taken from them.

What about parents who seriously neglect their children? What about children who are sexually abused? Shouldn't they be in custody? Wexler says those kids are a small percentage of all the children in custody. Federal stats for sexual abuse of children are about 25% —and haven't changed much in years. Non-government sources like National Children's Alliance say the number is 9%. The disparity seems to be different definitions of what constitutes physical and sexual abuse.

In any case, most kids don't have to be in custody. None of the children whose stories are told in this book needed to be in foster care. CPS investigators manufactured the threat of drug exposure and alleged neglect from their parents. A number of studies cited in these pages have shown that foster care is a cure worse than the disease of addiction.

When it comes to doing time for your parents' crime, whether or not they are addicts, DCS custody is worse than being in state prison. You don't have a fixed sentence to serve, and you don't get time off for good behavior. The rehabilitation of parents is a giant con DCS attorneys and caseworkers put over on parents and juvenile judges to keep children past the 15-month time limit so family bonds can be permanently cut.

Until 2022 DCS did not subsidize kinship placements at all. Relatives caring for youths between 18-21 can now get a monthly stipend equal to half of the foster care board rate.

Imagine the Good Samaritan owned a boarding house under a government contract. For their trouble, DCS fully reimburses the boarding house owner, i.e., foster parent, but discounts kindness by half when a relative shows mercy to a kinsman. A new law does not allow birth parents to live in the same house with the relative who has custody of the children.

One important thing the General Assembly could do to reform DCS is pass a 20-case limit for DCS caseworkers. It hasn't managed to do that in five years. It would stop workers from quitting in droves, result in better outcomes, and force DCS to be more accountable.

Another game-changer would be to mandate and support family advocates for parents caught up in DCS investigations and court proceedings. Without them parents are like deer caught in headlights.

Family advocates would go a long way to change outcomes in Tennessee. Unfortunately, bills to provide them have so far failed to pass. In Washington, Congressman Barry Moore is sponsoring the Advocates for Families Act of 2024. It would give parents an ally in juvenile courts. In about half the states they don't have one. A draft version of the bill can be found in Chapter Fourteen. It has Democrat and Republican sponsors.

For now, better child welfare is happening in states that have taken a two-pronged approach: better family defense in the courts coupled with social workers who have the agency to deliver services families need. That's easier said than done.

Richard Wexler is Executive Director of the National Coalition for Child Protection Reform. Wexler has been the nation's watchdog on child welfare for more than two decades. He said Alabama's child welfare system improved when a consent decree forced advocates and state officials to cooperate in making reforms. However, Wexler said since then, there has been some backsliding. That happens a lot in other states, too.

"During the time that they do better a lot of kids do better. They are spared from needless foster care and kids get safer. The fact that you can't necessarily keep it forever means you have to come back and fight for it again," he says.

The 2018 Families First Act has the right idea because it emphasizes supporting families instead of destroying them. But it doesn't fill the bill, according to Wexler.

"The range of prevention services that could be funded under Family Frist was tiny, and there were absurd restrictions on which programs within that range could get federal aid. And instead of limiting group homes and institutions, I argued that the bill was so weak that it actually strengthened them, creating a whole category of institution that would be, in effect, sanctified in federal law.

"So, it's no wonder that in 2016, the Congressional Budget Office estimated that only $130 million in additional federal funds would go to prevention each year – a drop in the bucket compared to the billions spent on foster care."

That is the case in Tennessee. The 2023-24 DCS budget was $1.4 billion. DCS asked for an increase of $156 million and Gov. Lee proposed adding another $193 million. Just $7.4 million had been earmarked for prevention services and that would increase with the extra money Lee proposed.

Family support services in 2021-22 cost $70 million, just 6.9% of the total budget. The lion's share of the department's budget is spent on foster care and residential services. About one third of the budget is spent on case management operations. So, Family First federal funding has not changed Child Welfare that much in Tennessee. Pending changes in Washington, it is not about to create major changes in DCS operations in Tennessee.

Some Things Other States Are Doing Right

Two things that would really help improve child welfare matters is, first, allow parent advocates a place in juvenile court proceedings and second, to institutionalize family defense by funding agencies to represent defendants instead of relying on court-appointed attorneys. Some states get better outcomes because juvenile court judges don't pay a rotating roster of attorneys who take indigent clients.

Wexler says Connecticut does a better job than most on dealing with substance use because they've pushed heavily for family-based drug treatment. He says New York City has done a better job than most places at keeping entries into foster care down because they have invested in high quality family defense.

"One of the solutions that helps cement reform in place, if you can get it, it is high quality is family defense. Because if you've got people who every day are in court with families fighting to keep them together, demanding help with poverty problems instead of the usual cookie-cutter service plans and so on, that serves as an on-going check against the abuses of family policing," Wexler says.

I asked him to describe the perfect child welfare system. Here is what he said:

"It would be one that focused on alleviating the worst stresses of poverty. Provide a guaranteed minimum income, plus, as needed, rent subsidies, childcare subsidies and universal health care and an enormous proportion of the cases agencies like DCS see would disappear. Second, where substance use really is an issue, make high-quality family-based drug treatment available on demand.

Where other help is needed, let community-based community-run agencies design the help, so it is geared to what families actually need.

Abolish mandatory reporting laws, so professionals are free to exercise their professional judgment, and families don't need to be afraid to reach out for help.

Provide high quality family defense to make sure families can get the help they need – or simply be left alone when DCS should never have been in their lives in the first place.

Shut down the group homes and institutions; replace them, for the very few youths who need them, with wraparound services and therapeutic foster care.

Do that and there will be plenty of good foster homes available for the few children who really need them."

The National Coalition for Child Protection Reform (NCCPR) has a website with a wealth of information and analysis about child welfare. Since 2000, NCCPR has issued more than 30 reports on 20 state or local child welfare systems.

A lot happens between the time children come into the system and when they leave. Several government departments and thousands of people are involved with child welfare and tens of thousands are impacted by it in the U.S.

Among his many issue papers, perhaps the most important is Wexler's take on due process in child welfare cases. Like a modern-day Martin Luther, Wexler posted an agenda for children and families and made 20 recommendations to transform child welfare in the U.S. It's not fixed to a cathedral door but can be found on the NCCPR website.

"NCCPR believes the only way truly to protect children is to demand civil liberties without exception. There can be no true child protection when a government agency is given virtually unchecked power, almost no accountability, and operates in secret. That is why enacting meaningful due process protections for families is even more important than improving the "services" they receive from child welfare agencies."

A Final Note

The addendum contains articles and resources for anybody in child welfare to educate themselves and advance their work. This collection is by no means exhaustive, but it contains both reformist and abolitionist perspectives.

There are similarities and points of agreement between these two camps. Many abolitionists would agree with changes reformers say are needed to improve child welfare in the U.S.

People like Richard Wexler and Dorothy Roberts know what's wrong with child welfare. Wexler is a reformer and Roberts is an abolitionist. In Wexler's view, child welfare is what it is and could be a lot better. In Roberts' view, child welfare agencies are doing what they are designed to do: namely, oppress poor people and especially Black people. She thinks the fundamental conflicts baked into the child welfare system can only be resolved by building something better in its place.

The question should always be: does it help or hurt? Does it add to the problem or help resolve it?

We know that child welfare has many problems that need fixing. Children are being damaged every day by a system that claims to be helping them. Huge sums of money are being spent to support a dysfunctional system while activists like Connie Reguli are trying to persuade politicians in Washington to change the way child welfare is funded. It's an uphill battle, one worth fighting, and one that must be won.

"The road to hell is paved with good intentions." —Anonymous.

Chapter Fourteen – Addendum: Child Policy Review

Here is a toolbox of articles and resources about child welfare. There is a critique of The Families First Act (2018) by Richard Wexler. There are two articles from the American Bar Association's Child Law Practice journal that describe a family-centered model of legal representation by Trine Bech, and another called *A Cut Above: What Makes a Parent Attorney Great* by Mimi Laver. Marie Cohen wrote an essay in the Child Welfare Monitor May 30, 2023, called *"Family First at five: Not much to celebrate."*

And there is a series on *The Weaponization of Whiteness in Child Welfare* by Maleeka Jihad, Jessica Handelman, Shayna Koran, and Sonja Ulrich from the National Association of Counsel for Children. There are articles by author Roxanna Asgarian, Dorothy Roberts, and Richard Wexler. There is also a draft of the *Advocates for Families Act of 2024*, sponsored by Congressman Barry Moore (R-Al) and Rep. Susan Wild (D-PA).

First up is Wexler's take on the Family First Act of 2018. He is Executive Director of the National Coalition for Child Protection Reform (NCCPR). There are many issue papers about child welfare laws and reports on subjects like due process available on the NCCPR website. There are also links to dozens of resources from government and other agencies there.

Friday, February 9, 2018

1. Don't believe the hype. The Family First Act is a step backwards for child welfare finance reform

Perhaps you've heard. Tacked onto the bill that averted another government shutdown is a child welfare finance "reform" measure called the Family First Prevention Services Act.

The bill was thought to be dead. It was killed last year by what one reformer who transformed his own institution years ago called the group home industry – the collection of private agencies typically paid for every day they hold foster children in the worst form of care, group homes and institutions -- and their public sector allies.

But it came back to life as part of the process of keeping the government open. Now it's law.

One might expect advocates of family preservation to celebrate, and some almost certainly will. The bill allows some federal money once restricted to funding foster care to be used for better alternatives. And, in theory, it curbs federal funding for group homes and institutions.

Some very good child welfare reformers favor the bill. The best case for it was made by one of those reformers, Jeremy Kohomban. He transformed what was once one of the nation's most regressive residential treatment centers, Children's Village, in New York, into a leader in emphasizing trying to help children in their own homes or foster homes. Here's his case for the bill.

Setting up Prevention to Fail

But I disagree. In 2016, I wrote that the range of prevention services that could be funded under Family Frist was tiny, and there were absurd restrictions on which programs within that range could get federal aid. And instead of limiting group homes and institutions, I argued that the bill was so weak that it actually strengthened them, creating a whole category of institution that would be, in effect, sanctified in federal law.

So, it's no wonder that in 2016, the Congressional Budget Office estimated that only $130 million in additional federal funds would go to prevention each year – a drop in the bucket compared to the billions spent on foster care. CBO also estimated that the proportion of foster

children in group homes and institutions would barely change –
declining from 14 percent to 11 percent – over ten years.

So, what the bill really does is set prevention up to fail. When these
minor changes don't do much to curb needless foster care, those
wedded to a take-the-child-and-run approach will say See? Changing
financial incentives didn't work, all those children must really need to
be in foster care. In fact, all those kids will still be in foster care because
there was almost no real change in financial incentives.

A "Presents for Pimps" Loophole

Nevertheless, the group home industry insisted that even the slightest
restriction on their ability to warehouse children in the very worst form
of "care" was more than they could handle.

Desperate to get something passed, supporters caved on issue after issue:

- They weakened a provision requiring institutions that supposedly
  engage in residential treatment to have actual clinical staff on site.

- They added a "presents for pimps" loophole – creating a whole
  new category of institution exempt from restrictions on federal
  funding.

That was in 2016.

The New Law

In one respect, the version that just became law may be a little better:
although the types of prevention that can be funded are as limited as
ever, the standards for specific programs don't seem to be as onerous.

But in at least one key respect, possibly two, the version that just became
law is even worse.

- There's a provision (Section 2661) allowing funds from a much
  smaller existing "family support services" program to be
  diverted to "supporting and retaining foster families for

children." (I'm not sure if this is new, or if I'd simply overlooked it in previous versions.)

- States can delay the minor restrictions on funds for group homes and institutions for two years (though if they did that, they'd also have to forego the limited new prevention funding). In fact, this is closer to a four-year delay. The bill's provisions concerning group homes don't take effect until October 1, 2019 – states opting to delay would not be affected until October 1, 2021.

This gives the group home industry lots and lots of time to weaken the law still further.

Goldilocks is wrong

And finally, as I wrote last year: Please, spare us all the Goldilocks defense; the one that goes, if some people think the law is too tough and other people think it's not tough enough, it must be juuuuuuuuust right.

No. The fact that some in the group home industry have the gall to claim this law is too tough just shows how spoiled they've gotten after all those years getting to eat all the porridge.

ABA National Project to Improve Representation for Parents

Investment that Makes Sense

The proof is in — providing parents with quality legal representation in child welfare cases isn't just the right thing to do. It's also the smart thing to do.

High quality legal representation for parents involved in the child welfare system reduces the need for foster care placement and saves public dollars.

Housed within the ABA Center on Children and the Law, the ABA National Project to Improve Representation for Parents is the only national legal organization with dedicated staff working to improve the practice of parents' attorneys, educating child welfare decision-makers, and building a national community of parents and parents' attorneys. The Project, guided by a steering committee of nationally recognized child welfare and legal experts, is the national leader of this important reform effort.

Whenever we see investment in quality legal services for parents, professionals working in all parts of the system see an improvement in the functioning of child welfare:

- More families receive the services they need to raise their children safely
- Fewer children suffer the trauma of unnecessary removal from home
- Taxpayer dollars are saved

"Parents' lawyers—particularly when they work in offices staffed with social workers and parent advocates—are now being recognized as vital allies in helping the child welfare system achieve its preferred objectives: keeping children safely with their families... Parent representation would not be where it is today without the support of the ABA and its Parent Representation Project."
-Professor Marty Guggenheim, NYU Law School

Better Outcomes for Children

Even the most well-intentioned interventions have unintended consequences. Unnecessary placements or prolonged stays in foster care can be detrimental.

Researchers at MIT found that compared to similarly situated children who remain at home, children placed in foster care face the following adverse outcomes:

- **Juvenile Justice.** Approximately three times more likely to be involved in the juvenile justice system
- **Teen Pregnancy.** More likely to become teen mothers
- **Employment.** As a young adult, less likely to hold a job for at least three months
- **Incarceration.** A two to three times higher arrest, conviction and imprisonment rate

Children who remain home with their parents, often who are engaging in services, have improved life outcomes.

A National Movement

The ABA has been integral in advancing representation for parents. Before 2006, there were no nationally recognized standards of practice for parents' attorneys and no source of technical assistance for practitioners. Today, through ABA work, there are:

- Widely accepted practice standards
- An active listserv connecting nearly 800 parent attorneys and parent advocates nationwide
- A biennial national conference focused exclusively on effective representation for parents' attorneys

The ABA is committed to this progress. Project staff continue to:

- Convene national and state parent representation leadership forums
- Help states assess current parent representation programs, create innovative pilot programs, and draft practice standards
- Organize regional parent attorney conferences
- Develop tools to evaluate and measure the impact of parent representation interventions.

National Project to Improve Representation for Parents

Much more must be done to support innovative and effective parent representation programs around the country. Many parents still lack meaningful representation in cases involving the well-being of their families, which can result in unnecessary and prolonged separation for families, sometimes permanently. A continued national voice is needed to lead this effort.

In too many communities without robust parental representation, the rate of children reunifying with family has been decreasing even though family reunification is the preferred and most common goal. Meaningful participation by parents and their attorneys is essential to a well-functioning child welfare court system.

"...[A] barrier to parents receiving quality representation is funding. We need to elevate this work and help people understand how quality representation for parents helps achieve reunification. Better funding of parent representation will result in cost-savings."
- Minnesota Supreme Court Justice Helen Meyer, ret.

When government entities and private funders invest in quality legal representation for parents, they see improved outcomes for the children and families the system is designed to serve. Programs across the country are showing that quality legal representation for parents is what's best for children.

What Works: A Multidisciplinary Approach

Reports from three different and unique methods of delivering parent representation prove that quality parents' attorneys, working as a team with social workers and parent mentors, can help reduce the need for foster care placement. !

New York: Center for Family Representation (CFR)
- Average 1.8 months in foster care for children of CFR clients, compared to a statewide average of more than 2 years

Michigan: Detroit Center for Family Advocacy (CFA)
- Avoided the filing of a petition in the child welfare court system in all but four of the 55 pre-petition cases it handled. None of the 110 children involved entered foster care

Washington State: Office of Public Defense (OPD) Parent Representation Program (PRP)
- A 36% increase in families' reunification rates since the implementation of the PRP

A Look Forward

Today there are relatively few established multidisciplinary parent representation programs. Yet we have learned that by investing in this kind of high-quality parent representation, we can reduce the number of children removed from their parents and for those children removed, shorten the time they spend in foster care. With the ABA's leadership, we can continue to work to ensure that parents and their attorneys always have a meaningful voice in the child welfare process.

Support for this work is needed. To date, the Project has been supported exclusively through foundation partnerships. With increased support, the ABA National Project to Improve Representation for Parents can continue working to:

- Help every state train their parents' attorneys and develop and implement standards of practice so that where a parent lives doesn't dictate the quality of representation she receives
- Support the development of law school clinics focused on parent representation so that there is a new generation of well-trained attorneys dedicated to this work
- Educate local, state, and national leaders about the impact of high quality parent representation so that there are leaders in every state ready and equipped to make positive change

For more information, contact **Mimi Laver** | Mimi.Laver@americanbar.org | 202-662-1736
www.americanbar.org/groups/child_law/what_we_do/projects/parentrepresentation

ABA National Project to Improve Representation for Parents

Legal Representation for Parents Facing the Loss of Their Children: The Right Thing to Do, The Smart Thing to Do

Models that Work

New York: Center for Family Representation (CFR)

- Every parent represented by CFR works with a team of lawyer, social worker, and parent advocate.
- Focus on helping clients access services, supporting them at case planning meetings, and working to facilitate frequent and meaningful family visitation.
- Representation begins at the first hearing of the case and continues until dismissal or reunification.

  Outcomes: Data starting in 2007 shows that more than 50% of the children of CFR clients avoid foster care placement all together. When foster care cannot be avoided, the average foster care stay for children of CFR clients is just 1.8 months compared to a statewide average of more than two years. Just 7% of children of CFR clients re-enter care, compared to a statewide foster care re-entry rate of 15%.

  Cost Savings: CFR's services cost approximately $6,500 per family over the case lifetime. That sum is vastly less than a single year of maintaining a child in an out of home placement, which in 2010 could range from $29,000 to as much as $200,000 per child per year.

Michigan: Detroit Center for Family Advocacy (CFA)

- Focus on serving residents in the Osborn neighborhood of Detroit, a neighborhood with one of the highest rates of removal of children to foster care in the state.
- Represents parents during the child protection investigation.
- CFA clients are represented by a multidisciplinary team of a lawyer, social worker, and parent advocate.
- Use legal mechanisms – such as guardianships, child custody or personal protection orders, education and landlord-tenant advocacy – to allow parents or their family members to care for their children without the need for foster care or child welfare court interventions.

  Outcomes: From 2009 through 2012, CFA handled 55 pre-petition cases involving 110 children. In all but four cases, CFA reached a resolution for the family and avoided the filing of a petition in the child welfare court system. Through its work representing parents, CFA prevented all 110 children from entering foster care.

  Cost-Savings: The average annual cost per family to deliver CFA services is $3,200. The average monthly foster care payment per child in Michigan, not counting court costs, is $2,248. Based on that average and the national average length of stay in foster care of 21.1 months, the cost for Michigan when a child enters foster care is $47,433. If we assume conservatively that 25% of the 110 children whose families received CFA representation would have entered foster care for the national average length of stay, the cost CFA saved Michigan for these cases would be $1,304,407.

Washington State: Office of Public Defense Parent Representation Program (OPD)

- Handles approximately 7,000 ongoing parents' representation cases and is wholly supported by state funds.
- Created on a pilot basis following investigative report showing indigent parents typically receive poor representation.
- Since 2000, the program has expanded from serving three counties to nearly all of the state's counties.
- Key elements of the program include case load limits, attorney practice standards, access to expert services and program social workers, oversight of attorneys, and ongoing training and support.

  Outcomes: OPD has been favorably evaluated numerous times. A 2011 review of court records and orders in 1,817 child welfare court cases filed before and after implementation found that the percentage of children who reunified increased by 36%. Another study by Dr. Mark Courtney and Dr. Jen Hooks at the University of Washington found that the program was successful in helping children move out of foster care and into permanent homes significantly faster, concluding that it should be expanded throughout the state.

  Cost-Savings: The PRP saves the state much more than it costs. In 2013, due to the increased reunification and permanency impacts, the state avoided $20 million in state foster care and adoption subsidy costs and spent only $12.5 million for the program.

Child Law Practice Vol. 27 No. 4

Better Lawyering

A Cut Above: What Makes a Parent Attorney Great

by Mimi Laver

What does high quality legal representation for parents look like? The ABA Standards of Practice for Attorneys Representing Parents in Abuse and Neglect Cases outline duties for attorneys. These include guidance about working with the client, preparation, involvement in case planning, courtroom activities, and post-hearing obligations. Following these standards would improve representation for parents across the country.

Effective advocacy, though, is about more than setting standards and trying to enforce them. The best parents' attorneys:

Spend time getting to know their clients. They meet with the clients regularly, and if their clients are out of contact, the attorney makes efforts to find and communicate with them. These attorneys form relationships with their clients so they can give the client hard-to-hear but necessary information like "if you don't participate in services, you really could lose your child forever." These attorneys then promise their clients assistance in accessing services and advocating for the client with the agency and the judge. The attorney understands that as a parent, the client generally wants what is best for the child and the attorney works to empower the client to make good decisions for the child. This may mean, for example, obtaining the child's medical and school records and discussing the records so the client can play an active part in decision-making about the child.

Know their work outside the courtroom is at least as important as in-court advocacy. They attend case planning meetings with their clients and help the client decide which services they can realistically participate in. They work with the agency to make the case plan workable for the parent. These attorneys emphasize the importance of frequent visitation in child-friendly places to the client and agency and ensure the agency schedules these visits, helping with transportation and supporting the parent during the visits. The attorney reminds the agency about reasonable efforts when necessary (enlisting the court when needed) and works with the client to comply with the efforts. The attorney may provide the client with a pocket calendar and help the client fill in important dates or map out directions to ensure the client knows how to get to meetings and appointments.

Know it is often best for the client to collaborate with the child welfare agency. The attorney still goes to court and seeks a judge's assistance when the parent is not receiving the help she needs. In addition, the attorney participates in alternative dispute resolution but will only agree to something if the client agrees. The client must be given the information and opportunity to make decisions in all aspects of the case, and the attorney must advocate the client's wishes. Counseling and open communication are key for this to work.

Know delay tactics rarely help the client because the "ASFA clock" is ticking. In some cases, asking for a continuance benefits the client, so the attorney asks. On top of everything else, the best attorneys are strong courtroom advocates. They know the case, they know what the client wants, and they put on effective cases to persuade the court to make specific orders that benefit their clients.

Don't try to do it alone. Some attorneys work with paralegals, social workers, investigators, interpreters, and parent advocates. This multidisciplinary approach allows the attorney to focus on the truly legal aspects of the case. These attorneys also network with each other. If they have supervisors or other parents' attorneys in their office, they discuss case strategy and ask for help identifying resources. If they are sole practitioners, they find colleagues in the courthouse to share ideas with, mentor newer attorneys, attend brown bag lunches or training and ask for assistance from attorneys around the country.

(To sign up for the ABA parent attorney listserv send a message to listserv@mail.abanet.org with "SUBscribe child-parent's attorneys

YOUR NAME" in the body of the message.) It is important for attorneys to have access to resources and other people who understand the challenges of representing parents.

Identify their clients' parenting strengths. They work with those involved in the case to build on parents' strengths to support the client in reaching a positive outcome. It takes a lot of work, but the results in cases in which the parent has an effective attorney are good for the parent and child.

Mimi Laver, JD, directs a project to improve parent representation in child welfare cases at the ABA Center on Children and the Law.

Family First at Five: Not Much to Celebrate

childwelfaremonitor May 30, 2023
By Marie Cohen

When the Family First Prevention Services Act (FFPSA) passed as part of the Bipartisan Budget Act of 2018, it was hailed by many as a revolutionary step in the history of U.S. child welfare. Five years after the Act took effect, child welfare leaders have been weighing in with statements like this one from Rebecca Jones Gaston, Commissioner of the Administration on Children, Youth and Families: "Following its passage five years ago, the Family First Prevention Services Act has transformed our approach to child welfare and benefited families across the many states that have used it to provide concrete support and services." But for those closer to ground-level and less invested in demonstrating the act's success, there's not much to celebrate.

FFPSA had two major goals: to keep children out of foster care altogether through services to families and to keep more of those who do have to enter care in family homes. In terms of the first goal, the law's impacts on services to families have been almost negligible. And in its effort to keep foster children in families, FFPSA has exacerbated the critical shortage of appropriate placements for our most troubled youth, many of whom may need placements in larger settings. In this post, I examine these two goals and their outcomes in greater detail.

FFPSA's Part I made it possible to allocate funds under Title IV-E of the Social Security Act, previously directed mainly to foster care, to services aimed at keeping children out of care. The law allowed spending on mental health, substance abuse prevention and treatment, and in-home parenting services, "when the need of the child, such a parent, or such a caregiver for the services or programs are directly related to the safety, permanency, or well-being of the child or to preventing the child from entering foster care."

As I explained in my 2019 post, Family First Axt: a False Narrative, a Lack of Review, a Bad Law, Part I was based largely on the false premise that current law, by allowing Title IV-E funds to pay for foster care and not for services to prevent it, incentivized states to remove children rather than keep families together. While it is true that IV-E funds were not available to pay for services to children and families in their homes, that does not mean that no money was available to help keep families together or that states had an incentive to place children in foster care.

In fact, states had long been using Medicaid and other funds for services to prevent the placement of children in foster care. In Federal Fiscal Year 2017, according to federal data, out of the children who received services after a CPS investigation or alternative response, only 201,680 were placed in foster care, while 1,332,254 (or more than five times as many children) received in-home services such as case management, family support, and family preservation services.

Disregarding the role that other funding already played in child welfare, the framers of FFPSA required that Title IV-E would be the "payer of last resort," so that any services already paid for by Medicaid could not be paid for by Family First. By doing this, they ensured that states with a generous Medicaid program would be hard-pressed to find any service already existing in the state on which to spend their Title IV-E money. If not for this provision, such states might have chosen to supplement Medicaid funding for some of these services.

Perhaps some states would have allowed Title IV-E funds to be used to pay high-quality providers who do not accept Medicaid funding due to the program's low reimbursement rates and high paperwork burden. (During my time as a foster care social worker in the District of Columbia, we had contracts with high-quality providers who did not accept Medicaid in order to provide therapy for our most complex clients).

The choice to fund only parenting, mental health and drug treatment services by the framers was another design flaw of FFPSA. The absence of a domestic violence service among the funded services is striking. It is universally acknowledged that drug abuse, mental illness and domestic violence are the "big three" factors that result in foster care placement.

But for some reason, the words "domestic violence" are nowhere to be found in FFPSA. Perhaps even more striking is the failure to include one of the most promising services to prevent foster care–high-quality childcare.

As I have written not only does quality early care and education prevent foster care placement through multiple pathways, but it also provides an extra set of eyes on the child in case of continued abuse or neglect– greatly needed if FFPSA is to achieve its goal of keeping children both safe and out of foster care. Think of what a difference Congress could have made by providing matching funds to provide quality childcare to all families with in-home cases!

Perhaps the most unfortunate feature of FFPSA's Part I is the requirement that all funds must be spent on "promising, supported or well-supported practices," with 50 percent of the total spent on "well-supported practices" — a percentage that increases after 2026. The law imposes strict requirements for designating a program as promising, supported, or well-supported. It set up a clearinghouse to assess the data on existing programs and approve those that met the criteria.

As Dee Wilson points out in one of his essential commentaries, the law gets it exactly backwards. We have very little evidence about what works to prevent foster care placement. What we need is to invest in innovative approaches to doing this safely. But FFPSA prevents the use of Title IV-E funds for this purpose.

Thanks to the various restrictions imposed by FFPSA, the clearinghouse is woefully incomplete. For example, Cognitive Behavioral Therapy (CBT), the therapy of choice for depression and anxiety, which has not been approved nor is it on the list of programs to be examined by the clearinghouse ("Trauma-Focused CBT," a newer and much narrower and short-term model, has been approved.) No residential drug treatment program has been approved or is even slated to be considered. The requirement that the practice have a manual may be at fault for the failure to include CBT and residential drug treatment programs, but I'd like to hear from readers who may be better-informed. Buphenorphine therapy for opioid use disorder, which is often preferred to methadone therapy (which is approved by the clearinghouse) because it does not require daily clinic visits, has not been approved and is not slated for consideration, according to the Clearinghouse. Of course, these popular programs are often funded by Medicaid anyway, so they would be ruled out by the last resort provision as well.

With all these restrictions on Title IV-E spending, it is not surprising that states have been hard-put to find useful ways to spend Title IV-E funds to keep families together. In an important article, Sean Hughes and Naomi Schaefer Riley cited the latest available federal data showing that just 6,200 children across the entire country received an FFPSA-funded service in FFY 2021, costing a grand total of $29 million. That is truly underwhelming given that about 600,000 children were found to be victims of maltreatment in FFY 2021.

The other major purpose of FFPSA was outlined in Part IV, entitled "Ensuring the Necessity of a Placement that is not in a Foster Family Home." The purpose of this part was to keep more children out of "congregate care," a term used to designate settings other than foster homes, such as group homes and residential treatment centers. FFPSA made it more difficult to place a child in a congregate placement by imposing conditions on Title IV-E reimbursement for such placements, and by limiting reimbursement after two weeks to facilities that qualify as "Quality Residential Treatment Programs (QRTP's), a new category defined by the act.

QRTP's must meet strict criteria that many facilities that were caring for foster youth at the time of FFPSA's passage could not meet without major changes. The act also (perhaps inadvertently) further restricted the number of congregate care beds available to foster youth by creating a conflict with a Medicaid provision called the "Institutions for Mental Diseases (IMD) exclusion" that prevents Medicaid paying the cost of care for children who are placed in facilities with more than 16 beds."

Like Part I, Part IV of FFPSA was in large part based on a false narrative. The myth this time was that every child does better in a family rather than in a more institutional setting. But as I described, there are many foster youths who cannot function in an ordinary foster home, at least until after a stay in a high-quality residential treatment program or group home. These are the same young people who bounce from home to home and end up in hotels, offices, jails, and other inappropriate settings, but FFPSA made no provision for them.

Even if too many children had been placed in residential care without sufficient clinical justification (which is probably the case in at least some states), it would not be responsible to shut down congregate care placements before ensuring that appropriate foster homes were available for all the children being displaced. But just as the DE institution movement of the 1960s closed mental hospitals before putting alternatives in place, FFPSA disregarded the question of where children would go when congregate settings disappeared.

As I described, FFPSA exacerbated trends that were already underway. Group homes and residential treatment centers were already shutting down due to growing publicity about abusive incidents at some facilities, failure of reimbursement rates to keep up with costs, and resignation of staff due to poor pay and working conditions.

Tragically, this reduction in residential capacity coincided with increased demand for care due to the youth mental health crisis and increasing levels of need in the foster care population due at least in part to delays in removing children from abusive and neglectful homes. The restrictions put in place by FFPSA added to the problem. As Hughes and Schaefer Riley put it, "If you want to understand why foster children across the country are being housed in a range of inappropriate temporary settings, including county and state offices, hospitals, hotels and shelters, FFPSA is a significant factor."

The trends just mentioned have contributed to a foster care placement crisis that has if anything worsened since I described it last October. In Illinois, the Department of Children and Family Services (DCFS) is being sued by the Cook County Public Guardian for allowing foster children to remain locked up in juvenile detention even after they've been ordered released. In Maryland, a disability rights group has just filed suit against the Department of Human Services and other agencies for keeping foster children in hospitals and restrictive institutions beyond medical necessity for weeks, months, or even as long as a year.

In a must-read article, Dee Wilson documents a 370 percent increase in hotel/office stays in his state of Washington since 2018 despite a federal court order to stop the practice. At an average cost of up $2,000 per night (including the cost of paying two social workers and a security guard), overnight hotel placements cannot possibly be cheaper than group homes or residential treatment centers. Similar problems are reported around the country, differing only in which inappropriate settings each state is relying on.

As is often the case, California paved the way for FFPSA by passing its Continuum of Care Reform, designed to curb the use of congregate placements, in 2015. A new article in the *Los Angeles Times* recounts the results. The number of children living in congregate care has dropped from 3,655 to 1,727 since implementation of the law, but the state has failed to find the foster homes to replace the congregate care settings.

As a result, Los Angeles County has placed more than 200 foster youths in hotels, sometimes for months. County officials report that two social workers have been assaulted by foster youths in separate incidents this year at hotels. Moreover, it appears that care at the existing congregate facilities has grown worse as larger numbers of troubled youths are placed together in fewer facilities.

The results of California's reform and of FFPSA were predictable and indeed predicted by some commentators (including this writer), but these predictions were ignored.

As Dee Wilson puts it, "The implementation of Family First legislation has accelerated the demise of residential care, which has decreased 25% nationally during the past five years. It has been the goal of the federal Children's Bureau and influential foundations to reduce the use of residential care (which has a bad reputation among advocates and most scholars) and they have succeeded; but without developing — or sometimes even proposing – viable alternatives."

Anyone who chooses to celebrate the "revolution" wrought by FFPSA is living in a dream world. It's time for Congress to recognize and correct the many errors it made in passing the law. At a minimum, Congress should add funding for early care and education and domestic violence programs to the models that can receive funding under Title IV-E, loosen the standards for evidence-based practices, modify the last-resort provision to allow payment for services to providers who do not accept Medicaid, eliminate some of the restrictions on congregate care, and provide incentives for states to boost their capacity of quality residential programs. Until such changes are made, there will be nothing to celebrate.

Child Law **Practice**

Vol. 19 No. 2   April 2000   *Helping Lawyers Help Kids*

Developing a new approach to parent representation in child protection cases was the goal of a conference held in South Royalton, VT, October 26-27, 1999. This conference, sponsored by the Annie E. Casey Foundation, joined child welfare experts and practitioners from Vermont and around the nation to create a parent representation model to address current system shortcomings. This article describes the model, the systemic and organizational structure needed to support it, and offers tips for creating an action plan to implement it.

A Family-Centered Model of Legal Representation for Parents in Child Protection Cases

by Trine Bech

Parents rating their trust for their lawyers:

[M]any attorneys have no experience, really don't have a clue and you are counting on this person 100%. It scares you to death to get an attorney who does not seem to know or be interested in what you need. 'We are human beings. This is our life and these are our children.' ... Many times you are told the day before to be at court. You don't even have an opportunity to meet your lawyer beforehand. ... This kind of lack of notice makes you feel totally hopeless. [1]

Vermont's Court Improvement Project identified inadequate parent representation as one major barrier to achieving better outcomes for abused and neglected children. Experience in Vermont and research of other states' parent representation systems show that representation is inadequate and sometimes harms parents' interests. Parents report that the adversarial nature of the courtroom pits them against their children. Their family histories, strengths and needs get lost in a system bent on finding fault and blame.

Unlike representation for child welfare agencies and for children, many states have no system in place to ensure competence in, and accountability for, parent representation. Although parent representation models vary, many states base them on the criminal defense model where *deny and delay* are seen as effective legal strategies. Such criminal defense tactics rarely meet the parents' objectives for the return of their children to their custody (see sidebar p. 23 for more shortcomings of parent representation models).

A Family-Centered Model of Legal Representation

This is a system in which the lawyers honor the family's integrity by taking time to understand the family's dynamics and relationships, explain the legal process and options, and engage the family in finding their own solutions. This "family-centered" problem solving representation model has its main focus in a forum outside the courtroom. This model is contrary to the current representation model where the court is often the only place where parents see their lawyers.

In defending the current model, lawyers argue that the courtroom is the appropriate forum when there has been a long history of violence against children; the alleged perpetrator is in denial, or shows no remorse; or there are criminal proceedings pending arising out of the same facts. Experience in the use of family-centered tools has shown, however, that parents, if given options, can choose what will work for them if they have competent legal counsel. [2]

A family-centered approach presumes that families have strengths, can change, are able to make responsible decisions, and can be accountable for their actions. When criminal

E-mail: childlawpractice@staff.abanet.org   ♦   Internet: http://www.abanet.org/child

proceedings prevent frank discussions or parents deny that they placed their child in jeopardy, the parents will likely choose the courtroom as the more appropriate forum. Thus, a family-centered approach includes traditional litigation as the forum.

Why Parents Need A Family-Centered Model

Effective legal representation for parents is crucial because the Adoption and Safe Families Act of 1997 (ASFA) 3 shortens the time parents have to remedy the problems which led to their children's removal. Under ASFA, to receive Title IV-E foster care reimbursement, the child welfare agency must petition to terminate parental rights to every child in custody for 15 of the last 22 months, unless the agency can show a "compelling reason" not to. With these shortened timeframes, the legal strategies for parents involved in child abuse and neglect proceedings need to shift to consult and create to assist them make changes needed for their children's safe return home.

Parents find that a structured dialogue among themselves, their children (if age appropriate), the social worker, service providers, lawyers and guardians ad litem, aimed at creating a timely safety plan for the children, is more likely to be successful in achieving the goal. Such dialogue, in contrast to the hurling accusations found in contested litigation, is also more conducive to creating a constructive relationship between the social worker and the family. After a plan is created, either through the dialogue or a contested hearing, the quality of the working relationship between the social worker and the family is crucial to the plan's success.

Characteristics of the Family-Centered Model

The following elements are essential to family-centered legal representation for parents in child abuse and neglect proceedings:

Educate and Guide the Parent through the Legal System

It is the lawyer's job to explain the options available and guide the parent through the legal process. The laws are not complicated, but the interwoven social services designed to change behavior to make children safe are complex and require interdisciplinary understanding and expertise. Understanding which social services program and treatment options work for specific parenting issues is a prerequisite to effective practice.

Counsel the Parent about Expectations and Consequences

The lawyer should counsel the parents about specific expectations and consequences for failing to meet expectations. This role is particularly challenging when parents are struggling with substance abuse and domestic violence.

Establish Trust

Parents in child abuse and neglect proceedings often must change their behavior to make their homes safe for their children. This takes time and usually many failed attempts. To be effective, the lawyer must have a trusting relationship with the parents. Establishing trust involves spending time listening and getting to know the parents. Parents appreciate small courtesies, like returning phone calls and promptly responding to requests. Such efforts help establish the trust required for the parent to listen and consider the lawyer's recommendations.

Be Accessible

The lawyer must be accessible to the parent geographically, culturally, and linguistically. A different language, lack of transportation to appointments, lack of access to the same lawyer at critical stages of the legal proceedings — all prevent the parent from trusting the help the legal process can provide.

Be Competent in the Conventional Legal Role

In addition to interdisciplinary knowledge and skills, the lawyer needs to have conventional legal skills to protect client confidentiality, and represent the parent's constitutional and other legal rights. The lawyer needs to ensure the legal and social services systems provide the protection and services the parent is legally entitled to receive. This may involve skillful negotiations with the other parties focused on outcomes for the family (i.e., ensuring the child's safety needs will be protected within the family), and conducted in a manner and at a time where choices are meaningful (i.e., not in a crowded courtroom hallway).

Be a Compassionate Listener, Interested in the Work

Representing parents whose children have been taken into state custody, or who are at risk of being taken into custody, involves more than giving advice for a short time. The lawyer needs to understand and show concern for the parent's circumstances, be willing to listen, and be committed to creating hopeful solutions.

At the same time, the lawyer needs to accept the parents for who they are and work from their perspectives. This involves:

- providing options based on the family history and relationships;
- engaging the parent in taking responsibility for making choices;
- sticking with the work through difficult periods while the parent struggles to change behaviors which brought the child into the child protection system;
- looking to other family members who can be resources to the parent in the change process.

Engage Family Members and Family Resources

Engaging family members or other family resources to help the parent find solutions and keep his or her children safe is the essence of family-centered representation. Courtrooms are not conducive to engaging families, and the solutions they propose usually have limited success addressing long-term behavioral issues and family relationships.

Advocates and social service providers have therefore begun to use tools, such as mediation and family group decision making. These forums let parents, children, and other family members tell their stories and plan for the children's safety. If these tools are not available, the lawyer should help create them so the parents and children (if age appropriate) can choose an alternative to litigation. The lawyer's role may be limited in these settings to ensuring all issues are addressed and preventing the parents' stories from being used against them in the court- room if the alternative forum does not produce an acceptable solution.

Be Part of a Support Team

Accomplishing all tasks needed to effectively represent parents is easier if the lawyer works as part of a team with paraprofessionals. For example, helping the parent understand how to maneuver through the legal system, and access social services, are tasks a paralegal or a community-based advocate could perform, leaving the lawyer free to focus on legal strategies, negotiations, case preparation, legal briefs, appeals, etc. These options are explored later in this article as part of the infrastructure needed to support an effective system of parent representation.

How to Ensure Parents Have Family-Centered Legal Representation

To provide the legal representation described above, the conference participants looked at what systemic support and organizational structure would be needed. Although needs varied across jurisdictions and de- pended on the type of system in place, conference participants agreed the following systemic elements are essential:

Hiring/Contracting of Lawyers Hiring practices for lawyers to perform this work must take into account lawyers' interest, experience, education, and commitment to public service work, family law, and child abuse and neglect proceedings. Since this work is taxing on lawyers, dedication is a needed ingredient to longevity. The family bar may be a better source for recruits than the criminal bar.

Training

Lawyers need substantial training in family law, substantive and procedural child abuse and neglect laws, and the social service delivery system. Ongoing training is necessary to address specific aspects of child abuse and neglect (e.g., sexual abuse of and by children; multiple victims of domestic violence; timing of substance abuse recovery in contrast to

ASFA timelines; concurrent planning), good practice, and innovations (e.g., family group decision making, pre-adjudication service "front loading").

Lawyers as Specialists

To give this work priority, lawyers should dedicate full time to representing parents in child abuse and neglect cases. Just like specialized lawyers who represent child welfare agencies and children, parents' lawyers should specialize in engaging parents in child protection, holding agencies accountable, and finding creative solutions to complicated family dynamics. Specialization will also foster continuity of representation where the same lawyer is available from the first custody hearing until permanency is achieved for the child, including the child welfare agency case plan reviews. Thus, the lawyer becomes invested in the long-term solutions for the family. Depending on the jurisdiction, to achieve specialization in rural areas, a regional model may be necessary to create full attorney caseloads. Neighboring counties can combine their caseloads and share the same lawyer in much the same way as some states have created "cluster" courts where one specialized juvenile judge travels from court to court.

Compensation

Lawyers for parents should be paid at the same level as lawyers for the state and for children in child abuse and neglect proceedings. This is a challenge in systems where the lawyers come out of the chronically underpaid public defense system.

One approach is to have separate appropriations for criminal defense and children, youth and families, even if both are housed under the same public defense system. Experience shows that legislators are more apt to want to support families than accused criminals.

Another approach would be to connect the system with specialized law school clinics, where a shared pool of blended state/county/university and private foundation funding could meet the need while training new lawyers in this work.

The funding could also come from Title IV-E through some creative application, such as the child welfare agency identifying parent representation as an essential child welfare service and contracting for these services.

Adequate compensation, including benefits, enables lawyers to choose this work as a career with upward mobility. It permits them to increase their skills and improve their representation, which ultimately benefits children. Better parent representation should decrease children's length of stay in out- of-home care, thus reducing foster care costs.

Capacity to Support a Parent Representation System

To ensure ample compensation, training, supervision, and accountability, a supportive organizational structure must be in place. The organization must establish performance measures that ensure goals are met. A case management and performance- based system will help achieve results, such as shortened timeframes between legal events, successful reunification, and successful use of alternative dispute resolution tools. It will also help managers analyze system improvements.

The organization will also be responsible for setting attorney caseloads that give lawyers enough time with each parent to create a trusting relationship, represent the parent in court, and follow up on social service delivery and effectiveness. The organizational structure should be linked either to a family advocate in the community or include paralegal support for the lawyer.

Family Advocates or Paralegal Support

Two different models of ancillary parental support were proposed:

1. Community-Based Family Advocates/Resource Consultants are parents who have gone through the system and are familiar with what works. They mentor parents from their first involvement with the child protection system to ensure they understand what is expected of them and the consequences for not following through. Because they have been through the system, family advocates are better able to form trusting relationships with parents.

The family advocate explains, supports, and assists/insists on communication between the parents and the other parties to the legal proceedings. The family advocate has equal status to the other "players" and helps educate the lawyers about family needs and perspectives, acts as a buffer or "simultaneous translator" for the parents, and ensures out-of-court tools like mediation and family group decision making are available. Once a case plan is approved by the court, the family advocate helps the family implement it. The family advocate has immunity from being subpoenaed for court proceedings.

The cultural acceptance within the jurisdiction for paying parents who have previously been involved in the system is a factor to consider when deciding whether to use a family advocate.

2. Paralegals fill many of the roles identified for the family advocate, but work within the lawyer's office, are available to parents, arrange for alternative dispute resolution options and monitor social service delivery.

Creating an Action Plan

Your jurisdiction may already have some of the elements for a family-centered model of legal representation for parents. If not, you will have to start from scratch. A good place to start is with your Court Improvement Project's Advisory Committee. If your state does not have one, consider forming a special task force consisting of child welfare agency leaders, representatives from the state/county court, the public children's and parents' representative, social service agencies, lawyers, and parents who have been involved with the child protection system. If consensus can be reached, such a collaborative group, despite its unwieldy nature, is powerful with the legislature or other body responsible for appropriations. An outside facilitator may help the group reach consensus.

The action plan should: identify why the current system acts as a barrier to safety and permanency for children; outline what steps will be taken to create an administrative structure which ensures parents' attorneys are trained, supervised, supported, and held accountable; identify possible funding sources; develop budgets; establish timeframes;

identify who is responsible for each step of the plan.

Shortcomings of Current Parent Representation Models

- Little specialized interest and commitment to child protection issues.

- Little understanding of family dynamics, child abuse and neglect laws, domestic violence, substance abuse and the community social service system.

- Little legal experience or only criminal defense background. Inadequate training, support, supervision, and accountability. Low compensation rate.

- High turnover rate (the Vermont Attorney General, responsible for the parent representation system, reported that there is an annual one-third turnover rate for parent attorneys).

- Lawyers practice in both criminal and family courts creating scheduling conflicts between courts.

- Lawyers not appointed until after the first emergency custody hearing. Lawyers do not meet with their clients until the adjudicatory hearing. Lawyers not available for agency case plan reviews.

- Lawyers relieved of their representation after the disposition, leaving parents unrepresented while they try to meet the requirement of the disposition order.

- Little continuity of representation from the emergency custody hearing through final permanency for the child, causing delays in permanency decisions for the child.

- Lawyers craft solutions which are either unattainable or not understood by the parents.

351

Conclusion

Parent representation in child protection cases in most states does not meet parents' needs, is not accountable for results, and is a barrier to permanency for children. Systemic changes are needed to improve outcomes for children, meet ASFA timelines, and ensure fairness. Incorporating a family-centered model with the characteristics described in this article will raise the quality and fairness of representation parents receive, and hopefully shorten the time children spend in foster care.

Trine Bech, Esq., was the Permanency Planning Director for the Vermont Court Improvement Project of the Vermont Supreme Court from November 1997 to April 2000. She is now the Deputy Director for the Delaware Division of Family Services.

Endnotes

1. St. Albans Consumer Advisory Board Meeting Minutes, November 5, 1998; see also William Mcgrath, MA and John Burchard, PhD, Process Characteristics of the Chittenden County Family Court, November 19, 1999, where 10 families were extensively interviewed and rated their trust for their lawyer as 1 on a scale from 0-4.

2. Casey Family Services, Vermont Division, currently facilitates Making Action Plans (MAPS) in court-related child protection cases in four Vermont counties. MAPS is a voluntary process for parents that consists of six steps that are facilitated by a neutral person: history, who you are, dreams, fears, current and future needs, and creation of a plan. An evaluation is in progress, but so far, no type of case has been found categorically inappropriate.

3. The Adoption and Safe Families Act, P.L. 105-89, signed into law in November 1997. It amended the federal foster care law, Titles IV-B and IV-E of the Social Security Act, making safety and permanency the primary focus of the law.

4. For a description of mediation and family group decision-making tools, see National Council of Juvenile and Family Court Judges. Technical Assistance Bulletin 2:7, November 1998; Hon. Leonard Edwards. "Dependency Court Mediation." Family and Conciliation Courts Review 35:2, April 1997, 160-163; American Humane Association, Children's Division. "The Practice and Promise of Family Group Decision Making." Protecting Children 12:3, 1996; National Council of Juvenile and Family Court Judges, Permanency Planning for Children Project. Diversion Project Matrix: A Report from Four Sites Examining the Court's Role in Diverting Families from Traditional Child Welfare Services into Community-Based Programs, 1998.

5. For training sources, contact the ABA Center for Children and the Law, 202/662-1720, the National Council of Juvenile and Family Court Judges, 775/ 327-5300; and the Child Welfare League of America, 202/638-2952.

6. ABA Center on Children and the Law. "Cluster Courts: Innovative Court Reform for Rural Areas." ABA Child Court Works 3:2, July 1999.

7. Friedman, Mark. A Guide to Developing and Using Performance Measures in Results-Based Budgeting. Washington, DC: The Finance Project, May 1997, for an example of a framework for establishing performance measures.

8. For further information, contact the Rutland County Family Court, 83 Center Street, Rutland, VT 05701, 802/786-5856.

9. For another example of effective use of ex-clients of the child welfare system, contact the Annie E. Casey Foundation, 410/547-6600, about the Sobriety Treatment and Recovery Team (START) project at the Cuyahoga County Department of Child and Family Services, Cleveland, OH.

10. In Vermont, the facilitated conference broke a longstanding impasse among the stakeholders and created consensus for a proposal for reform. This proposal includes all elements described in this article and is now being considered by the Vermont Legislature.

The Best Way to Reduce Child Abuse Fatalities is to Reduce Poverty

Richard Wexler
From Tennessee Lookout – July 15, 2024, 4:59 AM

The only acceptable goal for child abuse fatalities is zero. But how do we come closest to achieving that goal? Some have suggested that because child abuse deaths may have increased by 30% in 2023, Tennessee is doing too much to keep families together so we should tear apart even more families. That would only make everything worse.

For starters, there is no evidence for the claim that Tennessee is bending over backwards to keep families together. On the contrary, even when rates of child poverty are factored in, Tennessee takes children from their families at a rate nearly 50% above the national average. And it's easy to take the years you want to prove whatever you want. Between 2018 and 2020 entries into foster care in Tennessee declined by 15%. During that same period child abuse deaths also declined by about 15%. And if Tennessee's apparent increase in fatalities is evidence of the need to take away more children, why did fatalities drop dramatically in Texas after they passed new laws that reduced foster care?

But what about the fact that more than two-thirds of these children were previously known to the Department of Children's Services? How could all those warning signs be missed? That's easier to understand when one looks at the sheer number of children on DCS' radar.

As the *Lookout* reports, in FY2023 DCS received 100,000 calls and investigated 66,000 cases. Assuming an average of 1.84 children per family that means, depending on how you define it, somewhere between 124,000 and 184,000 children were known to DCS in some way. Of that number, about 127 died. That means of all the children DCS encountered 99.89% did not die. Nor is it reassuring that of those 127, 11 were already in DCS custody when they died.

355

Those deaths in custody are just the tip of the iceberg. Multiple studies find abuse in one-quarter to one-third of family foster homes and the rate in group homes and institutions is even higher.

The take-the-child-and-run approach practiced in Tennessee is typical of America's response to child abuse deaths for 50 years. It's given us a giant child welfare surveillance state in which more than one-third of all children, and more than half of Black children will be forced to endure the trauma of a child abuse investigation before they turn 18 — almost always in response to a false report or a case in which family poverty is confused with neglect. It's forced hundreds of thousands of children to endure being torn needlessly from everyone they know and love and consigned to the chaos of foster care.

All those false reports, trivial cases, and poverty cases cascade down upon DCS workers, overwhelming them so they don't have time to investigate any case properly. So it's no wonder they miss that one-tenth-of-one percent of children who subsequently die. Remember the children torn from their loving parents because the parents committed the "crime" of Driving While Black? In addition to what that did to those children, all the time, money and effort spent tearing this family apart was, in effect, stolen from one of those children in that one-tenth-of-one percent.

So, what can we do to bring the number of fatalities closer to zero?

Become laser-focused on the #1 cause of actual abuse and the #1 issue confused with neglect: Poverty. In Tennessee, 88% of children who enter foster care do so in cases where there is not even an accusation of physical or sexual abuse. In 60% there isn't even an allegation of drug abuse.

So, it's no wonder that study after study finds that even small amounts of additional money will reduce not only neglect, but even fatalities. (Such investment also costs less than foster care, and far less than group homes and institutions.) The child welfare think tank Chapin Hall at the University of Chicago estimates that every additional $1,000 per person living in poverty invested in public benefits, whether for medical care, housing, food or child care, causes a a 2.1% reduction in foster care placements, a 4.3% reduction in abuse and neglect reports – and a 7.7% reduction in child maltreatment fatalities.

For 50 years we've responded to tragedies that are needles in a haystack by making the haystack bigger. The result has been more tragedies. Isn't it time to start shrinking the haystack to make it easier to find the needles?

Richard Wexler is Executive Director of the National Coalition for Child Protection Reform in Alexandria, Va., www.nccpr.org

How the Child Welfare System Is Silently Destroying Black Families

A single call from an anonymous tipster is all it takes for the government to take children from their families

By Dorothy Roberts

Diamond Haynes tearfully discusses her seven children, all in foster care, on Feb. 13, 2018. Haynes, in her late 30s at the time, lived in a trailer outside Los Angeles before moving to South L.A. to work as a retail clerk.

The sun had just begun to rise over Manhattan on an August morning in 2013. Angeline Montauban was whispering into the phone as she crouched in the bathroom of her apartment. As her partner and their 3-year-old son slept, Montauban had tiptoed to the bathroom to call Safe Horizon, a domestic abuse hotline she had seen advertised in subway stations. She had decided it was time to stop the violence she was experiencing at the hands of her partner, and she hoped Safe Horizon could provide counseling or help her relocate with her son.

At first, the social worker who answered her call listened sympathetically to Montauban's story. But once Montauban mentioned the couple had a little boy, the voice on the other end turned harsh and began collecting information about the family's whereabouts.

That very afternoon, a caseworker with the city's Administration for Children's Services (ACS) arrived at Montauban's apartment, explaining she was there to investigate a report of child maltreatment. At first Montauban was confused; she and her partner took excellent care of their son and had never abused him. Then she realized the social worker at Safe Horizon had contacted child protection authorities based on Montauban's call for help.

"The minute she knocked on my door, she was building a case against me," Montauban would recall about the ACS worker. The caseworker inspected her son's body, as well as the entire apartment, finding no evidence of harm to the boy, yet she told Montauban that her family was under ACS supervision for the next 60 days. Twice a month, a caseworker would make an unannounced visit to inspect their home, looking for evidence that might warrant removing her son and putting him in foster care. Within a few week, Montauban obtained an order of protection for herself against her partner, and he moved out of their apartment. But the visits and order didn't satisfy ACS.

In a family court hearing, ACS insisted Montauban file for an order of protection for her son against his father as well. Montauban disagreed, explaining to the judge that she wanted her son to maintain a relationship with his father, who had never hurt him.

A few days later, Montauban's partner took their son to family court for an appointment. ACS instructed him to leave the boy at a daycare center on the first floor of the court building. It was a setup: ACS had filed a petition to apprehend Montauban's son on the grounds that he was neglected because Montauban allegedly had allowed him to witness domestic violence and declined to file an order of protection against his father. That evening, the caseworker called Montauban to inform her that ACS had snatched her son from the family court daycare center. Her toddler was in foster care—in the custody of strangers in the Bronx.

Instead of working toward reunifying Montauban with her son, ACS moved him to several foster homes, promised the foster caretakers he would be free for adoption, and retaliated against Montauban when she expressed concerns by suspending her visits with him. When Montauban faced termination of her parental rights, it was her son's insistence on being reunited with her that preserved their legal bond. It took Montauban five years to retrieve her son from what she calls the "labyrinth" of family policing.

A longstanding narrative has convinced the public that the child welfare system is a flawed but benevolent social service program that strengthens families and rescues children from abusive homes. Most people think of the child welfare system and the criminal punishment system as distinct parts of government. Child welfare is supposed to be based on civil law and therefore not entail the surveillance and condemnation that characterize criminal justice. Whereas police investigate crimes to arrest lawbreakers, child protection workers investigate allegations of maltreatment to keep children safe. Whereas accused defendants stand trial to determine criminal culpability and are punished if convicted, family courts determine what's in the best interests of the child and order services for their parents. Or so goes the official story.

In reality, the child welfare system operates surprisingly like its criminal counterpart. It is a $30 billion apparatus that monitors, controls and punishes families in the same Black communities systematically subjugated by police and prisons. It is more accurate to call it a family policing system. State-level child protective services agencies investigate the families of 3.5 million children every year, with one in three children nationwide subject to investigation by the time they reach age 18. Most Black children (53%) experience an investigation from child protective services (CPS) at some point while growing up. A 2021 study of large U.S. counties revealed that Black children had consistently high rates of investigation, reaching 63.3% of Black children in Maricopa County, Ariz.

Identifying children as at risk of maltreatment gives caseworkers the authority to probe into and regulate every aspect of a family's life.

All it takes is a phone call from an anonymous tipster to a hotline operator about a vague suspicion to launch a life-altering government investigation. Based on vague child neglect laws, investigators can interpret being poor — lack of food, insecure housing, inadequate medical care — as evidence of parental unfitness. Caseworkers search homes, subject family members to humiliating interrogation and inspect children's bodies for evidence, sometimes strip-searching them. Caseworkers can make multiple unannounced home visits at any time of day or night and request personal information from teachers, hospitals, therapists and other service providers. In some cities, caseworkers force parents to sign blanket release forms to obtain confidential records about them and their children

These investigations not only traumatize families but can lead to intense family regulation and years of separation between parents and children, and ultimately can result in permanent dissolution of families.

Every year, CPS removes about 500,000 children from their homes — half through judicial proceedings and half through informal "safety plans." The racial disparities seen in CPS investigations are mirrored in the national foster care population, with Black children grossly overrepresented. Although Black children were only 14% of children in the United States in 2019, for example, they made up 23% of children in foster care. More than one in 10 Black and Native children in America will be forcibly separated from their parents and placed in foster care by their 18th birthday.

Recent foster care rates for U.S. children, at 576 per 100,000, are about the same as incarceration rates for U.S. adults, at 582 per 100,000. Black and Native children are also more than twice as likely as white children to experience the termination of both parents' rights

Child welfare investigations are essentially stop-and-frisk family surveillance, without the safeguards of law and public scrutiny that are present in the criminal context. Because child welfare is classified as part of the civil legal system, CPS workers are not classified as law enforcement officers. The Fourth Amendment protection against unreasonable government searches still theoretically applies, but agencies and courts have created a child welfare exception—arguing that if the rights of family members pose a risk to children, then those Fourth Amendment protections can be waived.

The tentacles of CPS surveillance have reached across U.S. society, far beyond the walls of child welfare agencies. Family policing relies on an expansive network of information sharing that spans the school, healthcare, public assistance and law enforcement systems. By federal edict, every state must identify people who work in professions that put them in contact with children — such as teachers, healthcare providers, social services staff and daycare workers — and require them to report suspected child abuse and neglect to government authorities. These deputized agents are known as "mandated reporters." Since states began enacting these reporting laws in the 1960s, the categories of enlisted professionals have expanded, and some states have passed "universal" reporting legislation that requires all residents, with few exceptions, to convey suspicions to the state.

As mandated reporters, providers of social services direct state surveillance against poor and low-income families — especially Black families. And using social services, receiving welfare benefits and living in public housing subject families to an extra layer of contact with these mandated reporters. Public workers are far more likely to report suspicions about their clients (essentially, because they are poor) than their counterparts in the private sector (who work with a more affluent, paying clientele). Regardless of income, healthcare professionals, for example, are more suspicious of Black families than other groups who bring their injured children to the hospital.

What's more, mandated reporting drives parents away from the very service providers most likely to support them. Many parents are deterred from fully engaging with healthcare, educational and social service systems because mere suspicion from a service provider could lead to family separation.

Mandated reporting, then, thwarts the potential for schools, healthcare clinics and social programs to be caring hubs of community engagement that non-coercively help families meet their material needs. It also wastes millions and millions of dollars investigating baseless allegations — money that could have provided concrete assistance to children and their family caregivers. These funds would bear far better fruit for children if given directly to their parents as cash allowances or used to provide material resources that meet children's needs. Instead, these professionals divert struggling families into a system with the potential to destroy them.

The extensive, multisystem network of CPS informants, combined with their power to pry into a family's personal life and space, gives CPS access to massive amounts of information ordinarily beyond the government's reach. In recent years, CPS agencies have begun adopting novel technological tools that are expanding the scope of family surveillance even further. Governments are increasingly considering hiring technology and consulting firms — including IBM, SAS and Deloitte — to employ big databases and artificial intelligence to monitor families and automate decisions about interventions. Some of the nation's largest child welfare departments — in California, Florida, Illinois, Pennsylvania and Texas — are using computerized risk assessment technologies to police families. The contracts (lucrative for private enterprises) not only magnify government surveillance but eat up budgets that could be used to provide material resources that families need.

For families that are screened into the family policing system, the next phase of surveillance entails their forced compliance with mandated services requested by CPS agencies and rubber-stamped by judges. These "service plans" usually have nothing to do with providing the tangible things families need but instead consist of a list of requirements family caregivers must fulfill — or else they lose their children to foster care. Rarely are parents asked what services they would find helpful; instead, parents are asked to focus on fixing their perceived parenting deficits with skills classes and psychological counseling.

All it takes is a phone call from an anonymous tipster to a hotline operator about a vague suspicion to launch a life-altering government investigation. Service plans are akin to the probation orders and restrictions imposed on people convicted of crimes. In the criminal context, the violation of a single provision lands the offender in prison. In the child welfare system, parents who fail to fulfill some provision on their list in time risk having their parental rights terminated and their ties to children irreparably disrupted.

The public accepts this extraordinary infringement on freedoms and family relationships because it masquerades as benevolence — and because it disrupts the most marginalized communities. Precisely because it seems to operate outside criminal law enforcement, the family policing system has become an extremely useful arm of the carceral state. CPS has the power to intensively monitor entire communities, all the while escaping public scrutiny and bypassing legal protections by claiming to protect children.

It's time to tear off this veneer. The child welfare system oppresses poor communities and especially Black communities by policing families. Revealing the truth about the CPS system should force the public to question its purpose, design and impact — and to see the need to replace it with a radically reimagined approach that can actually serve families and keep children safe.

This article is reprinted with permission from *in These Times* magazine, © 2022 and is available at in these times.com.

In These Times October 2023
https://inthesetimes.com/article/child-welfare-abolition-cps-reform-family-separation

The Case For Child Welfare Abolition

By Roxanna Asgarian

Early last December, CBS Sunday Morning ran a 12-minute segment about the harms of the child welfare system. The report led with the story of Vanessa Peoples, a Colorado nursing student and mother of three who became the subject of an abuse investigation after her two-year-old briefly wandered away from a family picnic. A stranger saw the child and called the police, despite the fact that Peoples, who is Black, caught up with her son shortly afterward. The call initiated an investigation from child protective services (CPS). A month later, a social worker made an unannounced visit to Peoples' home; when Peoples didn't immediately answer (because she was doing laundry in the basement), the social worker called the police, who ended up violently hogtying Peoples and charging her with reckless endangerment of a child. Peoples won a settlement against the city of Aurora for using excessive force, but she was still traumatized — and left with a criminal conviction that makes it difficult for her to find employment.

While Peoples' story had received media attention before, the CBS segment represented a watershed moment, decades in the making. One of the country's most-watched news shows, with nearly 5.5 million viewers, was talking about systemic problems in the child welfare system that have long been relegated to niche activist and academic circles. The child welfare system has always been a neglected newsroom beat, and what little coverage there is has typically been reserved for blaming protective services agencies after the death of a child.

It's hard to overstate how little mainstream news attention has been paid to other problems with the system, which critics say is more akin to law enforcement than social services, given its ability to surveil parents and hand down the ultimate punishment — terminating the legal bonds between parent and child. Families ensnared in the system lack many basic due process rights in navigating a punitive bureaucracy, and they typically don't receive a lawyer until the state seeks temporary or permanent custody of their child in court. Regardless, children often aren't actually made safer; the rates of maltreatment for children in foster care are abysmal, and research has repeatedly found that children who enter the system fare worse on multiple measures than children left in their homes.

But in 2020, in the wake of George Floyd's murder at the hands of Minneapolis police, that started to change. As protests erupted across the country, the idea of police and prison abolition moved from activist and academic circles into the mainstream media. For the first time, much of middle America began arguing over questions of mass incarceration, the vast disparities in how communities get policed, and whether caging people actually makes anyone safer.

While watching the protests unfold, Dorothy Roberts, a law professor at University of Pennsylvania and author of two books on the harms of the child welfare system, became "increasingly concerned that family policing was absent from most calls to defund the police," as she told a conference audience the next year. "Some activists," she continued, "even recommended transferring money, resources and authority from police departments to health and human services agencies that handle child protection"—without recognition that those agencies fail and repress Black and other marginalized communities just as much as police do.

Within the world of social work, that issue was becoming a heated debate. In July 2020, responding to calls for social workers to become alternate first responders, Alan Dettlaff, then-dean of the University of Houston Graduate College of Social Work, wrote an op-ed in the Houston Chronicle noting that social work has its own abundant problems with racism, since social workers in the child welfare system already "over-surveil, over-police and over-remove Black children from their parents."

At the time, Dettlaff, a former child welfare worker, was helping launch the upEND Movement, an organization whose high-profile members had an explicit founding principle, similar to the calls for police and prison abolition: The child welfare system shouldn't exist. According to its founding salvo, the upEND Movement — based at the University of Houston — "works to create a society in which the forcible separation of children from their parents is no longer an acceptable intervention for families in need."

It wasn't first time the argument had been made. In her 2001 book Shattered Bonds: The Color of Child Welfare, a foundational text about racism in CPS systems, Roberts had argued for a complete overhaul of the system. But 20 years later, her hopes for reform had dimmed.

When she revisited the topic for her 2022 book, Torn Apart: How the Child Welfare System Destroys Black Families — And How Abolition Can Build a Safer World, Roberts reached the conclusion that the system should not be rebuilt at all, that what's needed is a "radically reimagined way of caring for families."

At the same time, the University of Houston was becoming a locus of the movement as upEND brought prominent prison and police abolitionist thinkers like Angela Davis to speak. While many grassroots activists affected by the system had already embraced abolitionist ideas — either as parents who lost children to foster care or former foster youth — upEND represented the first mainstream academic organization echoing their call. The group turned heads across the fields of social work and family law, and graduate enrollment for social work at the University of Houston leapt more than 30 percent as students increasingly sought a progressive social work education.

Underlying many neglect allegations is the fundamental problem of poverty. But when CPS intervenes in the lives of struggling families, it rarely addresses that root cause in helpful ways, such as helping families find stable housing.

Along with growing mainstream media attention to the injustices of the law enforcement and prison systems, a marked increase in critical investigative journalism about the harms of the child welfare system came after 2020. Where media once primarily covered CPS only in cases of horrific child abuse — a pattern that typically resulted in crackdowns, with increased removals of children from their parents — reporters began focusing on the overreach of the system itself, including unnecessary child removals, the systemic abuses of foster children, and harmful ties between medical professionals and CPS that result in wrongful family separations during children's health crises.

Then, in 2022, came the CBS segment on Vanessa Peoples' case, beaming these long-neglected issues into the homes of millions of viewers. Roberts and Dettlaff were each quoted extensively, explaining the punitive nature of the system and bringing abolitionist ideas to the most mainstream of audiences. It seemed like the movement's time had come. Nine days after the program aired, Dettlaff was abruptly removed from his position as dean of the Graduate College of Social Work.

Too Flawed to Fix

Abolishing the child welfare system is a bold demand. After all, don't CPS agencies save children from abuse? Who would protect them if those agencies no longer exist?

While CPS does intervene in cases of physical and sexual abuse, the vast majority of children involved in substantiated child welfare investigations — 76 percent in 2021 — experienced neglect, a catch-all term for children who aren't getting their basic needs met, from going hungry to being picked up late from school. Underlying many neglect allegations is the fundamental problem of poverty. But when CPS intervenes in the lives of struggling families, it rarely addresses that root cause in helpful ways, such as helping families find stable housing. What support the agencies do provide, advocates say, is often coercive — such as mandating parents, under the threat of losing their kids, undertake an exhaustive tally of classes, drug tests and meetings that, for poor parents juggling work and childcare, are very difficult to complete. In some places—like Colorado's Adams County, where Vanessa People's lives—parents have to pay for the services they're made to undergo.

CPS also operates as a fundamentally racist system, according to decades of research. A 2021 review of 37 studies found that Black children are disproportionately impacted every step of the way: They're more likely to have their families investigated for abuse, more likely to have those allegations substantiated, and more likely to be removed to foster care. Once in the system, they spend more time there than others, are less likely to be reunified with their parents and less likely to be adopted out. One large study found that 53 percent of Black children nationwide experience a CPS investigation during their childhoods. Black and Indigenous parents are also statistically more likely to be poor, and families in poor and non-white neighborhoods are reported to CPS at much higher rates than those from wealthier, whiter homes.

For decades, these problems led to calls to reform the system. After Dorothy Roberts released Shattered Bonds in 2001, she served on a task force established as part of the settlement of a case against Washington state's child welfare system, for inflicting emotional and psychological harm on foster youth shuffled from home to home. Nearly a decade later, the task force disbanded, having achieved few of its goals. Roberts came to believe that the small fixes they'd managed to make—such as better protocols for keeping siblings together and moving children around fewer times—only tweaked a system that was inherently racist and fundamentally flawed.

"I think the children's attorneys had good intentions; they wanted to end these horrible situations for children in foster care," Roberts told me in a 2021 interview for my book, We Were Once a Family: Love, Death, and Child Removal in America. "And our panel had good intentions; we wanted to improve foster care. But it can't be fixed that way—it can't be fixed at all, is my conclusion."

Dettlaff, who began his career as a CPS caseworker in Texas, had a similar path to abolition. In 2005, the Texas legislature directed the state's foster care agency to research racial disproportionality in its

369

system. It was part of a larger wave of acknowledgement around the country that child welfare had an outsized impact on children of color, particularly Black and Indigenous children. Over the next decade, Dettlaff and other researchers published data on the prevalence of, and reasons for, the inordinate number of Black children affected by CPS and the negative outcomes they experience compared with white children.

Tides shifted in the 2010s, in part because prominent conservative scholars, like Harvard's Elizabeth Bartholet, argued that focusing on racial disparities left Black children in greater danger of maltreatment. Funding for disproportionality research dried up; the agency tracking the Texas system was defunded and closed by 2018. Dettlaff was left discouraged: What was the point of all these task forces — working toward solutions, or just working to give the impression that something was being done?

Dettlaff, along with four scholars who had studied disproportionality with the nonprofit Center for the Study of Social Policy — Kristen Weber, Bill Bettencourt, Maya Pendleton and Leonard Burton — began reading prison and police abolitionist texts and discussing how similar structural inequities were actually baked into the child welfare system, rather than being a problem that could be reformed out of it.

In 2020, those meetings culminated in the creation of the upEND Movement, named for its goal to upend the narrative around child welfare, to shift the focus from troubled parents to a troubled system.

"The way I think about it now," Dettlaff says, "is that reforms ask the child welfare system to do the impossible. They ask the system to forcibly separate families in a way that's a little bit less racist, a little bit nicer and a little bit more palatable to the general public. And that's just not possible. Family separation causes harm every time. And until that ends, the system is never going to change."

A common argument against abolition is that people who want to dismantle the child welfare system are all-or-nothing — that they can't see the need for what child protection workers do, that vulnerable children will be hurt without caseworkers to protect them.

Some anti-abolitionist scholars even argue that Black families are disproportionately represented in the system because Black children are at greater risk of abuse, pointing to such factors as lower marriage rates in Black communities. As Naomi Schaefer Riley, a fellow at the right-wing American Enterprise Institute, argues, "If Black children are in greater danger of being abused or neglected than white children — child maltreatment is highly correlated with family structure, and two-parent, married couples are not evenly distributed across race in this country — then it is the job of the child welfare system to protect them regardless of the color of their skin."

The truth is that, while research on abuse rates and racial demographics is mixed, the single strongest predictor of child maltreatment is, in fact, socioeconomic status — poverty, not race. What's also ignored is how abuse findings are made by individuals with their own beliefs and biases.

Regardless, abolitionists understand that child abuse is real — many thanks to first-hand knowledge. Zara Raven, a Philadelphia-based abolitionist organizer, experienced abuse in her family home before she was removed to foster care. But Raven's time in the system was also traumatizing and abusive; she was separated from her siblings and placed in a foster home that doubled as an office, where she says she was repeatedly sexually assaulted. She ran away as a teen and became homeless — like thousands of older foster youth do each year — and had engaged in survival sex in exchange for places to stay while she completed her high school degree. "I wasn't given any choices at any point in this process," Raven recalls.

Raven's realization that she had suffered both interpersonal abuse — by her family — and state violence — in foster care — made her an abolitionist. "The state is not a tool that can create safety," Raven says now. "Instead, the state is another instrument of violence that tends to re-victimize survivors of abuse."

Other abolitionists, like Joyce McMillan, founder of the abolitionist group Just Making a Change for Families, note that the current system is overly focused on marginal cases, leaving caseworkers ill-equipped to recognize and handle more severe abuse. "The first thing [detractors] say is, 'What about the children that really need help?'" says McMillan, who experienced the system firsthand when CPS temporarily removed her children in the 1990s. But in a bloated child welfare system that takes too many children into state custody, where social workers routinely juggle too many cases, more serious abuse often falls between the cracks. "So it's not about 'what about the children who need help?' — it's about how to get the people who need help real help, and leave the other people alone."

The abolitionists' vision of an alternative is more nuanced than critics claim. They want to dismantle the surveillance and punishment aspects of the child welfare system — which research shows decrease neighborhood trust — and replace them with a robust support network that isn't punitive. The idea is that, when people have their needs met, they are less likely to harm those closest to them, and strong communities caring for children will provide better opportunities to intervene if and when harm happens.

For a movement that entered mainstream conversations just three years ago, there's been a huge amount of engagement with abolitionist ideas across the profession.

"We need childcare collectives," Raven says. "We need care teams. There's not one single intervention, but one important shift in the conditions that we need is whole communities taking responsibility for the care of children and youth, and building relationships with young people, so that folks have safe places to turn to if they're experiencing violence — and then we can listen to young people about how they want to respond."

The major distinction between abolitionists and reformers is abolitionists' insistence on changes that shrink, not grow, the system — similar to the recognition that flooding police departments with cash won't solve police brutality. Called "non-reformist reforms," these changes focus on increasing parents' rights in the process and removing fewer children in the first place.

Some of these items are big-ticket goals, like the push to repeal the Adoption and Safe Families Act (ASFA). Passed in 1997, the law starts a clock the day a child is removed; if a child remains in foster care for 15 of 22 consecutive months, states are required to initiate the termination of their parents' rights. The law was passed with the goal of getting more children who were languishing in foster care into permanent homes — with the understanding that those permanent homes would likely be adoptive families, not family reunification.

Advocates for parents involved in the system say that the issues they're struggling with, often including substance use and housing insecurity, aren't easily solvable on a 15-month timeline, particularly with the child welfare system's punitive approach. In most Texas counties, for instance, lawyers for the Department of Family and Protective Services automatically file a petition to terminate parental rights immediately after a child is removed. Although they also create a service plan (putatively intended to reunite parents with their children), if any item on that plan isn't completed within the federal ASFA timeline, or if parent's misstep, the petition for termination is ready to go.

Abolitionists are also pushing for the rollback of mandatory reporting laws. Every state requires certain professionals — usually teachers, social workers and doctors — to report suspected child abuse or neglect. A few state, like Wyoming, Texas and New Jersey, consider every resident a mandated reporter.

At first glance, it's hard to imagine how mandated reporting could be bad. Shouldn't we all be responsible for keeping children safe? In fact, research reveals that mandatory reporting laws do not identify more abused kids and that the laws disproportionately affect poor and Black families. "Mandatory reporting is about casting the net wide," McMillan says. The training that teachers, social workers and medical professionals receive as mandatory reporters is "vague and threatening," leading to a "better safe than sorry" approach that inflicts more harm than good.

Some non-reformist reforms are already being implemented in state and local jurisdictions around the country — and not always where you'd expect. In September, Texas will start requiring caseworkers to inform parents of their rights at the beginning of an investigation, something activists call "family Miranda." The state also banned most anonymous reporting of abuse and neglect to CPS, in an attempt to reduce the number of unfounded allegations made by ex-partners and others using the system as a form of harassment and retaliation. Nearly identical bills failed in New York this year amid pushback by New York City's child welfare agency. But Texas passed both bills with bipartisan support and little fanfare, with the extremely conservative legislature viewing the issue through the lens of parents' rights. This unlikely alliance — between the ideas of progressive activists and Republicans, each rooted in very different beliefs about family — has resulted in some conservatives using abolitionist language in support of limiting child welfare overreach.

"Having a child removed is one of the strongest police actions that we can take," Texas state Rep. James Frank, the Republican author of the state's new family Miranda law, told me earlier this year. There are abundant checks and balances for people facing criminal charges, Frank said, and rightfully so. But child removal? It has due process, but not nearly as consistent."

Then They Fight You

As calls for abolishing the child welfare system have gained steam, so too have ideological struggles among social workers, some also dating back to the transformational moment in 2020.

That summer, glowing media profiles of police-social worker crisis teams raised the possibility of increased collaboration as a way to reduce police killings of people experiencing a mental health crisis. Even former President Donald Trump echoed the reasoning when he signed an executive order that would incentivize more partnerships. "This is what they've studied and worked on all their lives," Trump said of social workers. "We will have the best of them put in our police departments and working with police."

Angelo McClain, then-CEO of the National Association of Social Workers, the country's largest social work membership organization, wrote an op-ed in the Wall Street Journal celebrating how "social workers are playing an increasingly integral role in police forces, helping officers do their jobs more effectively and humanely and become better attuned to cultural and racial biases."

But not everyone was on board. At the University of Houston, Alan Dettlaff viewed the prospect as short- sighted and further damaging to social workers' reputations in poor communities. "Social work has always had an inferiority complex — a feeling that we weren't recognized as a profession in the way we should be," Dettlaff told me. "And now, all of a sudden, some of the leaders in our profession were seizing on this moment ... jumping on this opportunity to be seen as the remedy for everything wrong with policing."

In July 2020, Dettlaff wrote his Houston Chronicle op-ed. He noted social workers' problems with racism in family policing and argued that social workers collaborating with police "is absolutely not" what they should be doing. "We cannot continue to be complicit in what we know to be a harmful, racist institution."

The piece kicked off an internal storm at the University of Houston. Three members of the Graduate College advisory council resigned. One of them, retired social worker Beverly McPhail, wrote an email to the advisory council, saying that Dettlaff's argument should be made "behind closed doors within the social work profession, not trumpeted in news headlines."

Addressing Dettlaff directly, McPhail's email lamented that Dettlaff "could have taken this opportunity as Dean to practically write an unpaid commercial for our school." Instead, she continued, he "focused on the racist past of the social work profession and dismissed the police as too racist to work with."

The University of Houston conflict speaks to a longer-standing, more fundamental division that has existed within social work since its earliest days: Are social workers meant to help individual poor people fix their problems and improve their lives? Or do social workers have a larger mission to challenge systemic forces that oppress poor people in the first place?

Prominent early social workers advocated for social programs that addressed poverty on a systemic level, like the 1800s settlement house movement to support new immigrants and poor people in quickly industrializing cities, or New Deal programs like Aid to Families with Dependent Children.

But much of that early work was limited to helping white families. Jane Addams, who co-founded Chicago's Hull House, was, like many of her contemporaries, a eugenicist; Black people weren't allowed to live in the settlement houses that Addams' work inspired across the country. The New Deal's Social Security Act created welfare programs, but the laws systematically denied support to Black families at the state and federal level.

After World War I, progressive social workers who advocated for systemic solutions to poverty were branded as communists. "During the Red Scares, social work [as a profession] aligned with the government, and basically ratted out a bunch of social workers that were teaching about equality, fairness — things that the U.S. government was saying, 'If you say these things, you're a communist,'" said Justin Harty, an assistant professor at Arizona State University who studies the history of social work.

"The state is not a tool that can create safety. Instead, the state is another instrument of violence that tends to re-victimize survivors of abuse."

History may be repeating itself. In many places, progressive social workers and academics are pushing to root social work education in abolitionist principles. Cameron Overton, who runs the master's social work program at Milwaukee's Alverno College, is attempting to build a completely abolitionist curriculum from the ground up — as far as he knows, the first master's-level social work program to do so. "I don't want this to be like diversity, equity and inclusion, where you take that one course on abolition, one course on cultural diversity," Overton says. "We're infusing this everywhere in our curriculum."

The program is admitting its first class of students this fall, and the titles of intro classes are telling, such as "Behavior and Unmet Needs" and "Clients are People."

Elsewhere, abolitionist-minded social work students have encountered staunch resistance. Elena Gormley was a graduate student in social work at the University of Illinois Chicago when, as part of a group project in 2020, she and her classmates created a guide called "Alternatives to Calling DCFS [the Department of Children and Family Services]." The guide details the vague nature of "neglect" and how biases affect who gets reported to child protection agencies. It includes local resources, like food banks and childcare assistance programs, to contact on behalf of struggling families, as well as an ethical checklist for cases when calling protective services is necessary.

Gormley's group project got an A, and the guide was disseminated far and wide. It's even being taught in other social work programs. But when Gormley emailed the guide to her school's listserv, the university initiated disciplinary proceedings, charging that "the content of the email encouraged students to commit a crime, which could lead to harm or the death of a child if the suggestion were followed." The official complaint calls Gormley's actions unprofessional and unethical and claims Gormley's "behavior indicates that she is unsuitable for the profession."

Gormley spent five weeks defending herself against a litany of conduct violations, the threat of expulsion looming over her. She successfully fought the proceedings and graduated in 2021, but the experience was harrowing.

Still, Gormley points out that abolitionist framing is taking hold at the highest levels of decision-making. Jerry Milner, head of the federal Children's Bureau under Trump, publicly advocated for "radical change and wholesale replacement of the current system," for instance.

"There is such a steep change now and it's coming from not particularly radical organizations," Gormley says. "So, I think it does behoove the entire profession to really look at, are there other ways we can do this? Are there better ways we can do this to actually keep families safer and be more supportive?" As industry leaders increasingly recognize that families should stay together whenever possible, it's clear that child welfare abolitionists are no longer on the fringe. But once an idea is taken seriously, its proponents become an actual threat.

When University of Houston interim provost Bob McPherson announced the decision to remove Alan Dettlaff from his post as dean, in December 2022, many students in the graduate school were stunned. Some had chosen the University of Houston for its explicit abolitionist stance, and—according to letters student groups sent to the administration—none had been consulted or addressed prior to the dean's removal. "Most people were blindsided—I was completely blindsided," says Eve Ryan, then a student in the program who organized protests against the decision.

In the announcement, McPherson wrote that he'd removed Dettlaff "to better align the college with the university's academic priorities, which include growing research expenditures and elevating the learning experience for all students."

According to Dettlaff, McPherson told him the ouster was tied to more specific complaints, like Dettlaff's decision to stop placing graduate students in local police departments and the district attorney's office, which some faculty felt had damaged the school's reputation. Additionally, McPherson claimed some faculty believed Dettlaff's abolitionism was jeopardizing their grant funding — specifically, a federal grant program that pays for some students' master's degrees if they commit to work for child protective services upon graduation. (Dettlaff says there's no evidence to suggest that's the case and the "grant continues to be renewed every year.") University of Houston representatives declined to comment, and McPherson did not respond to numerous requests for comment.

"Reforms ask the child welfare system to forcibly separate families in a way that's a little bit less racist, a little bit nicer and a little bit more palatable to the general public. And that's just not possible. Family separation causes harm every time."

Dettlaff remains a professor at the university, but his removal as dean sent waves across the field, and his ouster wasn't the only sign of backlash. Kristen Weber, another cofounder of the upEND movement, left her role at the Center for the Study of Social Policy in 2022, in part because she felt she couldn't be as vocal in support of abolitionism as she wanted. Some philanthropic funders won't support programs that use abolitionist language, Weber says, and other abolitionists in the field have been quietly pushed out or laid off.

In July, Angela Burton, a top advisor on child welfare issues to the New York state court system and an outspoken abolitionist, was scheduled to address Congress about problems in family policing but was denied permission to attend by her employers at the Office of Court Administration, who fired her when she pushed back. "This episode really shows the depth of resistance to change," Burton told national child welfare publication The Imprint. "[T]here's a recognition that this oppressive system is cracking, because the truth is being told about it."

Justin Harty, at Arizona State, says the current political climate feels reminiscent of previous eras of backlash. "I think that, right now, we're in the third Red Scare," Harty says. "I don't know how we're going to move forward through this because I think a lot of social workers are scared."

379

As discouraging as some of these developments are, they may represent a strange sort of success. For a movement that entered mainstream conversations just three years ago, there's been a huge amount of engagement with abolitionist ideas across the profession. "I've never seen this kind of quick pick-up—and also quick attack," says Weber, now at the National Center for Youth Law. "The backlash means that we are somewhat successful in challenging the dominant worldview and really shifting things. And when you are challenging and shifting things, there's a scramble to maintain power and relevance."

Dorothy Roberts, who has studied the child welfare system from outside the profession of social work, is skeptical that a field so closely tied to a system could support its abolition. "To me, it's this larger question of whether it's even possible to transform social work into a socially just profession," she says. "Even the idea that social workers solve social problems is part of this carceral approach that social problems are caused by the people experiencing them, rather than people in power."

Roberts believes in increased support for people living through poverty, but also that, as long as social work remains bound to the government, that support will be tied to a carceral approach to society's problems. She argues that "a precondition of radical transformation—which we can see hope for in the ways that some social work students and others have challenged that ideology—would be to end this tie to government and free social workers to reimagine and implement a new vision."

Eve Ryan, who received her degree this spring, sees some social work jobs as less harmful than others, such as working for holistic legal defense offices like the Bronx Defenders, whose social workers are protected from mandatory reporting laws by attorney-client privilege.

But reducing and dismantling a harmful system is only a first step. In order for abolition to work, it needs just as much of a push toward non-carceral community supports—most importantly, actual investment in our social safety net, which has been systematically stripped to the bones.

"There are communities that have, on purpose, been destroyed and disinvested in, poisoned," Weber says.

"And then we blame individual families for hurting or neglecting their kids, and we've created a legal scheme that makes it easy to remove those kids.

"I think some of the pushback is that, if you lose this narrative of individual families hurting kids, then you actually need to recognize and respond to these larger structural problems."

This article is reprinted with permission from *in These Times* magazine, © 2023 and is available at inthesetimes.com

Advocates for Families Act of 2024

The Advocates for Families Act of 2024 is a federal law aimed to enhance the child welfare system by ensuring that families have access to a family advocate throughout all levels of administrative and legal proceedings. We encourage bi-partisan support on this bill and ask for your co-sponsorship. Contact matthew.krall@mail.house.gov, for Congressman Barry Moore.

Objective:

The primary objective of the Advocates for Families Act of 2024 is to facilitate smoother and expedited navigation of the child welfare system for families. By allowing the participation of a family advocate, this bill intends to prevent unnecessary removals, and reduce the trauma and instability experienced by children who are temporarily removed from their homes and placed in foster care. Additionally, it aims to decrease the duration of out-of-home placements and ultimately reunite children with their parents or relatives in a timely manner where appropriate.

Key Facts:

- Each year, 600,000 children are removed from their homes and enter the foster care system.
- Nearly 50% of these children are six years old or younger.
- More than 60% of these children will eventually return to a parent or relative.
- These children will spend 15 to 17 months in out-of-home placement before being reunited with their families.
- NCMEC recently reported an explosion in children going missing from the child welfare system as well as children being sex-trafficked out of foster care.

  https://www.missingkids.org/footer/about/leadership/leadership-profiles

Importance:

The Advocates for Families Act recognizes the need for support and guidance throughout the child welfare process. By providing families with a dedicated advocate, this legislation aims to address several crucial aspects:

- **Improved Negotiation:** Family advocates will assist families in navigating the complex administrative and legal procedures, ensuring their voices are heard and their rights are protected.

- **Expedited Process:** With the aid of a family advocate, the bill seeks to streamline the child welfare system, minimizing unnecessary delays and expediting the reunification process.

- **Reducing Trauma:** By reducing the time spent in foster care, the bill aims to mitigate the emotional and psychological impact on children, promoting stability and preserving familial bonds.

- **Cost Savings:** Through more efficient processes and reduced out-of-home placement durations, the Advocates for Families Act aims to save taxpayer dollars by decreasing the reliance on federal funding for foster care.

Prolonged and Unnecessary Separation Causes Severe Emotional Trauma:

Clinical research shows that:

1. Children who are removed are "overwhelmed with feelings of abandonment, rejection, worthlessness, guilt, and helplessness."

2. Separation floods stress hormones throughout the child's brain and body, leading to: difficulty sleeping, developmental regression, heart disease, hypertension, obesity, diabetes, and decreased longevity.

3. Separation causes permanent architectural changes in the brain, including lower IQs. depression, more suicide attempts, and more problems with alcohol abuse and gambling.

4. Children generally suffer worse outcomes when removed than if they had been allowed to remain in marginal homes. In studies of similarly situated children, children who were removed (compared to those remaining at home): have two to three times higher delinquency rates; have higher teen birth rates; have lower earnings as adults; are two to three times more likely to enter the criminal justice system as adults; and are twice as likely to have learning disabilities and developmental delays.

   https://www.americanbar.org/content/dam/aba/publications
   /litigation_committees/childrights/child-separation-
   memo/parent-child-separation-trauma-memo.pdf

Conclusion:

The Advocates for Families Act of 2024 represents a significant step towards enhancing the child welfare system. By providing families with access to a family advocate, this legislation aims to promote smoother navigation, expedite reunification, and ultimately improve outcomes for children and their families. It is anticipated that this bill will reduce trauma, provide stability, and save valuable resources, all while prioritizing the best interests of the children involved.

Contact matthew.krall@mail.house.gov, for Congressman Barry Moore.

Glossary

A
AFCARS Adoption and Foster Care Analysis and Reporting System
APSR Annual Progress and Services Report

B
BPR Tennessee Bureau of Professional Responsibility investigates lawyers and censures them for misconduct

C
CAPS Child Abuse Pediatrician
CAPTA The Child Abuse Prevention and Treatment Act (CAPTA) was passed in 1974.
CASA Court Appointed Special Advocates
CFSR Child and Family Services Review
CPS Child Protective Services

D
DCF Florida Department of Children and Families
DCS Tennessee Department of Children's Services
DCYF Washington State Department of Children, Youth & Families
DEA Drug Enforcement Agency
DMHSAS Tennessee Department of Mental Health and Substance Abuse Services

F
FFPSA The Family First Prevention Services Act (2018)

G

GAL Guardian ad Litem is lawyer appointed by a judge to represent children

H

HHS U.S. Department of Health and Human Services
HIPAA Health Insurance Portability and Accountability Act (1996)

N

NCANDS The National Child Abuse and Neglect Data System
NCCPR National Coalition for Child Protection Reform

O

ORPC Colorado Office of the Child's Representative

S

SNAP Supplemental Nutrition Assistance Program

T

TennCare TennCare is the state of Tennessee's Medicaid program
TFACTS Tennessee Family & Child Tracking System
TPR Termination of Parental Rights

W

WOPD Washington State Office of Public Defense

Contents

Index

389